COME FOLLOW ME

To Paul Mueggenborg

My Father

COME FOLLOW ME

DISCIPLESHIP REFLECTIONS ON THE SUNDAY GOSPEL READINGS FOR LITURGICAL YEAR B

DANIEL H. MUEGGENBORG

GRACEWING

First published in England in 2017

by

Gracewing
2 Southern Avenue
Leominster
Herefordshire HR6 0QF
United Kingdom

www.gracewing.co.uk

The right of Daniel H. Mueggenborg to be identified
as the author of this work has been asserted in accordance
with the Copyright, Designs and Patents Act 1988.

ISBN 978 085244 878 6

Typeset by Gracewing

Cover design by Bernardita Peña Hurtado,
incorporating *The Sermon on the Mount*
by Carl Heinrich Bloch (1834–1890)

CONTENTS

INTRODUCTION

In 2003 Bishop Edward J. Slattery appointed me to serve as synod director for the Diocese of Tulsa. The synod process involves a series of meetings, which serve as listening sessions and provide opportunities for the faithful to share their concerns, insights, and recommendations for the future. Over the course of the succeeding two years we held more than thirty such sessions in various parishes and institutions throughout Eastern Oklahoma.

The three primary topics for the synod focused on the celebration of the Lord's Day, family life, and evangelization.

The synod was an enlightening process that fostered fruitful discussions and stimulated creative recommendations. Among the insights that left a lasting impression were the following.

First, the faithful had a strong desire to understand their Catholic faith from a biblical basis. At the same time, many people indicated they lacked sufficient knowledge of the scriptures which prevented them from pursuing a personal study of the sacred texts.

Second, the faithful indicated how good homilies were able to change their lives. This was especially true when the message of the scriptures was effectively applied to the practical situations of everyday life.

Third, the faithful expressed a sincere and authentic desire to grow deeper in their relationship with Jesus through prayer, the Sacraments, and daily discipleship. In order to facilitate this deepened relationship, they would need to develop a mature adult faith and solid spirituality. They would also need the support and encouragement of a parish faith community that could help them take the necessary steps to grow in that maturity through solid teaching and practical witness.

Although the diocesan synod process formally ended in 2005, these insights continued to inform and shape my life as a priest and my vision for parish ministry. In particular, these insights instilled within me a great desire to connect people with the scriptures in an effective and life-giving way. This series, Come Follow Me, was published as a tool that can help parishioners experience the Word of God in sacred scripture and grow in maturity as disciples of Jesus Christ.

This writing contains a series of exegetical, in-depth reflections based on the assigned Gospel reading for the Sundays of a given liturgical year. Each reflection contains a few insights that are explained and then applied to the lived experience of a Christian disciple.

I wish to acknowledge the various excellent biblical commentaries from which the vast majority of insights were drawn that are presented in these reflections. I strongly encourage anyone who wants to become a serious student of Scripture to consult these commentaries directly. In no way do I claim these biblical insights to be my own. I am utterly dependent upon the research of generations of scholars. These reflections do not so much represent an original work on my part as they do a composition of insights gained from studying three essential biblical commentary series and some online homily resources from a noted theologian.

The following biblical commentary series were used extensively and repeatedly in the compilation of these reflections. Each of these series has a separate volume for specific Gospels and other biblical writings. The reader is encouraged to consult these commentary series:

- The Anchor Bible (New York, Doubleday)
- The New Interpreter's Bible (Nashville, Abingdon Press)
- Sacra Pagina ("A Michael Glazier Book." Collegeville: The Liturgical Press)

In addition to these three essential commentaries, I also gained insights from homilies given by the Most Reverend Robert Barron and posted on the Word on Fire website. Bishop Barron is one of the most talented theologians and communicators in the Catholic Church today. He is also a man of great humility, authenticity, and fidelity. His homilies are an invaluable resource for all disciples and are readily available as part of the "Resources" section of the Word on Fire website (www.wordonfire.org). I researched the fifteen-year collection of his homilies in preparation for each of the weekly reflections contained in this book and used those insights, which especially pertained to the biblical text. The reader is encouraged to consult the Word on Fire website for further study of these resources and for the other excellent evangelization materials available from that ministry.

The primary purpose of this writing is to promote a personal, discipleship-focused study of the Gospels and to facilitate small group discussions. It is hoped that this book can be of benefit to parishioners, homilists, and parish ministry staff.

As you read through these reflections in preparation for the Sunday Mass, it will be important to use a Bible to consult the many scriptural passages. The New American Bible Revised Edition is referenced throughout the reflections. The abbreviation "cf." is used to indicate opportunities to confer or compare other relevant biblical texts. The abbreviation "v." is used to identify corresponding scriptural quotes and/or passages.

There is no substitute for the Word of God in Scripture. These reflections may shed light on the biblical texts but they should never replace those sacred texts in personal prayer and study.

When using these reflections for small group discussion, the following recommended process is simple and effective:

1. Start with an opening prayer.
2. Read the relevant biblical text.
3. Review one reflection at a time and focus the discussion on the application questions.
4. Proceed to review the next reflection and focus on those questions.
5. Continue this process until all the reflections for a given Gospel passage have been reviewed.
6. Conclude by praying for the members of the group and interceding for particular needs.

Acknowledgements

This book relies heavily on the scholarship and research of the essential sources that are listed in the bibliography. It also represents the cumulative effort of many people who assisted in the editing and composition process.

Most of all, I wish to acknowledge the following people who were involved in this publication:

Blake A. Hite, who provided final editing services.

Rev. Elkin José González, STD, who assisted in editing each reflection and provided references from the rich spiritual tradition of the Church to enhance and focus various topics.

Sue Karol Roach, for her proof-reading of the final document.

A. J. Tierney, MFA, for her work in formatting and reviewing the text to ensure consistency and conformity.

FIRST SUNDAY OF ADVENT

Our Scripture passage for the First Sunday of Advent comes from the Gospel of Mark 13:33–37. This section of Mark's Gospel is commonly referred to as the "Little Apocalypse" because of the many images and stories of judgment presented in it. As we begin a new year in the Church's calendar, this reading offers some important insights to help guide us in discipleship.

Advent is a time of preparation. However, no real preparation can take place until we first know clearly the event for which we are preparing. Most people think that Advent is the season in which we prepare for Christmas. According to that understanding, Advent helps us remember and celebrate the Birth of Jesus in Bethlehem as the Eternal Word of God became flesh and dwelt among us (see Jn 1:14). While that historical event of our salvation is worthy of celebration and reverence, it does not take much preparation to simply remember something from the past. Advent is really about preparing for a future event—namely, the coming of Jesus at the end of time. You see, Jesus first came to us as a babe in Bethlehem in fulfillment of God's promises to send a Savior (see Mi 5:2). Since God has demonstrated that He is faithful to His promises, we can be assured that our Lord will fulfill His Word in the Gospel to come again at the end of time. Thus, Advent is really about preparing for our Lord's future coming and not just celebrating a past event. That is why the Gospel reading for the First Sunday of Advent always points to the future. As we attend the succeeding Sundays of Advent, we will read how people prepared for the Lord's first coming in order to guide us in our preparation for the Lord's second coming. Because of this expectant faith, Christianity looks to the future with hope and confidence.

How do most people prepare during the time of Advent? How much time, effort, and resource do you put into decorating and celebrating Christmas?

What resources and practices can help you prepare for the Lord's second coming?

What would your Christian life look like if you put as much time, effort, and resource into preparing for Jesus' second coming as you do celebrating His first coming?

When we pray the Lord's Prayer, we say, "Thy Kingdom Come!" If you knew that the Lord's second coming would take place in twenty-five days, what are some specific things you would do in the next few weeks to be prepared for that moment?

In this Gospel reading, Jesus tells us that His second coming will be like a man who goes on a journey, putting each of his servants in charge of a specific task in his household. Note that the tasks are not self-selected by the servants but are clearly assigned by the man. Upon the Lord's return, the servants will be judged based on how well they have carried out those tasks entrusted to them. Jesus cautions us twice against attempts to calculate the exact time of His return when He says, "you do not know when" the time will come. Thus, because no one can know the time of return, the only way to be prepared now is by diligently carrying out the tasks the Lord has entrusted to us. This teaching is a caution to prevent us from erroneously thinking it is acceptable to passively wait for the Lord's return. This passage reminds us that Jesus has given us a mission to accomplish and we will be judged on how well we have carried out that mission.

What do you believe are the "tasks" or mission that God has entrusted to you?

What tasks (or mission) are you fulfilling well?

What tasks (or mission) are you not fulfilling well?

Sometimes we like to self-select our tasks in life. When we do so, we are telling God what we want for ourselves rather than asking God what the Lord wants of us. How can sanctifying your desires alter the way you approach your prayer and your daily life?

What temptation leads you to "fall asleep" in your faith rather than remaining diligent in fulfilling your tasks?

> *How do we try to figure out the timing of the Lord's coming*
> *instead of living in a state of constant preparedness?*

This chapter from Mark's Gospel provides an opportunity to learn about "Apocalyptic literature", a literary style which we see elsewhere in the Bible. The word "apocalypse" comes from two Greek words meaning to "un-veil" or "reveal". It is meant to give the reader insights into the meaning of current events and to foster hope of vindication in the future. This style of literature developed during times of great oppression when the people had no recourse against unjust persecution except for divine intervention. For this reason, apocalyptic literature is oftentimes referred to as the "language of the dispossessed". Both Christians and Jews used apocalyptic literature to give their people hope when they were in the midst of seemingly hopeless circumstances. This was certainly the situation during the reigns of the first century Emperors Nero and Domitian. Even today some people lack the ability to control the forces that affect their lives, which renders them at the mercy of the powers that be. When those powers are malevolent, a person's only hope for vindication and salvation is to wait for the Lord (Ps 27:14). The fundamental message of apocalyptic literature is that those who persevere faithfully to the end will be vindicated by God and that suffering is an inevitable part of God's plan for the establishment of His Kingdom. The personal Life, Death, and Resurrection of Jesus witness to the truth of this message.

> *Who are people in our world today who have no ability to*
> *control the forces that affect their lives?*
> *When have you had no recourse for help except for divine*
> *intervention in your life?*
> *What is a situation in your life that you would like to have*
> *"un-veiled" so that you could understand it from God's*
> *perspective?*
> *How are you being asked to persevere through a challenge*
> *of faith?*
> *Why is hope important for people who are suffering?*
> *How can you give hope to someone who is dispossessed?*

As we begin a new year in the life of the Church, it is always a good opportunity to stop and take inventory of our growth in faith and consider what has taken place in the past year as well as what we want to take place in the next year. In short, it's time to make a "New Year's Resolution" for discipleship.

> *What would you like to be different in your faith life one year from now?*
> *What steps will you take to make it happen?*
> *What have been milestones of your growth in discipleship this past year?*

This First Sunday of Advent is a good time to pray with eagerness and generosity for the gift of wisdom and insight so that we might know God's will for our lives. Saint Francis of Assisi prayed the following words before the Crucifix of San Damiano and received the commission from Christ to "Rebuild My Church." Imagine how blessed your Advent might be if you prayed this prayer every day.

> *Most High, glorious God,*
> *Enlighten the darkness of my heart*
> *And give me right faith,*
> *Certain hope, and perfect charity.*
> *Lord give me insight and wisdom*
> *That I may know*
> *Your holy and true will.*

SECOND SUNDAY OF ADVENT

O ur Scripture passage for the Second Sunday of Advent comes from the Gospel of Mark 1:1–8. These few verses are the very opening words of Mark's Gospel, and they are loaded with powerful and meaningful messages. Because we frequently hear the terms used in these opening phrases, we can sometimes fail to recognize or appreciate just how important they were when Mark intentionally wrote them for Christians of the first century. While there are many worthy points on which to reflect in these verses, it is the opening statement that is selected for this week's study: "Beginning of the gospel of Jesus Christ the Son of God." This phrase is not so much a sentence as it is a title, and as such, Mark intends it to capture our interest today even as it did for disciples in the Early Church. It is important to remember that Mark most likely wrote his Gospel in Rome, around the year AD 70, for a Christian community that was conscious of their Jewish roots and experiencing the first persecutions of the Roman Empire.

The first word Mark uses in his opening phrase is "Beginning" (Greek: *arche*). That is a very important term for several reasons. First, it echoes the first word of the Book of Genesis, and Mark's Jewish-Christian readers would have immediately recognized that connection. Thus, Mark is announcing that in Jesus, God is starting a new creation, a new order, a new revelation, and a new act of salvation. John's Gospel begins with a similar reference to the Book of Genesis in his opening verse as well.

Second, by identifying his writing as the "Beginning," Mark is telling the Christian community that this message is to always be the rule by which we measure our faith and discipleship. Today we sometimes speak about "getting back to the basics", but people in Mark's time would have spoken about "remembering their beginnings". Thus, the Gospel of Mark serves as an enduring rule of life for Christians of all time.

Third, Mark's writing is sometimes called the "Gospel of Beginnings" because of how frequently he states that Jesus "began" to do something (see Mk 4:1, 6:2, 6:34, 8:31, 11:15, 12:1, 13:8, and 14:33). Although these ministries may begin with Jesus, Mark never says that our Lord ended these ministries. Hence, the Church has the responsibility to carry on the ministry that Jesus began. The Gospel of Mark, then, is not only the story of what Jesus did, but also the "job description" of what disciples should be doing since we are the ones who continue that ministry. It is worth noting that Mark also includes the beginning of some actions that are detrimental to the ministry of Jesus and obstacles to the message of the Gospel (see Mk 1:45, 8:32, 10:41, 14:65, 71, 15:8, 18).

Lastly, Mark would have known that there was a great philosophical debate in Greek culture as to the origins of the world in the "Beginning". That debate led the ancient philosophers such as Anaximander, Aristotle, Thales of Miletus, and Anaximenes to consider the role played by the four fundamental elements of wind, fire, earth, and water in the process of creation. By starting his Gospel with the word "Beginning" and associating it with Jesus Christ, Mark is clearly saying that the true origin of all creation is not the mere interplay of basic elements of nature but the very person of Jesus Christ. In Him is our origin! These four meanings associated with the term "beginning" provide a profoundly rich way for Mark to start his writing. Jesus reveals to us the face of God, and through the establishment of His Kingdom shows us that a new order, a new creation, has indeed begun. The teachings of Jesus and His lived example serve as an enduring guide for Christians of all time. We are challenged by the story of Jesus when we realize that it is our responsibility to carry on what the Lord began. Finally, when we seek the deepest answers to life's questions and wonder why God created us, the answer is always found in a person—Jesus Christ.

Which of these four significances of the word "beginning" intrigues you the most and why?

In what part of your life would you like to have a new "beginning"?

In what part of your faith would you like to get "back to the basics"?

What is a ministry of Jesus that you think the Lord might be asking you to continue?

What are the philosophical questions you ask yourself, and how might you find your answers in the person of Jesus?

The second important word Mark uses in his title is that of "Gospel". This locution comes from the Greek words *eu* and *angellion* and means "Good News". Mark's community would have understood this term in two different ways. First, they would have understood it as a reference to the "Good News" promised by the prophet Isaiah in 40:9 and 52:7. These passages announced the "Good News" (also referred to as "Glad Tidings") that God would deliver the people of Israel from exile and lead them back to Jerusalem. In this action, God would manifest His mercy, redemption, and power to revive. Thus, Mark is announcing to the Christian community of Rome that Jesus is the one who fulfills the prophecy of Isaiah and redeems, restores, forgives, and leads God's people to new life through His ministry, passion, death, and resurrection.

Secondly, Mark's Christian community would have heard the phrase "Good News" in a secular sense as well. The term "Good News" was associated with actions of the Roman Emperor. For example, when Roman Emperors were victorious in battle they would send messengers to announce the "Good News" of victory. Also, an inscription from 9 BC referred to the birthday of the Emperor Augustus as being a cause of "Good News".

Now Mark is saying that Jesus, not the Roman Emperor, is the source and cause of all "Good News". This statement had powerful meaning for both religious and political reasons. Jesus brings to perfection God's redeeming, healing, restoring, and liberating work in our world, too. We are all exiled in a certain sense because sin can alienate us from our relationship with God and from becoming the persons God created us to be. Jesus can lead us back from our exile and alienation into the relationship and identity God desires for us all. That is good news! Also, while secular leaders and governments may affect our lives temporarily, Jesus is the one who accomplished an eternal victory over the forces of sin and death that tried to destroy Him—even the forces of imperial Rome. That too, is good news for those of us who know our need for a Savior.

When do you feel alienated from God?
When do you feel exiled from truly being yourself?

How can Jesus lead you to the fullness of life and integrity that both God and you desire?
When is it tempting to think that secular authorities can give us the good news for which we hunger?
If someone walked into your family and said, "I have good news for you and your family," what would you most want them to announce?
If someone walked into your professional life and said, "I have good news for you and your business," what would you most want them to announce?
If Jesus spoke to you in your prayer and said, "I have good news for you," what would you most want the Lord to say?
What is the Good News that God wants to bring to someone else through you?

The third important phrase Mark uses in his title is that of "Jesus Christ". The name of Jesus makes concrete and specific the person by whom God's redemptive re-creation will take place. It is important to remember that Christianity is not based on a philosophy, or historical event, or mythology (as was the case in pagan religions of the ancient world); rather, Christianity is based on a person—Jesus of Nazareth. In Jesus, the all-powerful God of heaven and earth became flesh and dwelt among us by becoming truly man. In Jesus, God is close to us and like us in all things but sin. The Christian message is always incomplete if it does not involve the person of Jesus. For this reason, relationship with Jesus is essential for a Christian disciple. The second part of this phrase is the identification of Jesus as the Christ. The word "Christ" in Greek, and "Messiah" in Hebrew," means "the Anointed One".

Mark is telling us that Jesus is the long-awaited Anointed One of God. The time of Jesus was ripe with messianic hope. Most of those hopes centered upon a Messiah who would be a new Moses liberating the people from the oppression of foreign powers, purifying their worship of God, and bringing about God's rightful reign. Mark is telling us that Jesus is that Messiah—not only in His miracles, successful teachings, and popular acclamation, but also in His betrayal, Passion, and Crucifixion. Jesus is the Messiah who leads us out of the slavery of sin by His obedience to the Father in all things, even the Cross (see Phil 2:8, Heb 5:8–9). Many people in Jesus' time were frustrated because He didn't act the way they thought the Messiah should act. Nonetheless, Mark assures us in this opening statement that Jesus is the Anointed One of God and that God has fulfilled His promise to send the Messiah.

> *Christianity necessarily requires a personal relationship with Jesus. How and when do you experience this relationship in your life?*
>
> *While people expected a Messiah, no one expected that God would become one of us (truly man) in the Incarnation of Jesus. Why do you think God chose to share in our human nature?*
>
> *Jesus offers us the gifts of freedom from sin, true worship in spirit and truth, and participation in divine life. Which of these Messianic gifts most appeal to you?*
>
> *How can our limited expectations of Jesus today prevent us from entering into relationship with Him?*

Lastly, Mark refers to Jesus as the "Son of God". While this title could have referred to a righteous person in Judaism, it was counter-cultural and politically charged in the environment of imperial Rome. Roman emperors claimed for themselves divine titles and believed that they were gods. Temples were erected to Julius Caesar, Caligula, Nero, Domitian, Hadrian, and others. It was a direct challenge to imperial authority to say that Jesus is the Son of God—and not the emperor in Rome! Jesus was not born in a palace; He did not command millions of soldiers, but He is greater than all the power this world can muster. He alone is the Son of God. His sovereignty will be made manifest in His complete surrender to the will of the Father, and His royal dignity will be found in His self-giving rather than His self-seeking. Indeed, Jesus will ultimately be correctly recognized as the Son of God by the Roman Centurion only when He offers Himself on the Cross for our salvation (see Mk 15:39). Jesus reveals the face of God who lovingly suffers for us and whose power is displayed in His forgiveness and redemption.

> *Who tries to take the place of God in our world today?*
>
> *How could the reminder that "Jesus is the Son of God" be a challenge to our current cultural or political world?*

Where in our world is the message of Christianity consid-
ered counter-cultural and even revolutionary, as the first
line of Mark's Gospel states?

Mark indicates that in Jesus the transcendent and omnip-
otent God, creator of Heaven and earth, is present. How
does this claim affect the way you will read the Gospel?

As you have reflected on the various terms Mark chose
to use in his opening phrase, which term do you want to
understand in greater depth and why?

Advent is a time of anticipation and preparation. How
does this announcement in Mark's Gospel increase your
anticipation and desire to meet Jesus or motivate your
preparedness for the Lord?

THIRD SUNDAY OF ADVENT

Our Scripture passage for this Third Sunday of Advent comes from the Gospel of John 1:6–8 and 19–28. This reading introduces John the Baptist and his ministry as a witness of faith. John is an effective witness because he possesses three essential qualities of an authentic disciple. He is honest about who he is not, he acknowledges who Jesus is, and he establishes his identity in relation to Jesus.

It is interesting that the first words spoken in the Gospel of John are in the form of a question: "Who are you?" That question hangs over the entire Gospel and challenges us for an answer as well. This fundamental question is part of the human search for meaning, identity, and relationship. As people of faith, disciples answer this question, not out of self-determination or social convention, but in the context of a living faith relationship with Jesus Christ. That is why the ministry of John is introduced as that of a "witness" who gives testimony about Jesus. These are legal terms (witness and testimony) and are present through the Gospel of John. Indeed, the Gospel of John is putting us on trial by presenting us with the Truth of Jesus. Our response to that Truth determines whether we are saved or condemned (Jn 3:16–18). Like John, we are called to be disciples who bear witness to Jesus in every situation we face. Sometimes we bear witness by allowing our decisions to be guided by the values of the Gospel. At other times we bear witness by sharing our faith and telling others about the movement of God in our lives. We also witness our faith when we confront what is contrary to the Gospel. Likewise, we end up denying the Lord when we fail to be witnesses in each of these circumstances. We are on "trial" every day!

> *When someone asks you the question, "Who are you?" how do you typically answer?*
> *When have you seen someone be a witness of faith in the most unlikely of contexts?*

11

*How can you practically, faithfully, realistically, or reason-
ably be a witness to Jesus in your family life and marriage?
How can you practically, faithfully, realistically, or reason-
ably be a witness to Jesus in your professional life?
When are you questioned about your values or decisions?
Have you ever answered in terms of your faith beliefs or
your relationship with Jesus?
The Greek word for "witness" is martyria, which gives us
the English word "martyr"; indeed, true martyrs are people
who are steadfast witnesses of Jesus even unto death. How
do people today misuse the term "martyr" and how are
authentic witnesses of Christian faith mistreated in our
world?*

John first answers the question "Who are you?" by stating clearly
who he is not. Just imagine how easy it would have been for John
to claim for himself this great role so as to gain the honor and
respect of the crowd as well as the messengers from Jerusalem.
John possessed an honest humility and those qualities allowed him
to dismiss false identities no matter how appealing they may have
been. The first important aspect of being a witness is to dismiss
our false senses of self and to clearly acknowledge who we are not.
Sometimes it is tempting to want others to believe that we are
more competent than we are, or that our lives (and relationships)
are without difficulty. It can also be tempting to want others to
see us as people who are somehow better than the rest in one way
or another—holier, wealthier, happier, or more successful. These
temptations can lead us to project and even believe in a false self.
We can also find ourselves believing in a false self because of the
erroneous messages we receive through the media, advertising,
magazine images, or other influences from the world around us.
These external influences can lead us to think that we are inherently
damaged or flawed in some way, and as a result, we can develop a
poor self-image that seeks material goods, products, relationships,
or physical beauty to be happy or loveable. Sometimes, too, people
can have a false sense of self that is based on weakness, failure,
or even an injury caused by another person—these, too, are false
identities. True and honest humility dismisses both false identities
of superiority as well as inferiority.

> *What are some of the false identities of superiority that delude people today?*
>
> *What are some of the false identities of inferiority that delude people today?*
>
> *When are you tempted to allow others to believe something about you that is not true?*
>
> *When have you been tempted to believe something about yourself that is not true?*
>
> *How can having a false sense of self prevent us from being a true disciple?*
>
> *What helps a person develop authentic humility so as to have the freedom and detachment expressed in the life of John the Baptist?*

The second thing John does is to correctly acknowledge who Jesus is. Earlier in the Gospel of John, Jesus was identified as the "Word" that became flesh and dwelt among us (Jn 1:14); Jesus was also referred to as the "Light" that shone in the darkness and the darkness has not overcome it (Jn 1:5). Now John calls Jesus the "Lord"—a title indicating Jesus' divine identity. John further indicates that Jesus is the "Master" whose sandal he is not worthy to untie. All these acknowledgements are true statements of who Jesus is. Throughout the Gospel of John, we will read about many people who will fail to recognize Jesus as the presence of God in their midst. Instead, they will only understand Jesus in limited terms as a king or prophet. John the Baptist cannot be a true witness unless he correctly acknowledges the fullness of Jesus' divine identity. Anything less would be a false witness and would impede his discipleship. The same is true for us. Sometimes we can have images of Jesus that fall short of confessing the reality of His divine identity. If we only see Jesus as a friend, teacher, or a miracle worker who is there to take away our difficulty, then we have misunderstood our Lord's deepest identity. It is even socially acceptable today to refer to Jesus as a great ethical leader, social activist, or philosopher. When our understanding of Jesus is formed only by these limited expressions of His identity then we have tried to "tame" and "contain" His person and message. The Lord cannot be tamed or contained! Jesus is the eternal Word of God who reveals the Father to us; He is the Light of God that shines in our darkness; He is the Lord who directs every part of a disciple's life.

When are you most aware of Jesus as the eternal Son of God?
How does Jesus reveal the face of God to you?
How does Jesus illumine your life with His Divine Light?
What part of your life is easy to submit to Jesus' Lordship?
What part of your life is difficult to submit to Jesus' Lordship?
What are the incomplete images of Jesus that can cause disciples to fall short in acknowledging Jesus' true divine nature?

The third thing John does is to define himself only in relationship to Jesus. Jesus is the Light of the World, and John is the lamp. Jesus is the Eternal Word, and John is the voice. Jesus is the Master, and John is the servant. Jesus is the Truth, and John is the witness. John's true self is found in relationship to Jesus, and that is what allowed John's testimony to be authentic and true. As human beings, we do not exist in isolation but in relationship. As Christian disciples, we are called to ground our identity in relationship to Jesus first and foremost. This is a relationship that exists beyond Sunday morning; it affects how we see ourselves in the office, with our friends, in the presence of our families, and even in our interaction with strangers. Sometimes we can be tempted to form our identity in other relationships instead. Some people allow their possessions, positions, or friends define who they are. Others allow their work or even hobbies and sports define who they are. Disciples are called to be clear about the fact that our true identity is formed only in our relationship to God. Every other part of our lives must flow from that divine source of meaning. If anything is more important than our relationship with God then we have become idolatrous. That is why John could only come to know himself by first shedding his false identity and acknowledging Jesus' true identity.

What does it feel like for you to form your identity only in relationship to Jesus?
What relationship in your life most forms your identity?

What can you do during this time of Advent to become more conscious of your relationship with Jesus?

John used the images of "Word/Voice", "Light/Lamp", and "Master/Servant" to describe his relationship with Jesus. What are images that you would use to describe your relationship with the Lord?

In the Gospel of John there are seven times when Jesus describes His own identity with the words "I AM" (The Bread of Life—6:35; The Light of the World—8:12; The Sheepgate—10:9; The Good Shepherd—10:11; The Resurrection and the Life—11:25; The Way, the Truth, and the Life—14:6; and The True Vine—15:1) Which of these identification statements of Jesus helps you to better understand your own identity in relationship to Him?

FOURTH SUNDAY OF ADVENT

O ur Scripture passage for the Fourth Sunday of Advent comes from the Gospel of Luke 1:26–38. In this reading we are presented with the person of Mary as a model for us in our Advent preparation. This passage is oftentimes referred to as the "Annunciation" because it tells of the angel Gabriel "announcing" to Mary the role she is asked to fulfill in God's saving work. As disciples who desire to hear the Word of God and do it in our own lives, we have much to learn from the faithful example demonstrated in the Blessed Mother of Jesus who said "yes" to the will of God in her life.

The opening line of this passage contains a sequence of names and places beginning with that of the angel Gabriel who is sent "from God". That is a powerful statement in itself: Somebody great is being sent from some place great. But then the passage continues to state that Gabriel was sent to a town of Galilee called Nazareth and to a virgin. We have to remember that Galilee was in a remote part of the Jewish world and that Nazareth was an absolute no-place village. We also have to remember that a woman in Jesus' time had a place in society through the men in her life (husband or children). Thus, to be a virgin living in Nazareth was to be a no-body in a no-place part of the world! The last thing we are told is that the virgin's name was Mary. This passage is good news for Mary and good news for us. What made Mary great and what makes us great is not the world in which we live or our own call to fame, but rather God's invitation and action in our lives.

The Gospel is about God and not about us. It's about what God can do and not what we can do. Sometimes we can expect God to have certain criteria for those whom He chooses and works through. We can think that God will choose the holy ones, those with special talents or significant accomplishments, or even those who hold special offices. Mary had none of that but God chose her to be His instrument of salvation by becoming the mother of His Son. That's the good news of this passage because throughout history God is going to call the most unlikely candidates to special roles in the work of salvation. Who could be more unlikely to lead the charitable renewal of the Church in the 20th century than a little nun teaching in Calcutta; by the way, her name was Mother Teresa. Who could be more unlikely to found the parochial school system in America than a poor widow and mother; by the way, her name was Elizabeth Ann Seton. In the same way, God wants us to be His instruments not because we deserve that role or have earned that role or are even qualified for that role; rather, God chooses us because in our lowliness His power can shine. The name "Gabriel" means "God is my strength"; Mary knew her lowliness and because of that humble self-awareness, she could give credit to God for the Lord's greatness in her life.

> *When do you feel undeserving of God's grace in your life?*
> *When have you felt poorly-prepared for something you sensed God was inspiring you to do?*
> *Why do you think God likes to choose no-body people from no-place parts of the world to be His instruments?*
> *How can you spiritually dispose yourself in the example of Mary so as to offer your life as an instrument of God's work in the world?*

The greeting of Gabriel is worthy of note as well. The archangel says to Mary, "Hail Graced One". This greeting prompts us to ask the question: Why was Mary the "graced one"? Gabriel explains his greeting by stating that Mary has found favor with God. This grace is not something she accomplished but a state of being with which the Lord gifted her. She was graced so as to be a worthy mother for the Son of God. God created her and "graced" her for a particular mission in the world and yet the Lord must ask her permission before entrusting her with that mission. That is the dilemma of discipleship. God graces us with talents, possibilities, opportunities, skills, and other blessings for a reason—namely, to accomplish a divinely intended mission in the world. Out of respect for our free will, God first asks our permission to use our lives.

It takes real courage to actually hear God asking something of us that is different from what we were already planning for ourselves. Think of Mary, she was betrothed to Joseph and had her life dreams all planned out; then God asked her to take on a special mission that would disrupt those dreams. She was graced not for her own self-pursuit but for the mission God wanted to accomplish. How easy it is for us to use our talents, opportunities, possibilities, and skills for our own desires and personal pursuits but how difficult it is for us to let those same gifts be used for God's will. Mary had the ability to be truly "obedient" to God. The word "obedience" means to listen with an attentive and responsive heart to the Lord. It means to hear the Word of God and to act on it. Gabriel tells Mary, "Nothing will be impossible for God." Indeed, if God can enter into the human world as a child, be raised from the dead, and empower the Church with the Holy Spirit then nothing will be impossible for God.

> *With what opportunities, skills, possibilities, or talents do you believe God has graced you?*
> *How do you relate to Mary who had to let go of her own dreams in order to do what God wanted in her life?*
> *What challenge or situation causes you to wonder whether God will act—or even can act—in the midst of it?*
> *God respects our free will and asks our permission to work in our lives and through our lives to accomplish His will. What do you think would have been the consequence if Mary had said "No" instead of "Yes"?*

The final response of Mary is to declare: "I am the servant of the Lord; be it done unto me according to your word." This is a meaningful statement on several levels. First, Mary identifies herself as a servant of God whose purpose is to do the Lord's will. Second, she opens herself so that the "Word" of God can act in her life. As a servant of the Lord, Mary is taking on the identity of God's Servant as expressed by the Prophet Isaiah (49:3, 50:4, 10, 52:13). She is assuming within herself the identity of the people of Israel and is placing her life in service of the Lord. This in itself is a powerful statement. So many times we perceive our relationship with God as a personal and private experience; Mary understood her relationship with God as intimately connected with all the people of Israel. She knew that the mission entrusted to her was not only for her own benefit but that all humanity would be blessed because of her service to God. When she opens herself to the "Word" of God, she agrees to be the mother of Jesus. But, her "yes" also signals a far greater commitment of faith. We know the greatness of this event because when Luke writes "[Be it done unto me] according to your 'word'", he indicates that using the Greek term *rhema* (thing or reality) rather than *logos* (word or message about something). This means that Mary is saying "yes" not just to being the mother of the baby Jesus but to the entire Jesus event which will include His Ministry, Death, and Resurrection. That is a tremendous assent! Indeed, Mary is basically writing a blank check of her life to God. Whatever God will ask of her in relationship to Jesus, she is now ready to accept—even though she doesn't know what that will be. Her assent to the angel Gabriel will eventually lead her to the cross of Calvary and beyond. What a powerful commitment of faith and what an inspiring example for us on this Fourth Sunday of Advent!

> *When have you received a challenge or mission in your life that was difficult to accept?*
> *In which situations are you constantly asked to say "yes" in spite of your own desires?*
> *What are the factors that motivate you to embrace a mission with great generosity?*
> *In what area of your life do you have difficulty letting go of your will so as to accept something you know is better— something that God wants for you?*
> *For whom have you written a "blank check" with your life?*

FEAST OF THE HOLY FAMILY

This Sunday we celebrate the Feast of the Holy Family of Jesus, Mary, and Joseph. Our Scripture reading comes from the Gospel of Luke 2:22–40. In this passage, we read about the Holy Family going to the Temple in Jerusalem for the appropriate religious rituals following the birth of a child. This passage offers several points of reflection for us as we apply its message to our own families and especially to the Church as the Family of God.

In this passage we are told that Mary and Joseph took Jesus to Jerusalem to "present him to the Lord." The quotation from Exodus 13:2 does indeed state that the firstborn male child is to be consecrated to the Lord. In practice parents were able to "redeem" their child with a payment of five shekels so as to receive the child back as their own (Nm 3:47–48, 18:15–16). What is missing from this passage is the payment of the five shekels. Jesus remains consecrated to God and is not "redeemed" by His parents. Scripture scholars differ on whether or not the omission of the redemption payment is intentional by the Gospel writer and the possible significance of that omission. It certainly is consistent with the rest of the Gospel that Jesus' life belongs to God the Father rather than to any earthly authority, including His own parents.

In the Sacrament of Baptism we become consecrated to God as well and are established as a Temple of the Holy Spirit. We are also adopted into the Family of God, and because of that adopted status we can call God our "Father" in the midst of the Church. Following our Baptism, we are then "entrusted" to our parents to be raised—but always as a child of God. Once children have been consecrated to God in Baptism, our challenge is then to raise them according to the will of their Heavenly Father. By allowing Jesus to live His life in an unending consecration to God, Mary and Joseph are giving all Christian parents an inspirational example for their families as well. We belong to God before we belong to anyone else.

Families who understand the significance of this enduring consecration to God will raise their children according to the values of
the Gospel rather than the values of consumerism and secularism.
These families will teach their children how to be children of God
rather than children of the world.

> *What does it mean for you to know that you were conse-*
> *crated to God in your Baptism?*
> *What are ways in which we try to "take back" our lives after*
> *we have been consecrated to God?*
> *How can we help our children know that God is their Father*
> *in a practical and meaningful way?*
> *How can we renew our consecration to God?*
> *What would be different about our participation in Sun-*
> *day worship if we were more conscious of our consecrated*
> *identity?*

While the Holy Family was in the Temple precincts, they encountered two people who praised Jesus: Simeon and Anna. Simeon
specifically identifies Jesus as the long-awaited Messiah, the Source
of Peace, the Glory of Israel, the Light of the Gentiles, and the
Salvation of the World. Anna is said to have praised Jesus with
similar words, and we are told that she "kept saying" these things,
which means that her communication was an ongoing action. That
means Anna talked about Jesus to others and helped to spread the
message of who He was to the world. Anna appears in the Gospel of
Luke as an evangelist and a missionary much like the women at the
tomb who spread the message of Jesus' resurrection (Lk 24:9–10).
Simeon and Anna give us examples of how to be good members of
the Christian community. They were able to "unwrap" the identity
and mission of Jesus within God's plan of salvation for the world.

Mary and Joseph marveled at these words that were spoken of
their son and pondered over these sayings. Simeon and Anna are
good examples of how members of the Christian community (the
Family of God) can help our youth grow in their understanding of
faith and identity as disciples through our interaction with them.
Indeed, we need people today who can help our youth understand
and unwrap their identity and mission within God's plan of salvation. As an ancient proverb reminds us, "It takes two to have a

child and a whole community to raise a child." Sometimes we lose sight of the responsibility we have to influence the lives of others in the ways of faith—even those members of our community who are not our family or friends. We are all called to help encourage one another to grow in our Christian identity and accept our life mission in Christ.

> *Who has helped you to understand the meaning of your life in Christ?*
> *Who needs you to speak a message of faithful encouragement and inspiration to them?*
> *What are simple ways in which you can encourage and support children in their Christian discipleship?*
> *Simeon pronounced his words in response to the movement of the Holy Spirit. What does the Holy Spirit prompt you to do or say for the good of others?*
> *Anna "kept saying" wonderful things about Jesus to others. How can you esteem members of the Christian community in your conversations with others?*
> *What is it that you "keep saying" to people; is it a message of faith, encouragement, and praise of God's will, or do you "keep saying" a different message?*

One of the most misunderstood parts of this passage is the communication between Simeon and Mary when he speaks of Jesus being destined for the fall and rise of many, as a sign that will be contradicted, and that even Mary will experience the "piercing sword". These events are all connected. In order to understand the message of what it means to "fall" and "rise", we have to imagine a stone that can either serve to trip people (fall) or to become the cornerstone of the Church (rise). Throughout the Gospel we see people who are "falling" and "rising" in their response to Jesus. Jesus will indeed be a sign that many will dispute, resist, and oppose and we see this opposition throughout the Gospel of Luke (4:29, 13:33–35, 19:44, 47–48, 20:14, 17). Indeed, everyone must make a decision of faith when confronted with the person of Jesus. That is why a "sword will pierce" even Mary. She too must experience a personal confrontation of faith so as to become a disciple and not just a mother. Luke develops a wonderful teaching about Mary in his Gospel by depicting her as both the mother of the Lord and an exemplary disciple.

The image of a sword as the instrument of decision and judgment is richly developed in the Old Testament (see Ez 5:1–2, 6:8–9) and in Christian spirituality (St. Augustine, St. Gregory the Great, and St. Teresa of Avila). Even for Mary, obedience to the Word of God must be more important than the affection of family ties (see Lk 12:51–53). Luke reaffirms twice in his Gospel that Mary's greatness is not primarily because of her maternal connection to Jesus but due to her discipleship (see Lk 8:21 and Lk 11:28). If Mary had to make a personal decision for discipleship and a commitment of faith to Jesus, then we certainly have to do so as well. Jesus will be for us either a stumbling stone to the life we choose for ourselves or the cornerstone upon whom we build a life consecrated to God. The message of the Gospel will either oppose the opinions we hold or it will be the means by which our opinions are formed. And we, too, will face moments when we decide in a deeply personal and radical way whether we will relate to Jesus as the Lord of every part of our lives or whether we limit that relationship to only one part of our lives.

> *When does the message of the Gospel become a stumbling stone that stands in* the way of something you want to pursue?
>
> *It is an act of God's mercy (and our salvation) to "trip us up" when we are on the wrong path. What does this statement mean to you?*
>
> *As you have grown in your commitment to Jesus, how has the Lord and the message of the Gospel become a cornerstone in your life?*
>
> *What did you have to re-arrange in order for the Lord to occupy the central place in your life?*
>
> *What have been some of the moments in your life when you were pierced by the sword of discernment and had to make a radical decision for or against Jesus?*
>
> *As you apply the sword of God's Word to situations you face now, how does that sword of discernment help cut through the complexity of decisions you face?*

One of the final things to note about this passage is how frequently Luke tells us that the Holy Family took great care to fulfill the Law of the Lord (see also: Lk 22, 23, 24, 27 and 39). This was not a blind obedience to religious rules but rather a conscientious observance and integration of God's will into their daily lives. For Jesus, Mary, and Joseph, being a family of faith meant living out that faith in religious practices, customs, and other observances. Their actions were an expression of their love for God. Our contemporary culture tries to disassociate faith from expression. This trend can be observed even in these holy days of Christmas when greetings of "Happy Holidays" are expected and greetings of "Merry Christmas" can bring about a moment of awkwardness. We see this cultural disassociation further manifested when faith is reduced to a matter of mere sentiment or opinion rather than a matter of conviction with clear guiding principles that affect a person's personal, social, and professional life. We can even see this cultural disassociation manifested when freedom of religion (how a person lives through the week) is reduced to freedom of worship (how a person prays on Sunday). The lived example of the Holy Family of Jesus, Mary, and Joseph encourages us to observe the Lord's will in all that we do whether in the private world of our family or in the public world of our professional lives.

> *How often do you evaluate your actions in light of God's Law?*
>
> *What religious practices, customs, or other observances are a part of your family's expression of faith?*
>
> *What religious practices, customs, or other observances most help you remain connected to the presence of God in your life?*
>
> *When have you seen families ridiculed for their religious observance of the Law of the Lord?*
>
> *The Holy Family had a truly remarkable day when they went to the Temple in Jerusalem. How does your regular attendance at Sunday Mass enrich and bless your family?*

SOLEMNITY OF THE EPIPHANY

Our Scripture passage for this Sunday comes from the Gospel of Matthew 2:1–12. In this passage, we read the well-known story of the Magi who visit the child Jesus in Bethlehem and bring gifts of gold, frankincense, and myrrh. This passage offers some good points for our reflection and prayer.

One of the first things to note is that this passage contains the first words actually spoken by any person in Matthew's Gospel. The Gospel writers were careful to use the first words to establish a theme for their writing. Thus, the first spoken question, "Where is the newborn King of the Jews?" is a theme that will resonate throughout Matthew's Gospel. To be a king in the Jewish world was not just a political position of power. The Jewish people believed that God alone was their king and that any human regent had the responsibility to represent God. The people looked to the king to manifest God's justice, mercy, wisdom, and protection. The Magi were seeking the face of God in human representation, and they didn't find it in Herod.

Herod represented ruthless power and political cunning (he even executed three of his own sons). Throughout the Gospel of Matthew, Jesus will show us the face of the Father and in doing so He will authentically serve as God's perfect representative to the people. In witness to that authentic and complete representation, Jesus will properly be hailed as "King of the Jews" when He dies on Calvary. Through his self-centered, untamed, and ambitious pursuit of power, Herod caused others to suffer. Jesus suffered for others and opened the doors of God's mercy and forgiveness through His death and resurrection. Each of us in our baptism has received the commission to carry on the kingly ministry of Jesus. That means we are to be God's authentic representatives to the people with whom we interact.

Do people see Herod or Jesus in us?
Who represents the face of God to you?

Who looks to you to be a minister of God's justice, mercy,
truth, wisdom, or protection?
In what settings are you a good representative of God?
In what settings do you find it most difficult to live out the
royal mission of your baptism?
If someone approached you and asked, "Where can I find
the King of the Jews?" what would you say to them?

Another interesting thing to note is that the wise men do not come to visit the babe in the manger. Rather, we are specifically told that they come to visit the child Jesus. That is a very significant difference between searching for a babe and searching for a child. The Greek word used for "child" (Greek: *paidon*) refers to someone three to seven years old, not an "infant" (Greek: *brephos*). That means that the wise men were journeying for years! That took perseverance. They did not go on a weekend pilgrimage or visit for just an hour on Sunday morning. What they did was a journey of life and faith that required commitment and resolve. For years they were wandering, looking for Jesus until they found Him. They were seekers who were not deterred by the lack of immediate results for their efforts. That is an important message for us because sometimes we can become frustrated in our faith life if we do not sense immediate results to our prayer or at least the effects of God's presence. We live in a culture of immediate gratification and can easily lose patience or interest when our efforts are not immediately successful. The example of the Magi should inspire and edify us to examine our own lives as disciples and identify ways in which we have allowed our expectation for immediate results to deter us from our commitment to Christ. If the Magi could search for years, certainly we can persevere during difficult and dry times of prayer as well. The Gospels are full of stories of people who persevered in their desire to encounter Jesus. Many of these people had to overcome the objection of the crowds, the cultural expectations of others, and even their own shame in order to finally meet the Lord. Certainly the example of these Magi and the people of perseverant faith are presented for good reason, so we will not give up or lose hope in our discipleship.

> *When has the expectation for immediate results affected your resolve in prayer or discipleship?*
> *What is a grace or gift from God that you have been seeking for years?*
> *Who is an example of faithful perseverance for you?*
> *How can a faith community help people who struggle to find Jesus?*
> *Why do you think it took the Magi years to find the Lord?*

The gifts the Magi brought are all symbolic statements of who Jesus is. Gold is the gift proper for a King. Frankincense was offered during sacrifices by the High Priest to God in the Temple of Jerusalem. Myrrh was used as a perfume in the burial preparation of a body. Thus, the identity of Jesus is manifested in these three gifts: He is King, God (and/or High Priest) and Man (someone who will die). In one way or another, each of us makes the statement of who Jesus is to us based on the gifts we offer from our lives. For some, Jesus is a small part of their lives whose reign extends only to an hour on Sunday morning. Such a limited understanding of Jesus will be reflected in an equally limited gift of one's life to the Lord. For others, Jesus is the Lord of their lives twenty-four hours a day and seven days a week. Such a comprehensive understanding of Jesus will likewise be reflected in an all-encompassing gift of one's life to the Lord. We tend to give a person the gift that is appropriate because we believe they deserve it and that they can use it.

> *When it comes to Jesus, what does the Lord deserve from your life?*
> *Who is Jesus to you?*
> *How do you manifest your faith in Jesus through the gifts you offer Him?*
> *What are the gifts you offer to the Lord for Him to use?*

The star has historically been interpreted as a symbol for the light of faith leading people to Christ. For each person the path to Christ is unique and personal yet there are some common elements. For example, some people are led to seek God through the wonder of nature (the natural sciences). Others are led to seek God through events of salvation in their lives. Still others are led to seek God because of the influence of another person of faith. God reveals

Himself to us in a variety of ways, but there comes a point where we need to consult the Scriptures to really learn who God is through the person of Jesus. A story is told about St. Francis of Assisi who took Lady Poverty to a hill and said to her, "This, Lady, is our cloister."[1] By this he meant, "The world is the place where we encounter God." Regardless of what events may have initiated our journey of faith, Scripture is a necessary step in the growth of our faith and knowledge process of completing that journey and fully grasping the truth of who God is. That is why the Magi could not complete their journey until the Scriptures were consulted. The Word of God in Scripture sheds light on our experiences of faith and more clearly reveals to us the reality of God working in our lives. When we read the Scriptures, we grow in understanding and our eyes are opened to see clearly the character of God. We also unleash the power of God's Word in our hearts when we read the Scriptures. The Letter to the Hebrews attests that the Word of God is alive and powerful and that it can accomplish great things in our lives when we encounter it (Heb 4:12).

> *How has the study of Scripture opened your heart and mind in new ways?*
> *What have you learned about God through your reflection on the Word that you did not previously understand just based on your personal experience or the experience of others?*
> *What was the "light" that led you to desire to meet Jesus in a deeper and more personal way?*
> *Who is someone you know that is searching in the darkness, and how can you be a light to them?*
> *What can you do to foster your love for the Word of God in Scripture and share that love with your family and friends?*

Lastly, one cannot help but think about the contrast between the Magi and Herod. Herod had all the knowledge of Scripture but did not seek Jesus. The Magi were gentiles who searched in the darkness without the knowledge of Scripture but were willing to

---

1.   *Sacrum Commercium sancti Francisci cum domina Paupertate,* Ed. Stefano Brufani (Assisi: Edizioni Porziuncola, 1990), chap. 30, ed. 173.

travel far distances to meet this newborn king of whom they only had vague knowledge. Herod saw Jesus as a threat to his way of life. The Magi saw Jesus as the source of a new and deeper life. Herod lived comfortably in his palace in Jerusalem. The Magi wandered through cold nights and long days to fulfill their journey of faith. Herod had so much but gave nothing. The Magi had only what they could carry, but they gave everything they had. When it comes to our life of faith, Herod represents that attitude that tries to put God in the passenger seat while we control our own destinies. As the saying goes, "If God is your co-pilot, then it's time to trade places." Herod had no interest in trading places. The Magi, on the other hand, were eager to pay homage to the true Lord and King of their lives. Herod was unchanged by the birth of Jesus. The Magi were transformed by their encounter with Jesus and even returned home by another way from the way they came.

When does the message of the Gospel become uncomfortable or challenging for you?

When have you gone outside of your comfort zone to serve the Lord?

What do you admire most about the Magi and their journey of faith?

What aspect of Herod do you find most troubling?

What experience of God in your life has most changed you such that you became a different person because of that experience?

Jesus offers Himself to us in every Eucharist we celebrate. How can the attitude of Herod creep into our thoughts and prayers at Mass?

It's interesting that one of the most common images of early Christian art in the catacombs of Rome is that of the three Magi worshiping Jesus. Why do you think the early Christians of Rome identified with the Magi so strongly during the times of persecution?

FEAST OF THE BAPTISM OF THE LORD

This Sunday we celebrate the Feast of the Baptism of the Lord. Each year we read a different version of this moment in the life of Jesus and gain distinctive insights from the Gospel. This year our Scripture reading comes from the Gospel of Mark 1:7–11. This passage tells us of Jesus' Baptism by John in the Jordan River. There are some significant elements to this passage that are worthy of our reflection so we can have a deeper appreciation of our own Baptism as well.

It is significant that Jesus came from Nazareth while John was in the desert (Mk 1:4) and baptizing in the Jordan River. One of the expectations of the Messiah was that he would lead the people through a new Exodus and establish a new relationship with God. The first Exodus occurred when Moses led the Hebrews out of Egypt, and for forty years they wandered in the desert before reaching the Jordan River and entering the Promised Land. Now, John has gone to the desert to prepare a people for the new Exodus. It is in this context that Jesus appears on the scene and joins with the people so as to lead them into that new relationship. Jesus is Baptized not because He needs forgiveness of sins (see 2 Cor 5:21) but as an expression of His solidarity with our sinful human condition. Jesus is the Messiah who leads by example and who paves the way for us to follow. Throughout the Gospel we will read about how Jesus associated with the sinners and tax collectors so as to lead them in a new way of life and a new relationship with God. It is not surprising that Jesus initiates His ministry by standing in solidarity with those who are being Baptized in an act of repentance.

When have you chosen to stand by someone who was undergoing the difficult task of leaving behind a sinful or destructive way of life so as to enter into a new relationship with God?
What does it mean to you that Jesus stands with you even in your sinful condition?

Where in your life do you sense the Lord trying to lead you into a more committed discipleship?

Jesus leads by example and expects us to follow. What parts of Jesus' life do you desire to follow and which parts do you find yourself not wanting to follow?

Our Baptism is meant to be our incorporation into the new People of God, the Church.

What happens when people try to live their discipleship individually rather than as part of a community of faith?

Mark tells us that at the moment of Jesus' Baptism our Lord saw the heavens "tear open". That is a significant statement. It means that in the Baptism of Jesus, there is a new possibility of communication between God and Man (see Ez 1:1 and Jn 1:51). The Prophet Isaiah foretold that one day the heavens would be "torn open" and that God would descend to be with His people (Is 64:1). Indeed, Jesus has opened a new possibility of communication by bringing the compassion and forgiveness of God to the world. We now have an access to God that was not possible before Jesus' life and ministry. So many people who met Jesus only saw the actions of a wise teacher, miracle worker, prophet, or inspirational leader, but Christians see in Jesus the very actions of God in our world.

When do the heavens open for you in such a way that you experience a privileged communication and communion with God?

What is the connection Jesus makes in your prayer life with God?

For whom do you pray the heavens will open so they can be in deeper communion with God?

In our Baptism, we are united with Jesus in His relationship to the Father. What particular part of Jesus' mission do you think God has entrusted to you to be carried out in our world?

Baptism causes a permanent change in our relationship with God, but this new relationship has to be lived out and realized each day. How do you express and deepen this gift of new relationship with God?

Finally, there is a symbolic relationship between the Baptism and the Jordan that is worthy of reflection. Geographically, the Jordan River connects the Sea of Galilee and the Dead Sea. These two great bodies of water could not be more different from one another. The Sea of Galilee is a place of abundant life, commerce, and community while the Dead Sea is stagnant, lifeless, and isolated (although the Dead Sea today is a bustling place of industry and tourism, it was mostly deserted during the time of Jesus and when the Gospels were written). The Sea of Galilee receives its water from the surrounding land and then gives that water to create the Jordan River. The Dead Sea, on the other hand, receives the fresh water of the Jordan but keeps it for itself. While the natural processes of water flow do not involve free will, it does not take much effort to see in these two bodies of water a certain symbolic lesson of discipleship. We can be like the Sea of Galilee or we can be like the Dead Sea. Ultimately we stand somewhere in the Jordan River—the place of our Baptism—and must make the decision to either "go with the flow" and end up following the self-centered destructive secular values of greed, hedonism, and indifference or to "fight the current" and follow the values of the Gospel that teach generosity, self-sacrifice, and fidelity to the will of God. It's easy to end up in the Dead Sea; it takes real dedication, perseverance, and intentionality to arrive in the Sea of Galilee.

> *How does this reflection challenge your discipleship?*
> *When does your Baptism call you to "fight the secular current" you face?*
> *What are ways in which people can "go with the flow" in their marriages, families, and professional lives and end up where they do not want to be?*
> *How do you realize that you are beginning to 'drift' in to the Dead Sea?*
> *What are the tell-tale signs you are not where the Lord wants you?*

FIRST SUNDAY OF LENT

Our Scripture passage comes from the Gospel of Mark 1:12–15. In these verses we read the simple yet meaningful message of Jesus being tempted in the desert. As we begin our Lenten Time of prayer, self-denial (fasting), and good works (alms-giving), this text offers some important insights to direct our spiritual growth during the next forty days.

By going to the desert to be tested for forty days, Jesus is participating in a well-established tradition of Israelite history. The Hebrew people themselves were tested in the desert for forty years and it was through that experience that they learned fidelity, trust, and how to live as a people who have a covenant relationship with God. However, the Exodus in the desert was not an idyllic experience for the Hebrew people. It was also a place where they manifested periods of rebellion, idolatry, and disobedience. Moses went to the desert and fasted for forty days on Mount Sinai (Dt 9:18). Elijah also fasted for forty days near Mount Horeb (1 Kgs 19:8). The testing that Jesus experienced in the desert was a test of character. He had to demonstrate His resolute preparedness to be the Anointed Son of God and carry out the Good News of God's presence in the world. Thus, the desert (or wilderness) is the place where prophets prepare for their mission (testing), where the people learn to overcome their rebellious tendencies and where God's love is renewed through revelation and covenant relationship. By triumphing over Satan's testing, Jesus shows that He is the Just One who remains faithful rather than the one who gives in to sin and rebellion in the face of trial or temptation (see Wis 2:12–20, 5:1–23). The fundamental temptation of the Old Testament is commonly presented as lack of trust in the Word of God. We see this fundamental temptation surfacing in the original sin of Adam and Eve in Genesis and in the Israelites wandering in the desert when they thought that God had led them there to die. By going to the desert immediately after His Baptism, Jesus is teaching us that as Christian disciples we are to prepare ourselves by turning towards

God, trusting God's Word, and finding our security in our fidelity
to the Lord rather than in our earthly success. For all disciples,
when we turn "towards" the Lord, then we must inevitably turn
"away" from sin and all other influences that would lead us away
from God. The desert is the place where God reveals Himself, tests
His servants to strengthen them, and manifests His providence
and love; the desert is also a place of vulnerability and aloneness.

> *How have you experienced these dimensions of the "desert"*
> *in your life?*
> *What growth in discipleship do you want to occur in your*
> *life during these Forty Days of Lent?*
> *When is your character as a disciple tested?*
> *From what is God asking you to turn away in your life so*
> *you can grow closer to the Lord?*
> *What practices help make Lent a fruitful, spiritual time*
> *in your life?*
> *How can you create a "desert" in your life during these forty*
> *days of Lent?*
> *The number "forty" is symbolic more than chronological*
> *and it means a time of preparation and learning. Some-*
> *times God leaves us in the "desert" as long as it takes for*
> *us to learn the lesson the Lord knows we need. When have*
> *you felt like God has left you in a desert, and what was the*
> *lesson the Lord wanted you to learn?*
> *Jesus had to be "driven" into the desert. When have you*
> *felt God led you to a situation you did not want to face*
> *and why?*

One of the distinctive elements of Mark's Gospel is that he tells
us the interesting fact that Jesus was among the wild beasts and
that angels ministered to Him. This information is very important
for our understanding of this passage. These details also emerge
in various parts of the Old Testament. Psalm 91:11–13 connects
care by the angels with safety among beasts. In Genesis 1:28 and
2:19–20 it states that there was an original peaceful coexistence
with the various animals. Elijah is said to have received the ministry
of angels. Even Daniel in the lion's den relates the story of someone who coexisted among wild beasts and was ministered to by

angels (Dn 6:22–23). These passages speak not only of God's care for His chosen ones but also of God's intentionality for creation. Although the original peaceful coexistence was destroyed by sin, Jesus shows us through His obedience in the desert that He is able to restore what was lost and to bring about a new creation, a new beginning for humanity. Mark's Gospel will reiterate this hope of a new creation in 13:24–27. Thus, Jesus' obedience is able to overcome the disobedience of Adam and Eve and to once again establish right relationship with humanity. Saint Paul will use this contrast between the disobedience of Adam and the obedience of Jesus in His own writings to show how we receive this new life through Jesus. The Prophet Isaiah intensified the hope of a new creation when he wrote of how the wilderness will be transformed into paradise (see Is 11:6–9, 32:14–20, 65:25). Jesus will manifest His ultimate obedience to the Word of God on the cross of Calvary. In this great sacrifice, He will definitively accomplish the work of our redemption and offer healing to a wounded world. As our Lord carries out His ministry leading to Calvary however, He will encounter many people who will challenge Him and many people who will help Him. Those who challenge and help are sometimes interpreted as the ongoing presence of wild beasts (those who oppose) and angels (those who help through their ministry as in the example of Simon Peter's mother-in-law). So the message for us is to persevere and to help one another persevere in fidelity, obedience, and victory as we follow the Lord.

> *What strikes you most about this passage and why?*
> *What does it mean to you that Jesus overcame the dis-obedience (fundamental sin) of Genesis and how do we as disciples share in the Lord's victory of obedience?*
> *It is no accident that Jesus experienced temptation/testing immediately after being identified as the "Beloved Son" of the Father in Mark 1:11. What are the ways today in which people are tempted to not fulfill their roles (father/mother, son/daughter, husband/wife, business leader, or Christian)? Who are the "wild beasts" that try to deter Christian disciples from being faithful?*
> *Who are the "angels" that help Christian disciples persevere in fidelity, obedience, and victory?*

*When is it difficult to tell the difference between those who
are the beasts and those who are the angels?*
*What practices or tools help you remain faithful when you
are being tested in your discipleship?*
*How would your life look if God restored it to the way He
intended, before sin?*
*How can this Lenten Time be an opportunity for you to
enter more deeply into the redeeming grace of Jesus?*

Lastly, this Sunday is a good opportunity to reflect on the three
primary spiritual practices associated with the Time of Lent: prayer,
self-denial, and works of charity. While these practices are always to
be essential components of a disciple's life, the forty days of Lent are
a time when we are asked to intensify them so as to become more
faithful to God's Word as did Jesus in the desert. Deepened prayer
helps us to hear the Word of God more clearly and to become
more responsive in following the Lord's will in our lives. Prayer
also increases our love of God by deepening our relationship with
the Lord. Self-denial frees us from being enslaved by our appetites
or dominated by wasteful practices. Self-denial, especially fasting,
also awakens us to the needs and sufferings of others and allows
us to experience the frailty of the human condition so as to grow
in compassion for those who live in constant need. In performing
charitable works (almsgiving), we express our love of God in our
love of neighbor and begin to make a practical difference in the
lives of others as a witness of our discipleship. Charitable works
(almsgiving) also challenge us to let go of the false security of our
possessions and the illusion of self-sufficiency by our responsible
care for others. Thus, these three practices are interconnected:
prayer, self-denial, and good works all lead us into a practical and
more profound love of God and neighbor. Lent is not so much
about what we "give up", but rather what we "give to" God and
others. Thus, each of these three practices (prayer, fasting, and
almsgiving) is meant to deepen and sanctify our relationship with
God, relationship with self, and relationship with others.

*How can you deepen your prayer life during these forty days
of Lent so you can hear the Word of God more clearly as it
is being spoken to you?*

*What are some of the enslavements you experience, and
how can the practice of self-denial help free you from being
governed by those enslavements? ("Do you control your
desires or do your desires control you?")*

*Who needs to experience your mercy and charitable works,
and how can you express your love of neighbor in a practical
way during this Lenten Time?*

SECOND SUNDAY OF LENT

Our Scripture passage comes from the Gospel of Mark 9:2–10. This is the scene of Jesus' transfiguration and it is a fascinating revelation to the disciples of Jesus' inner identity and mission. This interesting event is contained in the three Synoptic Gospels (Matthew, Mark, and Luke), as well as the Second Letter of Peter (2 Pt 1:16–18). This multiple attestation means that the Transfiguration was a significant event in the life of Jesus that is important for our lives of discipleship as well. For that reason this account was carefully preserved by the 1st Century Church. There are several points for our reflection.

The story of the Transfiguration tells us that Jesus was seen in the company of Elijah and Moses. There are several possible explanations that give reasons for the association of these two religious figures with Jesus. First, Moses and Elijah represent the Law and Prophets of the Old Testament. The moment of the Transfiguration demonstrates that Jesus (and the Gospel) is both in accord with and the fulfillment of the Old Testament writings. It is Jesus who gives the Law and Prophets their meaning. This is an important message because there were some people during the first years of Christianity who doubted the enduring value of the Old Testament and even considered it unnecessary to read the Old Testament— Marcionism was a group who held this belief. This passage affirms the inherent value and enduring inspiration of the Old Testament while establishing its proper relationship to the Gospel and other New Testament writings: They are not in opposition to each other, but need to be understood in terms of "promise" and "fulfillment." With this understanding, it is important for Christians to read the Old Testament through the "lens" of Jesus Christ since He gives those writings their very meaning.

Second, Moses and Elijah are classic examples of divinely appointed people who suffered greatly for their fidelity to God's Word. Moses even prayed that God would take back the mission the Lord had entrusted to him! Certainly, fidelity to God's will can mean going against the world, and Jesus experienced suffering for His fidelity as well. Christian disciples are not exempt from such faithful suffering. Rather, Jesus has already instructed His disciples that they, too, must take up their cross and follow Him (Mk 8:34).

Third, Moses and Elijah are also people who were believed to have been saved from death and destruction and were believed to be "alive" in the presence of God. You might recall that Elijah was taken up into heaven in a fiery chariot at the end of his ministry (see 2 Kgs 2:11). Moses was popularly believed to have been assumed into heaven as well (see the inter-Testamental writing entitled, "The Assumption of Moses"). Thus, Jesus is standing with the two great leaders in the Old Testament who were saved from utter destruction and now live in God's presence.

Their experience of salvation is a preparatory sign of our Lord's resurrection. For all these reasons, Moses and Elijah are not only people of faith but they tell us a great deal about Jesus' life and mission.

> *During this Time of Lent, how can you grow in your appreciation and understanding of the Old Testament?*
> *Why is it important to know the Old Testament prophecies that are fulfilled in Jesus?*
> *Who today is suffering because of their fidelity to God's will?*
> *What stories of salvation (for example, being saved from utter destruction) give you courage to face adversity and overwhelmingly unfavorable odds?*

It is significant that Jesus goes up to a high mountain with His closest disciples for this moment of revelation and insight into His divine nature. It is also significant that God speaks from a cloud. In the Old Testament (and in other ancient cultures), mountains were places of communication between God and humanity. This was certainly true of Mount Sinai and the communication between God and Moses, as well as the Mount of the Jerusalem Temple. In pagan cultures, they also sought communication with the gods on mountains like Mount Olympus. The presence of a cloud had particular meaning for agrarian societies of the ancient world that depended upon rain for the success of their crops. Clouds bring rain and rain brings life. Since God is the God of Life, then a cloud is the perfect symbol for the divine presence as the Author of Life. We see the divine presence accompanied by a cloud in Exodus 40:34–38 when it covered the tent of a meeting. Also, in 1 Kings 8:10–11 a cloud filled the House of the Lord during the dedication of Solomon's Temple in Jerusalem. Psalm 68:4 states that the Lord "rides upon the clouds." All these texts affirm that the Transfiguration is a moment of revelation where the disciples are going to hear and recognize the voice of God and the presence of God in Jesus.

Such recognition may be easy in a moment of glory, but we need to remember that there will be another mountain Jesus will climb and that it will not be easy to recognize the voice of God and the Lord's presence on that mountain—it is the Mount of Calvary. As disciples, we may not go up to high places to meet the Lord, but we do have privileged places of encounter where we meet God more readily than in other settings. These privileged places of encounter may be the sacred space of a church, a prayer space in our homes, or other quiet area. We need to encounter the Lord wherever we can and whenever we can because for each of us there will be moments when it will be difficult to find that encounter or to recognize the presence and voice of God in the midst of a challenging or painful situation. The disciples needed to have this moment of revelation on the mountain of Transfiguration so they could remain strong when they faced the mountain of Calvary. We read this passage on the Second Sunday of Lent because we are praying for the grace to faithfully follow the Lord to Jerusalem and to accompany Him through His Death and Resurrection.

> *What is your privileged place of encounter with God? Where do you go to meet the Lord?*
> *When have you faced moments in which you needed to rely on a previous experience of God's grace because you could not recognize God's presence in the midst of your difficulty?*
> *The cloud passed away and the disciples eventually came down from the mountain. They never forgot that experience. What is an experience in which God has changed your life and given you lasting courage as a disciple?*

One of the final lessons this passage teaches us concerns the need for patience when we are trying to interpret what the Lord is saying to us. Peter demonstrates the opposite of prayerful patience in this scene. Notice how we are told that, "Peter spoke up and said…" That verse is trying to emphasize Peter's preference to speak before he correctly understands. Peter is afraid and in his fear he is trying to interpret the moment for Jesus rather than letting Jesus interpret the moment for Peter! We see Peter's mistaken interpretation when he refers to Jesus with the title, "Rabbi". Jesus is much more than a Rabbi and Peter has to be corrected of his misunderstanding. Peter thinks that Moses and Elijah are the great ones and that Jesus is being honored by their presence; Peter has to learn that Jesus is the greatest one who gives honor and meaning to everything Elijah and Moses ever did. Peter also thinks that this moment of glory is the real destination of a life of faith and discipleship as opposed to the suffering, betrayal, and death that awaits Jesus in Jerusalem as already foretold by our Lord in Mark 8:31. That's why Peter wants to build three booths, staying there to prolong the experience rather than continuing. Peter is suffering from distorted faith because his fear has led him to incorrect and false conclusions in his quest to understand. The voice from the cloud is a public instruction by God the Father to clarify the true identity of Jesus the Son. This instruction informs Peter's misunderstanding and challenges him to "listen" when he is fearful rather than filling the silence. During this Second Sunday of Lent, we are invited to consider the ways in which we have allowed fear to lead us to false conclusions in our faith as well.

Why do you think Peter was overwhelmed in that moment of revelation?

How does God get your attention when you are making a mistake?

How do people today try to answer the question, "Who is Jesus?" without listening to the revelation of God, and how can that process lead them to incorrect conclusions?

How much of your prayer is spent listening rather than talking?

Peter wanted to understand what was happening at the moment it was occurring, and his fear led him to erroneous conclusions. What fears cause trouble in your life as a disciple, and what habits or virtues can help you overcome those fears?

How has God interrupted your situation to reveal greater meaning and purpose in your life and help you see more clearly the presence of Jesus?

When we are in a fearful moment it can be tempting to grasp for certitude and security. For what security do you grasp when you are in a fearful situation?

THIRD SUNDAY OF LENT

Our Scripture passage for the Third Sunday of Lent comes from the Gospel of John 2:13–25. This is the story of Jesus Cleansing the Temple. Although Matthew, Mark, and Luke all place this moment at the end of Jesus' ministry, John places it at the very beginning and as one of our Lord's first public actions. In doing so, John is telling us that the cleansing of our temple has to be one of the first actions we experience as disciples of Jesus. This is an important message for us during this Lenten Time.

The first thing to note about this passage is that Jesus uses three words in reference to this Holy Place of Jerusalem. First, he uses the word that properly means "temple" (Greek: *hieron*). That term refers to the entire building complex of the Temple Mount and focuses primarily on the physical reality of the facility. Jesus further instructs the crowds that this physical building has a purpose—to be the House of the Father. By using the word "house" (Greek: *oikos*), Jesus is stressing that a physical place of worship (temple) must become a place where God lives in the hearts and souls of faithful men and women (house). Thus, the temple building is meant to be a place where people come so as to enter into an indwelling communion with God. Finally, Jesus then states, "Destroy this temple and in three days I will raise it up." The actual term he uses in this verse means more than "temple"; in fact it means "sanctuary" and referred to the Holy of Holies (Greek: *naon;* Hebrew: *debir*). The sanctuary (or Holy of Holies) was the innermost part of the Temple complex where the Presence of God was believed to have dwelt. We are later told that Jesus was referring to the sanctuary of His body. The presence of God that once resided in the Temple will be perfected in the resurrected body of Jesus. It is in His resurrected body that the Lord will then send the Spirit into the disciples and commission them to carry on His mission (see Jn 20:22).

In that moment, the Church becomes a living sanctuary as the Body of Christ bearing witness to God's love in the world. This granting of the Spirit of Jesus is only possible through our Lord's glorification, which is the "Hour" of Calvary. In the writings of Saint Paul, the theology of the Church as the Body of Christ is developed extensively (see 1 Cor 12:12–31, Col 1:18, 2:18–20, Eph 1:22–23, 4:13). John's progressive use of the terms "temple", "house", and "sanctuary" is intentional and challenges us to move deeper in our discipleship with the Lord. Sometimes disciples can remain on a surface encounter with God that takes place only in the sacred space of a church building. While sacred space is a privileged setting for the encounter with God, the Lord wants that encounter to have an enduring effect in our lives so that God dwells with us (house) even after we have left the sacred space of a building. Finally, the indwelling presence of God is given to us for a reason—so that we can become the Body of Christ, that is, the spiritual edifice in which the love of God and the living presence of Jesus are made known to the world (sanctuary). Disciples today must be able to say with the words of Saint Paul, "It is no longer I who live but Christ who lives in me" (Gal 2:20). For this reason, disciples are challenged not only to make room for God in our lives but also to actually become a living sanctuary of His presence. That means surrendering full control of our lives to the Lord. Jesus' action of cleansing the temple is showing us the divinely intended path of discipleship.

> *We come to the temple so that we can become a living sanctuary. What can take away (thieves) or distract us (busyness) from following this path to its divinely intended destination?*
>
> *Where are you on this progressive path: limiting your encounter with God to sacred space, giving only some space in your life to God, or surrendering your whole life to the Lord?*
>
> *What interior reasons can we have for stopping short at each of these various levels? For example, are we satisfied to just come to the temple or content to just give God some space in our lives?*
>
> *What busyness is going on in our faith community that distracts or prevents you from entering more deeply into communion with God?*
>
> *How can you prayerfully remove the obstacles that hinder you from becoming a living sanctuary of God's presence?*

The passage ends with the statement that many people came to believe in Jesus because they saw the "signs" He was performing but that our Lord would not entrust Himself to them because He knew the human heart. That is an interesting passage. It speaks about the flawed nature of sign-based faith. Sign-based faith relies upon confirming and intelligible manifestations of God to convince us of the Lord's presence or will for our lives. It is the kind of faith that expects or requires God to "prove Himself" to us. Jesus knows that disciples who follow Him with a sign-based faith have a shallow commitment and will be disappointed or disillusioned when the Lord does not act according to their requirements. Jesus wants us to be disciples who can accept God's revelation (Word) when it goes beyond our ability to understand. Because of our human condition, our ability to understand the mysteries of God will always be limited. The challenge of faith is not only to accept what we can understand but also to accept all that God reveals. The antagonists in this passage demonstrate the misunderstanding that takes place when we reduce faith to only what we can understand. They thought Jesus was speaking about the destruction and raising of the facility of the Temple while the Lord was referring to His physical body. Jesus reveals to us great mysteries of faith that go beyond our ability to fully comprehend based on human reason—the mystery of the Church as His Mystical Body, the mystery of the Eucharist as His Risen Presence in the form of bread and wine, the mystery of the Trinity as a communion of divine life and love, and the mystery of the Sacraments as the effective invisible grace of the Lord offered to us.

How does sign-based faith cause us to falter in our faith lives today?

What mysteries of Christian faith do you have difficulty accepting and why?

What happens when a person tries to reduce faith to only what they can understand with human reason?

When have you wanted God to prove His presence through signs?

What are unexpected signs that have confirmed God's presence in your life?

The Church chooses this Gospel reading during the Lenten Time for several reasons. It can certainly challenge us to move deeper in our discipleship and it can motivate us to accept the revealed mysteries of faith. This passage is also important during our Lenten Time because it encourages our preparation for the Passover of Jesus that includes His Passion, Death, and Resurrection. It is no accident that the opening verse of this passage mentions that Jesus cleanses the Temple during the time of Passover preparation—that is our Lenten Time! It is the cleansing of the Temple which initiates the process that eventually leads to Jesus' Passion (see the passage of Ps 69:9 recalled in Jn 2:17, "Zeal for your house will consume me", where the term "consume" refers to Jesus' consummation on the Cross as stated in Jn 19:30), and this passage serves as an excellent Lenten preparation for Holy Week.

Additionally, the passage is an encouragement for all disciples who face sacrifice because of their commitment to the honor of God (especially Moses and Matthias as well as others—Nm 25:11, 1 Kgs 19:10, Sir 48:1, 1 Mc 2:24). Finally, this passage is appropriate because it invites all disciples to cleanse the temple of our own lives during this Lenten Time. In our Baptism we become a temple of the Holy Spirit but over the course of time our lives can become cluttered with unholy deals, noises, and idols (values, actions, behaviors, and attitudes) that should not be there. Lent is a great time to take an inventory of the many ways in which we have allowed sin and distractions to compromise our Christian discipleship and to remove them.

The Ten Commandments are presented to us in the first reading for this Third Sunday of Lent for a reason; we are being invited to cleanse the temple of our lives by evaluating carefully our thoughts and actions in light of these revealed mandates of God's will (see Ex 20:1–17). In addition to the Ten Commandments, there are other excellent self-reflections known as "Examinations of Conscience" which can help a disciple recognize previously overlooked or unrealized situations of sin and weakness. By identifying and addressing these obstacles to growth in discipleship, we are able to become more fully the people God desires us to be—Living Sanctuaries of His Presence in the world. The Sacrament of Reconciliation is an especially important part of a Christian's life and Lent is a great time to celebrate this Sacrament.

> *How often do you use the Ten Commandments to evaluate your life?*
>
> *What are some of the distractive efforts that have become part of our contemporary faith communities that can take away from our authentic encounter with God?*
>
> *Who suffers today because of their commitment to the honor of God? Who is "consumed" with zeal for the Lord?*
>
> *When have you taken a stand of faith even though you knew it might lead to unpleasant consequences in the future?*
>
> *Why do you think John placed this passage at the beginning of Jesus' public ministry rather than at the end?*
>
> *What are some of the unholy deals, noises, and idols that need to be cleansed from the sanctuary of your heart and home?*

One final interesting note is worthy of our consideration. Although the cleansing of the Temple is contained in the other three Gospels (see Mt 21:12–13, Mk 11:15–17, and Lk 19:45–46), only John includes extensive details about how the cleansing took place. John specifies in particular that those selling pigeons were ordered to take them away (see Jn 2:16). That is because the pigeons were caged and could not fly away on their own; they would have been harmed in the overturning of the tables and other items. This detail is telling us that Jesus has an unbounded zeal for the Father's house but that His zeal does not cause injury to those around Him. He expresses His anger in a way that motivates and instructs but not in a way that harms the vulnerable. This is an important insight for us as disciples. If we are passionate about our faith and the values of the Gospel, then we, too, will experience a righteous anger at everything that opposes those values. However, our passion, like Jesus', must never harm the vulnerable.

> *How does this insight challenge you in carrying out your tasks?*
>
> *Who has been harmed by your passion or zeal?*
>
> *How do you balance passion for a just cause with respect for others who do not share your values?*

Fourth Sunday of Lent

Our Scripture passage comes from the Gospel of John 3:14–21. This passage contains one of the most famous and frequently quoted passages in the Bible—John 3:16). The focus on this singular verse can sometimes cause us to miss the rich meaning in the surrounding verses. Several central themes of John's Gospel emerge for the first time in these verses and so they are an important resource for understanding the central message and ministry of Jesus. These themes include "eternal life" and "salvation".

The first verses of this passage introduce the theme of "eternal life". In order to fully understand this message we need to back up two verses to John 3:12–13 where Jesus identifies Himself as the unique revealer of God; the one who descended from heaven, the Son of Man. It is one thing for Jesus to be the Revealer, but the question as to how Jesus accomplishes His revelation of God remains. That is the purpose of the first verse of this Sunday's passage: Jesus will carry out His great work of revelation as the Son of Man when He is "lifted up". The term "lifted up" (sometimes translated as "exalted") is a reference to His Crucifixion. Thus, Jesus, the revealer and Word of God, will communicate to us most clearly who God is when He is on the Cross of Calvary. This revelation on Calvary is given for a purpose—so that we can have eternal life by believing in God present in the Crucified Jesus.

Eternal life, then, is the primary purpose of Jesus' mission; it means being drawn into the revealing love of God and united to the Lord now and forever. Eternal life, then, doesn't begin at our death; rather, it begins when we "believe" in Jesus' revelation on the Cross. It is important to note that the words "faith" or "belief" never appear as nouns in John's Gospel. Instead, the terms faith or belief only appear as verbs. That's because John wants us to know that faith is not just a collection of intellectual precepts. Faith is an active and dynamic immersion in the life of grace. To "believe" doesn't mean that we simply memorize a creed; it means that we are active participants in the life and love of God.

What do most people think the term "eternal life" means?
John's understanding of "eternal life" is that it begins now
through our active participation in God's life and love. How
does his understanding inspire you?
What do you think of the fact that John never presents faith
or belief as a noun but only as a verb?
What are some of the many ways in which Jesus carried
out His work of revealing God?
Why is the revelation of Calvary considered to be the high
point of Jesus' revealing work?
How do people tend to reduce faith today to mean merely
a collection of memorized precepts?
The Church offers us this reading during the Lenten Time
so that we will understand and appreciate the salvific effect
of the Cross of Calvary. How does this text increase your
desire to spend time with the Crucified One?

Having established that Jesus is the unique revealer, that Jesus will
reveal God to us on Calvary, and that we are invited to respond
to that revelation by actively participating in the revealed life and
love of God (believe), the Gospel then goes on to address in the
next five verses how eternal life occurs. These verses speak about
how God's love is revealed in His actions of "giving" and "sending".
Thus, God's love is not an emotion but a dynamic action for the
salvation of the world. This is the first time the word "salvation"
appears in John's Gospel. Jesus was sent to make God known, and,
in order to do that, Jesus had to make love known because God is
love. This mission was perfected and accomplished on the Cross
of Calvary, and Jesus acknowledges the fulfillment of His mission
when He utters His final words, "Father, it is finished" (Greek:
telestai really means "perfected", "accomplished", "fulfilled", rather
than "finished"). Indeed, Jesus accomplishes the purpose for which
He was sent. God also loves by "giving". The word "give" in Greek
(didomi) is important because a variation of it means to "betray"
(literally to "give over" paradidomi). Thus, God's giving of the Son
is an action of His great love, but not all will receive it; some will
betray it instead.

To believe in God's love is to participate in the actions of God
by carrying on the mission of Jesus and giving ourselves to others

as He gave Himself to us. Thus, eternal life involves not solely receiving the life of God but also allowing the life of God manifested in Jesus to flow through us to the world. That participation in the life of God is salvation. Not all will accept the gift and choose to participate in that saving gift of life and love. God invites us to do so—He doesn't force us to do so. When we accept the invitation and "believe," we are saved through our participation in divine life. However, when we choose not to accept the invitation, and, thus "do not believe" by becoming an active conduit of God's life and love to others, we condemn ourselves because of our rejection. That is one of the interesting aspects of John's Gospel—he teaches us that we are our own judges. Hence, it is not God who judges us but we who judge ourselves by our decision to enter or not to enter into the revelation of God in Jesus on Calvary and allow that revelation to continue through our lives.

> *God's love is manifested in His actions of giving and sending the Son. How do you manifest that love of God in your actions?*
>
> *Who needs to experience the generous mercy of God (giving) through you?*
>
> *To whom in need is the Lord sending you to bring His divine love? For John's Gospel, salvation occurs when we become a conduit of God's life for others. How does this understanding of salvation differ from other popular meanings?*
>
> *How does the teaching that "we are our own judges" affect the way you will respond to opportunities to be a conduit of God's love?*

Jesus teaches us in the final verses of this passage about the necessary connection between faith and actions. This connection is expressed through the images of light and darkness. It is important to remember that Jesus has already been described as the "Light" in the opening verse of John's Gospel (Jn 1:5–9). Therefore, deeds that are done in "Light" are deeds that are done in Jesus as a sign of our participation in the active love of God. If we want to know whether we are really "believing" in Jesus, we only have to look at our deeds. If they are deeds that manifest the very love of God as witnessed on Calvary, they are truly done in the "Light." If our deeds reflect our own love of earthly pursuits, self-gain, and self-preservation or self-promotion, they are being done in darkness and necessarily apart from the "Light." Thus, the measure of our believing is in our doing. Deeds done in the "Light" of Jesus continue to manifest the revelation of God's love in the world; they are deeds done in God. In John's Gospel, the power of evil is manifested as darkness—all that opposes the Light. Any deed not done in the Light must necessarily be a manifestation of darkness.

> *What are deeds you have seen that manifest the love of God as witnessed on Calvary?*
> *What are deeds that typically manifest self-centered or worldly love instead?*
> *If the measure of our believing is in our doing, how do you measure up based on the past twenty-four hours of your life?*
> *When a deed is done in "Light", it continues to manifest the love of God in the World. Who manifests God's love to you most clearly and how?*

One final detail to note is the comparison that Jesus makes—Moses lifting up the serpent in the wilderness and our Lord's own exaltation on the Cross (see in Jn 3:14). As you may recall from Number 21:9, the serpent was sent as a punishment for the Israelites who had rebelled against God. They became ill from the serpent's bite and were healed only when they looked upon the bronze serpent Moses crafted onto his staff. The message is this: It is only when we examine, acknowledge and take responsibility for the source of our woundedness that we can experience healing. This is a powerful statement especially when we apply it to the emotional, psychological, and spiritual dimensions of our lives. Jesus tells us that we can only experience eternal healing (salvation) when we look upon the Crucified Lord in the same way: examine the love of God made visible, acknowledge His eternal sacrifice, and take responsibility for our sinfulness, which He died to forgive. Indeed, when we look at the Cross with the eyes of faith then we can say with John the Baptist in John 1:29, "Behold the Lamb of God who takes away the sins of the world." It takes real maturity for a disciple to look at the Cross of Jesus with such honesty, humility, accountability, and faith. However, those qualities are what allow a disciple to reach out for the transforming grace of God which brings both healing and conversion. We do not overcome our sin by denying it but only by acknowledging it in the context of God's loving mercy. That's why the Father sent the Son—so that the world might be saved through Him. During this time of Lent it is especially appropriate to pray for those qualities that will allow us to gaze upon the crucified Lord and to see in His loving sacrifice the forgiveness of our sins.

> *What is the emotional, spiritual, or psychological wound in your life that is not yet healed?*
> *What part of your life does God want you to "gaze upon" so as to examine, acknowledge, and take responsibility?*
> *How can prayer before a Crucifix help you to experience more deeply the graces of Lent?*

Fifth Sunday of Lent

Our Scripture passage comes from the Gospel of John 12:20–33. In this passage we see that the long-awaited "Hour" of Jesus has finally arrived. This hour was first alluded to in John 2:4 and further commented on in 7:6, 8, 30 and 8:20. The "Hour" of Jesus is not a chronological hour of 60 minutes, but rather signifies the culminating experience for which He was sent into the world: The "Hour" of Jesus is the event of His Passion, Death, and Resurrection.

Jesus knows this because the "Greeks" come to Him. They are Gentiles (foreigners) being drawn to God in Jesus. That gathering of the whole world (including non-Jews) is something that can only occur when Jesus is "Lifted Up" on Calvary. Thus, when Jesus sees the Gentiles coming to Him, he knows that the time for His being "lifted up" is at hand. His "Hour" has come. It is significant when John tells us that the "Greeks" come to Jesus by way of Philip and Andrew.

There are two important reasons for the choice of these specific disciples as the catalysts for the Greeks to encounter Jesus. The first reason is because "Philip" and "Andrew" are both Greek names, whereas the other twelve disciples all went by their Jewish names. This means that the "Greeks" feel a relationship exists with Philip and Andrew because they have something in common—Greek names.

The second reason why Philip and Andrew are the appropriate disciples to serve as catalysts is because they were the first disciples called by Jesus when He initiated His ministry (see Jn 1:40, 43). These two disciples received the gift of faith and now are introducing others to it as well. This connection is an important message for us. We each have interests, personalities, and social worlds that connect us with a wide variety of people. Part of our role as disciples is to use those "points of connection" as vehicles by which we invite others in and facilitate their encounter with Christ. Maybe it's a similar professional background, common sports interest, favorite hobby, or something as simple as living in the same neighborhood—we all have points of connection that can become the means of evangelization. In order to be missionaries like Philip and Andrew, we need to also remember that the invitation to discipleship wasn't given to us to keep to ourselves. Instead, God calls us to be disciples so that God can call others to discipleship through us.

> *What are qualities, interests, or involvements that we have today that are "points of contact" by which others can relate to and through us to connect with Jesus?*
> *Every shared interest or commonality can be a moment of invitation to lead others to Christ. How have your shared interests with others been a point of contact leading them to faith?*
> *Who have you invited into the relationship of faith in God?*

In this Gospel passage, Jesus makes a powerful statement when He says, "Whoever would serve me, must follow me. Where I am, there also will my servant be." It is a strong statement because John's Gospel was written during the age of persecution when many Christians were "following" Jesus in laying down their lives and being martyred for their faith. It's one thing to follow Jesus in His daily teachings of doing good and avoiding evil; it's another thing to face the decision of sacrificially laying down our lives in witness to Him. The image of the seed falling into the ground and dying gives meaning not only to the Death and Resurrection of Jesus but it also gives hope and meaning to us as Christians when we are called to embrace sacrifice as well. Jesus is teaching us that faithful sacrifice always brings forth "fruit." The term "fruit" will be further developed in John 15:1–8 when Jesus will explicitly identify it with the growth of the Christian community of faith. We are the fruit of Christian sacrifice! We have received a great deal thanks to the courageous witness of others. By being recipients, we are also called to pass on that gift so that more fruit can be harvested in the future and others can come to know Jesus through us. That fruit of additional disciples only happens when we choose to lay down our lives in love for others even as Jesus laid down His life for us. Indeed, as Jesus said, "Where I am, there also will my servant be." Today we're not necessarily called to be martyrs who are put to death for our faith, but there can be a real "martyrdom" when Christians suffer because of their public witness of faith. In those moments, it is important for us to remember the image of the seed falling into the ground and dying so that a rich harvest can be brought forth. We are responsible for imitating the example of Jesus; God is responsible for the harvest. Sacrifice is always difficult to accept. In those moments of difficulty, it is important to remember that the role of a disciple is to follow Jesus and not to get Jesus to follow us. Sometimes in our prayer we can wonder why "God isn't with us" in particular situations we face. It's interesting how easy it is to pray for "God to be with us" rather than "for us to be with God".

> *What discriminations or punishments take place in today's American culture and society when Christians publically witness their faith and adherence to Jesus and "follow him"? In what ways do you see yourself as the fruit of others' faithful sacrifice?*
>
> *Jesus said, "Where I am, there [also] my servant will be." He did not say, "Where my servant is, there I am also." When it comes to praying as a disciple, do you pray for the guidance to be where God is leading you, or do you pray for God to accompany you where you want to go?*
>
> *Who is in charge of your prayer?*

When the Father responds to Jesus' prayer about glorifying His name, the Father says, "I have glorified it and I will glorify it again." The crowds interpret this event only in terms of earthly realities (thunder) or misinterpreted heavenly events (angel). What they do not see or understand is that God is present in Jesus in an unmediated way—not through natural events or as in a messenger). They interpret the events only in terms of what they know, and refuse to accept the revelation Jesus has offered which is the key to understanding the things of heaven. Thus, their "life", which they love and hold dear, is a life defined by their narrow perspective. They are incapable of accepting Jesus for who He is: the presence of God in their midst. Of itself "this world" is neutral, but it is possible for us to make it into an end in itself. This happens when people begin to live as though all their meaning, satisfaction, and purpose must be found in the here and now (power, pleasure, prestige, wealth, or accomplishment). In doing so, a person becomes enslaved to limited and shallow pursuits. In the Gospel, Jesus presents Satan as the "ruler of this world" because the power of evil always tries to influence and tempt us to settle for less than God, and the attractions of this world are the tempter's instruments. The "Hour" of Jesus reveals that humanity's true destiny is not found in "this world" and so it frees us to seek the things of heaven.

> *What have been some of the "freeing moments or experiences" of your life that allowed you to let go of the allure of "this world" and have helped to un-slave you?*
> *How do people today continue to misinterpret the beauty of God's teaching and revelation so as to only understand things (issues) in terms of their narrow, limited, earthly perspective?*

One last reflection concerns the brief conversation between Jesus and the Father when Jesus says, "Father, glorify your Name." The Father responds by saying, "I have glorified it and I will glorify it again." To properly understand the importance of this exchange, we need to see how God (represented by His "Name") has already been glorified in John's Gospel. Several passages have already indicated that Jesus' actions have revealed God's glory. These actions begin with the miracle at Cana (water being turned into wine), continue with the cleansing of the Temple, and are further developed in the multiplication of the loaves and fishes, forgiveness of the woman caught in adultery, healing of the blind man, and finally culminate in the raising of Lazarus from the dead. God's glory has been revealed through the actions of Jesus in each of these moments. The Father's words are true when He says, "I have glorified it." The Father's name will continue to be glorified in the actions that continue to unfold in John's Gospel through Jesus and will reach perfection in the revelation of God's glory on the Cross of Calvary. The glorification of God's Name does not stop with Calvary, however. In John 17:22 Jesus prays during the Last Supper Discourse and asks the Father to give His disciples the glory which the Father gave Jesus so that the world might believe through the love of Christians. This means that the Father is glorified not only in the works of the Son but also in the lives of all faithful Christians who continue to manifest the love of God. Thus, an essential part of our discipleship is to glorify the name of God in our thoughts, words, and actions. The Father will continue to glorify His Name through us! When we allow the self-giving, sacrificial love of God to flow through us to others, even as Jesus did on the Cross of Calvary, then we give glory to God's name and reveal the love of God to the world so that the world might believe.

> *Who is someone you know who brings glory to God's Name through their manner of life and witness of Christian love?*
>
> *How can you glorify God in the midst of a particular situation in your life right now?*
>
> *Who has come to know the love of God through you?*
>
> *Who in your family, friendships, or professional relationships most needs to experience God's love right now, and how can you glorify God's Name by being the conduit of that love?*
>
> *How can self-centeredness get in the way of giving glory to God's name?*
>
> *How do you actually give glory to God in a practical response to God's love? What does it look like for you to give God glory?*
>
> *We can't give God the glory unless we realize that the blessings of our lives come from the Lord. What causes us to fall short of giving God glory, and to whom or what do we give the glory instead?*

PALM SUNDAY

Our Scripture passage for this Sunday is extensive and covers two entire chapters of Mark's Gospel from 14:1–15:47. In this reading, we hear of Jesus' Last Supper, betrayal by Judas, trial both before the Sanhedrin and Pilate, Suffering, Crucifixion, Death, and Burial. Various details are immersed in this account of our Lord's final hours of earthly ministry. Our reflection this week will focus on only a few of these details and how they affect our lives as disciples.

Mark begins his Passion narrative with the story of the woman who anoints the head of Jesus with a jar of expensive perfume (see Mk 14:3–9). This action of generosity, love, and sacrifice evokes the indignant response of others in the room who question why she did not sell the perfume and give the money to the poor rather than pour it on Jesus' head. Jesus addresses their statements by pointing out her good intentions and the ever-present opportunities they have to express generosity for the poor, which they apparently are not taking advantage of. In doing so, He is not diminishing the importance of practical charity for those in need but esteeming the sacrificial love of God manifested in this woman's action. Our Lord is also pointing out the hypocrisy of those who criticize this woman because they themselves could be helping the poor if they truly desired to do so. The implication is that they were more interested in a reason to discredit the goodness of her action rather than carry out their own works of charity. (Remember the quote of Mark Twain, "Few things are harder to put up with than the annoyance of a good example.")[2]

Judas, on the other hand, is presented in stark contrast to the woman. He goes to the chief priests and offers to betray Jesus for which he is promised money (see Mk 14:10–11). Judas is presented as an example of someone who uses Jesus for his self-gain rather than as the opportunity for loving, sacrificial self-giving. Not only

---

2. M. Twain, *Pudd'nhead Wilson and Those Extraordinary Twins* (New York: Harper and Brothers, 1894), p. 182.

does Judas not care about the poor, he doesn't care about Jesus either. The contrast between the woman and Judas could not be more dramatic. Throughout history there has always been a necessary relationship between our love of God and our love of neighbor. It is only through our love of God that we can truly love those in the distressing disguise of the poor and suffering. Our love of God is not to the exclusion of the poor, but rather the first step in our ability to serve the poor. As Jesus approached His Passion, the woman responded with generosity, commitment, sacrifice, and abundant love of God; Judas responded with self-preservation, self-protection, self-gain, and self-interest.

> *In what ways can people be critical today of others when they express their love for God through works of lavish generosity? How can criticism of others for their failure to serve the poor become the excuse by which we are tempted to exempt ourselves from serving the poor?*
>
> *When you are in a distressful situation like the Passion of Jesus, do you respond more like the woman (generous sacrificial commitment) or like Judas (self-preservation and self-interest)?*
>
> *During Holy Week, how can you be lavish in your love of God through your gifts of time and talent?*
>
> *How do we seek to discredit other people's good actions in an effort to exempt ourselves from the challenge of doing good?*

When Jesus is in the Garden of Gethsemane (Mk 14:32–42) we see less than stellar examples of discipleship in the persons of Peter, James, and John. In fact, they all appear as examples of failure. Just a few verses before this chapter Jesus had warned His disciples on the need to "Stay awake!" in Mark 13:37. Now they all fall asleep at the most critical hour. Those who were Jesus' closest friends and had been with Him from the very beginning of His ministry (see Mk 1:16–20) and had been part of His inner circle (see Mk 5:37 and 9:2), now appear disinterested in His distress. James and John, who were so confident that they could "drink from the cup Jesus would drink" in Mark 10:39 now sleep while Jesus prays that the cup may pass Him by. Peter, who claimed that he would be willing to die for Jesus (see 14:31), now appears unwilling to sacrifice even one hour of sleep for the sake of the Lord. It would be bad enough if they had failed once and been reprimanded for their lack of attentiveness and disinterest, but they failed three times in a row. Although they may have been close to Jesus by their physical proximity, their hearts were far from Him in this moment. The reality is that Peter, James, and John are not very different from any of us. It is easy to have great and noble ideas of how we will live out our commitment to God yet find it difficult to do so in daily circumstances. The Good News is that Jesus does not reject the disciples for their failure and disappointing progress. Rather, the Lord gives them a second chance and a third chance, and so on. Sometimes we believe that we are not capable of being great disciples but that is a lie; the only thing that prevents us from being great people of faith is our lack of desire for such greatness. Peter, James, and John will eventually become heroic examples of faith and committed disciples but only because they keep trying. The same is true for us. In our moments of weakness, short-sightedness, and failure, we should not lose hope, but rather realize our need for God's mercy, forgiveness, and grace and renew our commitment to follow the Lord.

> *How can people today excuse themselves from discipleship because of a personal failure of faith?*
>
> *Sometimes we only realize the magnitude of our failure in retrospect. How can the practice of honestly reviewing our lives serve to motivate us to deeper trust and committed discipleship?*
>
> *How does the Sacrament of Reconciliation help you to renew your commitment to discipleship despite a moment of failure?*
>
> *What self-doubts do you think Peter, James, and John experienced as they looked back on this moment, and how do you think the power of evil tried to manipulate their self-doubts to prevent them from becoming better disciples?*

Jesus' final words in Mark's Gospel are a quotation from Psalm 22:1 when He cried out, "My God, My God, why have you forsaken me?" These are not so much words of complaint and abandonment, but rather the prayer of a just man who suffers. By praying with the words of the Psalms, Jesus is reminding us of some very important truths that we need to know as disciples. These truths are contained in the rest of Psalm 22 that follow after this first verse. Although Jesus only quotes the first line of this Psalm, He is pointing us to it so that we can remember the entirety of the Psalm. In vs. 3 we are reminded that even in suffering, God remains "enthroned as the Holy One". In vs. 4 and 5 we are reminded that those who put their trust in God are not disappointed. In vs. 22 we are told that even in suffering we are to praise the Lord. In vs. 24 we are assured that suffering is not a sign that God despises us and that God does listen to our cries for deliverance. In vs. 28 we are reminded that God is in control of all kingdoms, all nations, and all history. Finally, in vs. 31 we are taught that whatever takes place, even in the suffering of the just, it is to be understood as part of God's plan. There could not be a better prayer to summarize and interpret the death of Jesus on the Cross than Psalm 22.

Jesus' Death is part of the mystery of God's unfolding plan. The Salvation the Lord offers us isn't always realized in the situations of this life; sometimes our deliverance from the forces that oppose and oppress us occurs in the Resurrection. Nonetheless, this prayer helps us to find meaning in our suffering, to have confidence in our trials, and to re-affirm our faith when things don't go our way by remembering that God is in ultimate control. When we pray the Lord's Prayer, we end by asking that we not be led into temptation and that we be delivered from evil. The temptation we most want to avoid is that of believing that God has abandoned us, God hates us, or that God doesn't care about us. When we pray to be delivered from evil, we are not praying to be preserved from it (that is unrealistic in a world infected by sin) but that we will not be overcome by it; that means we pray for perseverance, deliverance, vindication, and salvation from the evil situations we endure.

Read the prayer of Psalm 22. How does reading the prayer of Psalm 22 by Jesus on the Cross affect the way you understand our Lord's Crucifixion?

How does this understanding of the final verses of the Lord's Prayer and the lived experience of Jesus change the way you will pray that prayer?

What are the temptations you experience when you suffer unjustly?

What situations in our world today give the false impression that the forces of evil are victorious?
How can the experience of this Holy Week invite you to deepen your trust and confidence in God in the midst of adverse circumstances?

One of the most important elements of Mark's Passion narrative is the proclamation of faith by the Roman Centurion as Jesus dies on the Cross. The centurion exclaims, "Surely this man was the Son of God!" This is the first time in Mark's Gospel that such faith has been proclaimed by a human being. Mark told us in the opening verse of his Gospel that Jesus was the Son of God. That insight has been re-affirmed in significant sections of the Gospel by the Father (see the Baptism of Jesus in Mk 1:11 and in the Transfiguration of Jesus in Mk 9:7). The previous announcements by the Father were given during manifestations of heavenly glory as a proclamation of the Divine Presence. It is easy to see Jesus as the Son of God when the heavens open and the Spirit descends at the moment of our Lord's Baptism. It is also easy to see Jesus as the Son of God when He stands in the shining presence of Moses and Elijah. However, it requires exceptional faith and insight to see Jesus as the Son of God as He dies on the Cross of Calvary. That is why the proclamation of the Centurion is so important—he expresses the faith of a true disciple who can see that God is present in moments of suffering. The proclamation of the Centurion brings to fulfillment the very first verse of Mark's Gospel. As disciples, we are challenged to have the same faith as the Centurion. It is easy for us to acknowledge the presence of God in moments of great success and blessing, but it is even more important for us to be able to profess our faith in God's presence in moments of suffering and seeming defeat. The Cross of Calvary is not a sign of God's abandonment but a promise of God's presence.

When, in the midst of someone's suffering, has that person's faith inspired you?
In what moments of your life do you find it difficult to recognize and acknowledge God's presence?
What do you believe the other bystanders thought when they heard the Centurion's profession of faith?

What do you think the Centurion did as a result of his new-found faith?

The Passion narratives are full of surprises as we see how different people respond in various moments. Certainly we are surprised to see Jesus' closest disciples fall asleep and abandon Him after having spent three years following our Lord. We are also surprised to see that one of Jesus' own friends turns into a traitor while another of His friends denies Him three times. There are other surprises as well, like when we see a woman offer her precious gift of perfume to anoint Jesus, or when we read of Joseph of Arimathea coming forth to claim the body of Jesus for burial, or even when we hear the Roman Centurion—who had brutally treated Jesus and crucified Him—now profess his faith in the Lord. Indeed, the mystery of discipleship is full of surprises. A person's background doesn't indicate their future response. No one can ride on the laurels of their past fidelity and no one can rule out future holiness based on past sinfulness or rejection of the Gospel. We continue to experience this mystery of discipleship today as well.

Those we expect to be predictable examples of holiness sometimes let us down, while those from whom we expect little faith response can inspire us with their insight and courage. This message is a source of both hope and challenge for us as disciples. It gives us hope because it reassures us that no one—including ourselves—is beyond the invitation of God's grace no matter what our background or social affiliation. It gives us challenge because it cautions us against presuming our standing in the eyes of God based on some past witness or status; like Peter, James, and John, we are only one step away from infidelity.

How do you experience both hope and challenge from this reflection?
Who has surprised you with their witness of faith despite their seemingly difficult background?
Who has let you down in their witness of faith despite their privileged background of discipleship?
What helps a disciple remain faithful at each step of the journey?

SOLEMNITY OF EASTER (VIGIL)

This Sunday we celebrate the great Solemnity of our Lord's Resurrection (Easter). The primary liturgy for this celebration is the Easter Vigil. Our Scripture passage for this liturgy is taken from the Gospel of Mark 16:1–7. The New Testament accounts of the Resurrection of Jesus are well known to us. Due to our familiarity with these texts we can easily overlook significant details by which each of the Gospel writers wished to communicate particular meaning. The Gospel of Mark offers numerous insights that are meant to inspire, encourage, and guide our lives as disciples.

One of the first things to note about Mark's account of the resurrection is the emphasis he places on the stone (Greek: *Lithon*) used to seal the tomb of Jesus. This emphasis is demonstrated by the frequent use of the word "stone" (four times) in these short verses. The stone that was rolled in front of the tomb is a real preoccupation of the women who go to anoint Jesus and who wonder who will roll it back from the "entrance". It is described as being "very large". Mark is emphasizing the stone because it serves a symbolic function: the stone is the obstacle that separates the women from their friend and Lord. The key to understanding the symbolic role of the stone is that it obstructs the "entrance" preventing those who wish to enter from doing so. If we were told that the stone closed the "exit", that would indicate that it was an obstacle for Jesus' Resurrection, but that is not the case. The stone is not an obstacle for experiencing Jesus; rather, the stone is the obstacle that disciples encounter, which prevents them from entering into the tomb (dying with Christ) so as to be transformed by His risen life (Resurrection).

To enter the tomb and be transformed was an image of Christian Baptism in the Early Church. The stone becomes a symbol for all the obstacles of faith we must overcome in our journey to embrace and live out our Baptism as disciples of Jesus. For the early

Christians during the age of persecution, it was difficult to make the decision to become a disciple of Jesus because that decision might cost them their lives, their friends, or their possessions. Yet still so many overcame that obstacle. For the early Jews, becoming Christian could mean being "cut off" from their families and loved ones and declared "dead" with no further contact or relationship or inheritance. That rejection was a tremendous obstacle (stone) that prevented many from making the decision of faith. Our world of discipleship is different from that of the first century Christians. Some of our obstacles are more ideological instead of practical.

> *What have been some of the "stones" you have had to over-come in your journey to Jesus?*
> *What internal fears can prevent someone from being willing to "die with Christ"?*
> *How does the message of the resurrection address those fears?*
> *Mark's Gospel does not tell us who rolled back the stone for the women, but someone did. Who do you think was the instrument that removed their obstacle of discipleship?*
> *Who do you know that is struggling with the ability to sur-render fully to Jesus, and how can you be the instrument that helps remove the obstacles holding them back from embracing and living the fullness of Christian Baptism?*
> *The women in this passage went to the tomb despite the fact that they believed the stone would still be there (prevent-ing them from entering). Why do you think they did that and how does their witness of faith motivate you to face a situation in your life as a disciple?*

The second detail that Mark includes is that of the women's names. Mary Magdalene, Salome, and Mary (the mother of James, known as the lesser), and Joses from Mark 15:40 are no new-comers to Jesus' family of disciples and friends. They have been a part of the Gospel story for some time. In fact, some of them had rather diverse and even turbulent backgrounds. Salome is the mother of Zebedee's children as we can infer from Matthew's account of this event (see Mt 27:56). She is also the author of that impertinent petition to have her sons sitting with Jesus—one on His right and one on His left—in His Kingdom (see Mt 20:20–21). Mary Magdalene will be identified in Mark 16:9 as the one from whom Jesus cast out seven demons. These references tell us that at least two of these women came from less than holy or healthy backgrounds! We were also informed in Luke 8:3 that these women ministered to Jesus in Galilee. We were further told in Mark 15:40 that they witnessed Jesus' death. Finally, Mark 15:47 mentions the two Marys as having witnessed the burial of Jesus. Mark tells us the names of these women at various points in the Gospel story for a reason; He wants us to see in them examples of people who care for and minister to Jesus until the end.

Relationship with Jesus doesn't just mean assisting Him for a moment and then sending Him on His way. Instead it means being there to serve Him as His needs warrant at different moments and stages of His life—and our lives. Relationship with Jesus means that we are never exempt from the duties of discipleship so long as Jesus needs our loving service. The women served our Lord by supporting His ministry, standing by Him in His agony, and caring for His crucified body. They were with Him when He was popular and welcomed by the crowds in Galilee, as well as when He was jeered and despised on Calvary. They are examples of perseverance and thoroughness to inspire us. It was not a glorious task to serve Jesus by anointing His body, but it was the task the women thought Jesus needed and so they were willing to do it. The love they had for Jesus motivated them to go early in the morning with a humble and caring attitude to seek Him. As a result, something happened to them. Not only did they become disciples who received the news of the Resurrection but they were also sent to proclaim that news to others. Those who had cared for Jesus in His earthly ministry are now told to bring others to the Lord through their witness of faith. The example of the women offers us some guidance for our lives as disciples as well.

First, we need to look at our service to the Lord and evaluate how well we live out the qualities of perseverance and thoroughness. Sometimes we can limit our discipleship to doing the things that are easy or the things we enjoy rather than responding to whatever the Lord's needs are in a given moment. (Remember: The needs of Jesus are presented to us in the lives of others—those who bear His name as Christians.) Sometimes, too, we can find it easy to follow the Lord when it is popular or non-threatening but difficult when it means standing alone with the Crucified One abandoned on Calvary. We can also find it difficult to live out our discipleship in obscure hidden actions like caring for the details of a proper burial. When disciples enter into a committed relationship with Jesus, then nothing is more important than being with the Lord in every moment no matter what the cost or the reward.

Second, like the women, we need to be reminded that there is a point in our discipleship when we are called to be witnesses who invite others to Jesus rather than keeping our relationship with the Lord only to ourselves. Discipleship may be a deeply personal experience, but it is not a private experience. Just as the women were sent to share the message that transformed their sorrow into joy, so, too, we are sent to do the same.

> *If someone were to ask, "Are you a committed Christian?" how would you respond and what reasons would you give?*
> *What are ways in which people can be tempted to limit their discipleship to only doing what they want rather than doing what Jesus needs (present in the lives of those who bear His name)?*
> *Which action of the women do you find most challenging to live out in your life as a disciple (supporting Jesus through their resources, standing with Jesus on Calvary, going quietly to care for His body in the tomb, or becoming witnesses of the Resurrection to others)?*
> *Salome and Mary Magdalene show us that people from distressed backgrounds can become incredible disciples. How does this insight give you encouragement?*

The third detail that Mark gives us in this account is when he refers to the timing of the women's visit as being on "Day One". Some translations read "first day of the week" but that is not really accurate. Mark uses the phrase "Day One" for a reason—because it alludes to Genesis 1:5 as it is written in the Greek copy of the Old Testament also known as the Septuagint. References to Genesis have been present in other areas of Mark's Gospel as well (see Mk 1:1). By including this phrase in the context of the Resurrection,

Mark is telling us that a new creation is taking place and that the disciples are becoming a new reality. Indeed, through Baptism (immersion into the Death and Resurrection of Jesus), we are transformed from our human nature into Children of God and we become a new creation. Day One is a powerful day for Christians! The Gospels relate that on Day One many other things happen as well. This is the first day that Jesus' disciples truly understand the fullness of the "Good News" (lit. Gospel). It is the day on which the women become witnesses of the resurrection—the first disciple missionaries who share the good news with others. The other Gospels relate additional important elements that take place on the first day of the week. For Luke it is the day on which disciples recognize, celebrate, and receive Jesus' hidden presence offered to them in the form of broken bread (see Lk 24:35). In John, it is the day on which the Apostles receive the Holy Spirit and are sent to carry on the mission of Jesus in the world (see Jn 20:22).

Day One for us as Christians is Sunday. It is the day on which we gather each week to experience, celebrate, and receive each of these graces in our lives. In our liturgy, we hear the message of the Gospel and receive the hidden presence of Jesus in the Eucharist. We are also commissioned to "go forth" at the end of our worship to be missionaries who share what we have received with others. The liturgy is where we are regenerated and renewed in our Baptismal identity as the Body of Christ in the Church. What an awesome privilege to experience Day One each and every Sunday! Unfortunately a misunderstanding of, or lack of appreciation for, these graces can reduce our ability to receive and experience them when we gather for the liturgy on Day One of the week. If we are not seeking to hear the Good News of God's action in and through Jesus, we will not listen well to the Scriptures and the homily. If we are not seeking to live our lives more fully in Christ, we will not welcome the graces that challenge us to become the Body of Christ. If we are not seeking ways to be more generous with our time and talent, we will not understand how we are being sent to bring Christ to others. If we do not believe that Jesus truly offers His "Real Presence" to us in the Eucharist, we will be indifferent to an opportunity for a life-transforming encounter every time we receive Communion.

*How does this understanding of Day One, as experienced
by the women, challenge you in your experience of Day
One each week?*

*For which grace of Day One do you need to have a deeper
understanding and appreciation?*

*What can a faith community do to help all people expe-
rience the diverse and enriching graces of Day One in the
liturgy?*

Lastly, Mark states that when the women enter the tomb they see
a young man dressed in a white robe. That detail is intentional and
Mark is trying to tell us something by it. In order to understand the
message, we need to recall that in Mark 14:51 we were told about a
"young man" who fled Jesus as our Lord was being arrested in the
Garden of Gethsemane. When that young man fled, he left behind
even his garment and ran away naked. In the ancient world and in
Christian symbolism, clothing was a statement of a person's identity.
The young man who fled Jesus was casting off his "identity" in order
to detach Himself from the Lord in a moment of fearful suffering.
Now we are told that a young man is sitting in the tomb dressed in
a white robe. The white robe is a symbol of the Christian's Baptismal garment—our identity in Christ. The young man in the tomb
represents a disciple who is committed in Baptism and is able to "die
with Christ and be buried with him" (see Rom 6:3–5 and Col 2:12).
White is the color of the Resurrection, and the robe of the young
man symbolizes that he also shares in Christ's Resurrection. It is this
young man who now announces the Gospel message to others. He
has come a long way! His journey of discipleship has led him from
being someone who would discard his Christian commitment as
soon as it involved personal sacrifice, to becoming someone who
could not only die with Christ and be buried with Him, but also
share in our Lord's resurrected eternal life. He is no longer afraid
of rejection, persecution, association, or any other sacrifice; he is
now a courageous witness of how God's grace can transform us
into a new creation when we consciously and intentionally "clothe
ourselves" with Christ in the waters of Baptism.

*Do you identify more with the young man in the Garden of
Gethsemane or the young man in the tomb of Jesus?*

What are significant milestones in your life of discipleship that have demonstrated your ability to remain steadfast in faith and not falter in fear?

What do you think were the significant factors that helped transform the young man's faith from one that faulted in fear to one that courageously witnessed the resurrection?

SECOND SUNDAY OF EASTER

O ur Scripture passage comes from the Gospel of John 20:19–31. The Church provides this same reading for us each year on this Sunday and so we have ample opportunities to reflect on the many rich aspects of this passage.

It is interesting to note how much attention is given to the wounds of Jesus.[3] In John 20:20 we are told that Jesus showed the disciples His hands and His side. When Thomas enters into the scene, he insists to probe the physical wounds of Jesus (see Jn 20:25), and Jesus later offers Thomas such an experience (see Jn 20:27). The attention given to the physical wounds of the Crucifixion serves a variety of purposes. First, the presence of the wounds leaves no doubt whatsoever that the person who is appearing to the disciples in the upper room is indeed the same person whom they saw die on the Cross just a few days earlier. The wounds serve as attestation of identity. Second, the wounds serve as proof that the Resurrection of Jesus was not just a spiritual phenomenon or apparition of a non-physical being. Rather, the wounds serve to provide physical evidence that Jesus has risen in His very body yet His corporeal reality is no longer bound by time and space; Jesus is able to physically pass through locked doors. This second purpose is important because some disciples thought Jesus might have been a "ghost" in His Resurrection; the invitation to probe His physical wounds proves that He is flesh and blood and not a ghost (see Lk 24:37). Third, Jesus chose to keep the marks of His Crucifixion for a reason—because they are a sign of His triumph and not of His defeat. Jesus proudly bears the marks of the Crucifixion because it was the means by which He accomplished His mission and manifested the love of God to the world on Calvary. In doing so, Jesus made God known. The wounds of His Crucifixion are the trophies

---

3.   Thoughts for this reflection on the wounds of Jesus were taken from a homily by C. H. Spurgeon entitled, "The Evidence of our Lord's Wounds" from www.spurgeon.org/sermons/2061.php.

our Lord bears in eternity that show all the powers of heaven and earth how great God's love is for humanity. Lastly, Jesus bears the marks of the Crucifixion as a reminder of the great price He paid for our sin as the "Lamb of God who takes away the sin of the world" (see Jn 1:29). Jesus bears His wounds as a reminder and invitation to us that we might turn away from sin and choose life (Salvation) by believing and being drawn to in the Crucified One who was lifted up (see Jn 3:14, 8:28, 12:32).

The wounds of Jesus, then, are an enduring reminder to us that He has been given the power of judgment, and our response to Him is the basis of that judgment (see Jn 5:21–29). It is interesting how these last two purposes have been expressed in Christian iconography over the centuries. If you study carefully Michelangelo's fresco of the Last Judgment in the Sistine Chapel, you will note that Jesus prominently bears the marks of His Crucifixion as He comes in power to judge the world. You will also note that the great saints who surround the Lord in heaven are depicted holding the instruments of their martyrdom and the marks of their persecution. Like Jesus, the great saints and martyrs proudly display their wounds and the instruments of their torture, like trophies of their triumph over the forces of sin and death that tried to destroy them. By their faithful perseverance they were victorious, and the marks of their persecutions now serve as the sign of how great their love was for God. Lastly, Jesus bears the marks of His Crucifixion to give the disciples courage to face the suffering and persecution that will come into their lives as well. The disciples are locked in the upper room because they are afraid; they need to overcome their fear and know that nothing is more powerful than Jesus who has triumphed even over the forces of death. This message gives the disciples courage to go out and become fearless witnesses of the Gospel. They can face death themselves knowing that the Lord has gone before them, knows their suffering, and will not turn away anyone the Father has given Him. Finally, He will raise them on the last day (see Jn 6:37–40).

How do the above reflections help you better appreciate the marks of Jesus' Crucifixion?

> *Sometimes Christians today must pay a price for their faith.*
> *What are some of the "trophies" we should celebrate as*
> *signs of faithful triumph rather than indications of defeat?*
> *There are few realizations more dramatic than when we*
> *become conscious of the injury we have caused another*
> *person by our actions. How do the wounds of Jesus, by which*
> *our sins are forgiven, help you desire to turn away from sin?*
> *Jesus was no longer bound by time and space; He could*
> *be present to the disciples by passing through doors in his*
> *physical body. How is the crucified and risen presence of*
> *Jesus offered to you? (hint: It is on the First Day of the week!)*
> *How does the suffering of Jesus give you consolation, con-*
> *fidence, and courage when you are facing rejection or per-*
> *secution?*

Another interesting point about this passage is how disciples take different routes in the process of coming to faith in the Resurrection of Jesus. We see this process in the experience of Mary Magdalene in John 20:11–18 when Jesus must call her by name to awaken the realization that He is risen. Peter goes to the tomb in John 20:6 but there is no indication that he believes. The Beloved Disciple is the only one who does believe as a result of his visit to the tomb (see Jn 20:7). The disciples in the upper room obviously did not believe the news of the Resurrection as related to them by Mary Magdalene. Jesus reached out to them and offered them signs of His Resurrection in order to elicit their faith and overcome their fear. Thomas is really no different from the others. He, too, is in a state of disbelief and places basically the same conditions on what is necessary for him to accept the message of the Resurrection (as the other disciples received during our Lord's first appearance to them in the upper room).

As Jesus did for Mary Magdalene and the other disciples, our Lord now does for Thomas. Thomas does indeed come to believe and even makes the greatest profession of Jesus' identity in the Gospel of John when he exclaims, "My Lord and My God." It's important to note that we are never informed of Thomas actually touching Jesus. Rather, the implication is that Jesus' gracious offer and invitation was sufficient to elicit Thomas' faith. Jesus so desires that we believe in Him that the Lord reaches out to each of us like the Good Shepherd who calls His sheep by name and cares for their weaknesses. The Lord cares for us in the same way. Jesus continues to invite us into a relationship of trusting surrender, and He leads us by giving us what we need even if it is not what we want. We experience the presence of Jesus, the Risen One, in various ways including the quiet of prayer, the Sacraments, the lives of faithful Christians, and the gift of the Holy Spirit. All of these are means the Lord uses to help us believe in and be conformed to His living presence in our lives.

> *What have been some of the events or means that God has used to help you believe?*
> *What are some of the common conditions people put on their faith today?*
> *When the disciples believed in the Risen Jesus they were filled with peace and joy, and were no longer afraid. How does the experience of coming to faith change people today in a visible way?*
> *Why do you think John provides several examples of people who had to pursue their own personal and unique journey of faith?*

The scene ends with Jesus pronouncing a blessing on those who can believe without the necessity of "seeing". This beatitude is both consoling and challenging. It is consoling because it assures us that Christians of subsequent generations are at no disadvantage when it comes to faith. Rather, Jesus cares for us without limit and our faith can be just as great if not greater than that of the disciples in the upper room. Each of Jesus' closest disciples required some sign to confirm their faith. Not only can our faith be as great as that of the early disciples, but John is also telling us that our faith can be even greater than theirs! That may surprise us, but throughout the Gospel of John we have been called to believe in Jesus' Word rather than demanding signs to convince us. We encounter the Word of Jesus in Scripture and prayer as well as in the living experience of faith passed on through the centuries (Tradition). When our hearts are attuned to the voice of God then we can hear the Lord guiding and challenging our lives. John wants us to do more than just hear Jesus; John wants us to listen, to believe, and to do whatever the Lord tells us (see Jn 2:5). When God does bless us with signs or external confirmation of our faith, it is not because we are somehow privileged or more special than others. Rather, it is because our faith is weaker than others and Jesus is caring for us as the Good Shepherd who is helping His wayward sheep! More blessed than those who have received external confirmation of their faith are those who have faith without having received external confirmation.

> *Who is an example for you of someone who has great faith in the Word of Jesus?*
>
> *How can the experience of signs and external confirmation falsely lead someone to consider themselves "privileged" in their discipleship?*
>
> *What happens when someone puts great emphasis on a particular sign of faith they have experienced?*
>
> *Sometimes it is in the midst of difficult situations that our faith is weakest (tragedy, terminal illness, or broken relationships). Do you know someone who has been a witness of unwavering faith in the midst of hardship?*
>
> *What would your life be like if you acted on every inspiration in prayer without requiring confirming signs of God's direction?*

THIRD SUNDAY OF EASTER

Our Scripture passage comes from the Gospel of Luke 24:35–48. In this reading we heard of the two disciples returning from Emmaus and relating their encounter of the Risen Lord to the others gathered in Jerusalem. It is in this context that Jesus appears, opens their minds to the Scriptures, and commissions them to preach repentance to the nations. We continue to experience these same effects of the Risen Christ in our lives. As disciples, it is important for us to study this passage so as to better understand our encounter of the Risen Lord as well.

It is interesting to note that the two disciples specifically relate how Jesus was made known to them in the "Breaking of the Bread" (see Acts 2:46 where the "Breaking of the Bread" was the ritual meal for the early Christian community). This is a reference to the Eucharist. The passage then goes to state that it was, "...while they were still speaking about this, He [Jesus] stood in their midst and said to them, 'Peace be with you'". Luke is telling us something by connecting the actions of sharing one's faith experience with the manifestation of the Risen Lord. Something happens when people talk honestly and openly about their experience of God. Suddenly others begin to realize how God has been active in their lives as well and then they acknowledge that presence as an authentic faith encounter. In short, when we share our stories of faith it helps build the faith of others. In Matthew 18:20 Jesus told His disciples, "Where two or three gather in my name, there am I in their midst."

In this Sunday's passage from Luke we see similarly how disciples who share their faith suddenly do experience the Lord in their midst. Sharing our faith experiences can bring about other beneficial effects as well. It can help clarify for us how God has acted in a particular way and become the opportunity for us to express our gratitude. It can help encourage people to persevere when they are wavering in their commitment. It can even offer consolation when someone is going through a period of spiritual dryness or doubting God's presence in their life. God always reveals

Himself for the common good—even when that revelation takes place in individual lives and personal circumstances. When we share our personal experiences of God, we are contributing to the spiritual good of others. Sometimes we can mistakenly think that it is prideful or arrogant to let others know how God has worked in our lives, but those are mistaken thoughts. It is an act of faithful and humble witness when we share stories of God's presence. This experience of faith awakening happened in the context of the "Breaking of the Bread" and it should happen in the context of our celebration of the Eucharist as well.

> *How has someone's sharing of their experience of God brought about a spiritual awakening in your life?*
> *When have you felt deep peace while in the context of faith sharing?*
> *In what distinctive way do you experience the presence of the Risen Lord in the "Breaking of the Bread" of the Eucharist?*
> *What are some of the fears or concerns that can prevent people from sharing their experience of God with others?*
> *Who in your life is still waiting to experience Jesus in a personal way, and how can your experience of God help open their hearts and minds to the Lord?*
> *The disciples were gathered in Jerusalem when they started sharing their stories. What are ministry contexts today that provide great opportunities for faith sharing and faith witness in your faith community?*

When Jesus stood in the midst of the disciples, our Lord first "opened their minds" to the meaning of His words and to the Scriptures. It is significant that this appearance of Jesus to the disciples occurs in the midst of a meal (note that Jesus asked for something to eat and they provided Him with a piece of fish) while they were discussing their experience. The combination of Jesus' words, the Scriptures, a meal, and the Breaking of the Bread are all elements of our current Eucharistic Liturgy (Liturgy of the Word and Liturgy of the Eucharist). Luke is giving us an insight into what should be happening every time we gather to experience the Risen Lord in our community prayer: We should recognize Him both in the Word of

God proclaimed in the Scriptures and in the Eucharist celebrated on the altar. The Real Presence of Jesus in the context of the Mass is one of the significant teachings of Luke's Gospel because he is trying to encourage his community to find Jesus in the present, rather than only remembering Him as he was during His earthly ministry or how He will be when He comes again.

Luke wants us to realize that we can hear the Lord speaking to us every time the Scriptures are proclaimed, and we can experience deep communion with Jesus every time we break bread in the liturgy. It is important to note that the disciples could not grasp the meaning of Scripture on their own. Rather, understanding required that the Lord interpret the Scripture for them through the lens of His Death and Resurrection. Only from the perspective of Jesus' Passion can the Law and the Prophets (Old Testament) be properly understood. With Jesus' instruction, the disciples are now able to see how the words of the prophets were fulfilled in Him. As disciples, we are called to continue using the interpretative lens of Jesus' Suffering, Death, and Resurrection any time we read the Old Testament or the New Testament. Such a clearly defined perspective protects us from taking Jesus' words out of context or interpreting other passages of Scripture in ways that are not divinely intended. This is an important message for us as disciples because it helps us properly unlock the Scriptures and properly teachings of the Lord for our lives.

> *How can the Suffering, Death, and Resurrection of Jesus change the way you will read or understand your favorite passages of Scripture?*
>
> *What principles or interpretative lens other than the Suffering, Death, and Resurrection of Jesus can people be tempted to use when interpreting Scripture?*
>
> *What is the danger of reading Scripture through the lens of only one part of Jesus' Paschal Mystery? For example only viewing Scripture through His Suffering, Death, or Resurrection, but not all of it?*
>
> *How do you experience the presence of Jesus in the Liturgy of the Word?*

What can we, as a faith community, do to help "open the minds" of people to understand the meaning of the Scriptures for their lives?

How do you think the disciples were trying to interpret the Scriptures and Jesus' words before our Lord opened their minds to the correct way?

How do we know when someone is quoting or interpreting Scripture in a way that goes against the divine intention?

After the Risen Lord revealed Himself to His disciples and opened their minds to the meaning of the Scriptures, He then simply says to them, "You are my witnesses". This is a very powerful statement for three reasons. First, we usually understand "witness" in a passive sense meaning that a witness is someone who sees something occur. While it is true that the disciples did "see" Jesus teach, heal, lead, forgive, suffer, die, and rise, there is more to being a disciple than just being a spectator. Being a witness means communicating to others the reality of Jesus that we have been blessed to experience. It is an active role, not a passive role. Eyewitnesses must become Ministers of the Word for others (see Lk 1:2). Second, being a witness of Jesus means that we live out the same radical love and trust in our lives that Jesus demonstrated in His Passion, Death, and Resurrection. The word for "witnesses" in Greek is martyres that gives us the English word "martyr". Indeed, martyrs are people who witnessed their faith in Jesus' Death and Resurrection at the cost of their own lives. Virtually all of the disciples who encountered the Lord in this Scripture passage were put to death because of their faith. By remaining faithful and being united to Jesus in a death like His, they manifested their hope to share in His Resurrection as well. We may not be called to physically die because of our faith, but there are lots of ways in which we are called to be courageous witnesses of Jesus' Death and Resurrection each day. Third, Jesus tells His disciples that they are witnesses and that their witnessing is to have a practical effect in other people's lives. Namely, Jesus is commissioning the disciples and sending them forth with the great task of proclaiming the Gospel to all nations so that the nations might repent and share in the forgiveness of sins.

The message of Jesus has a purpose and that purpose is to change our lives (repentance) and lead us to holiness (forgiveness of sins). This Great Commission is not an invention of early Christians, as some contemporary adversaries of the Church claim. This Great Commission of Jesus is actually part of the fulfillment of Scripture just as much as the Death and Resurrection of Jesus is the fulfillment of Scripture (see Is 52:13–53:12 foretells the suffering Messiah; Hos 6:2 foretells the Resurrection on the third day; Is 49:6 foretells the message of Salvation and Repentance to all nations). With Jesus' Commission, the early Christians understood that being a disciple required three things: that we share with others what we ourselves have received, that we live out in our lives the mystery of Jesus' Death and Resurrection, and that we show the world what a life conformed to Christ looks like so others can be inspired and invited to become disciples as well.

> *How does this understanding of being a "witness" change your reading of this passage?*
>
> *How can people witness the Death and Resurrection of Jesus?*
>
> *What would it mean for you to move from being an eye-witness to becoming a Minister of the Word?*
>
> *If Jesus told you in your prayer that He wanted you to be His "witness", what would your first thought be?*
>
> *When have you been inspired to grow deeper in your faith life because of another person's lived example of faith?*
>
> *Why do you think Luke connects the forgiveness of sins to the experience of repentance (change of life) and what does that require of you?*

FOURTH SUNDAY OF EASTER

O ur Scripture passage comes from the Gospel of John 10:11–18. This is the famous passage in which Jesus identifies Himself as the Good Shepherd and for this reason this Sunday is always referred to as "Good Shepherd Sunday". As disciples who desire to follow the Lord's lead, this passage offers us some important insights and challenges for our faith. It should be noted that the term "good" really means "model" or "true" and so Jesus is presenting to us a definition of who we should be as we fulfill our shepherding responsibilities as disciples.

Describing God's care for His people with the image of a shepherd is nothing new in the Scriptures. Psalm 23 and others introduced this image into the religious view of the Jewish people centuries before Jesus. The most extensive and important Old Testament passage that speaks about God's shepherding care for His people is found in Ezekiel chapter 34 (God cares for the sheep, rescues them, gathers them, feeds them, and tends them). Examples of bad shepherds are also presented in the Old Testament (see Jer 23; Zec 13:7–9). These passages tell us that Jesus is drawing on a rich image when He identifies Himself as the Good Shepherd as opposed to the bad shepherd (hired hand).

Before explaining the qualifications that make Him the Good Shepherd, Jesus first defines the activities and motivations of the bad shepherd. The bad shepherd is primarily concerned for his own well-being at the expense of the flock's well-being. The bad shepherd's lack of protective action allows the flock to be scattered and devoured by aggressive and hostile forces. The bad shepherd is more concerned about being paid than relationship with the flock. Jesus, on the other hand, is willing to lay down His life for the sheep. This is a significant statement because nowhere in the Old Testament does it ever imply that God (as shepherd), or the Messiah, would go to the extent of laying down His life for the flock. That is the most radical part of this passage: Jesus is so committed to us and in love with us that He would die for us and so He did.

We all have influences that try to guide our lives and values. These influences are the "shepherding" forces. They may be members of our family and friends or even messages from the media. These influences may also be cultural expectations or even civic, corporate, or religious leaders.

> *How does the contrast between the qualities of the Good Shepherd and the characteristics of the bad shepherd help you to sort out the various influences in your life?*
> *Who exemplifies for you the qualities of the Good Shepherd?*
> *Who or what are some of the bad shepherds that try to influence you every day?*
> *Whose lives do you influence and how does the contrast between the Good Shepherd and bad shepherd challenge you?*

In the second part of this passage Jesus goes on to explain how He is the Good Shepherd, but this time the explanation is in reference to the Father and the flock rather than in contrast with the bad shepherd. There are four primary factors that make Jesus the Good (model or true) Shepherd. Let's look at each of these four and reflect on each one.

- First, Jesus is the Good Shepherd because of His relationship with the Father. This relationship is expressed in terms of "knowing". Throughout the Gospel of John, Jesus has repeatedly expressed His deep communion with the Father and has clearly stated that He speaks the Father's Word (see Jn 7:16, 8:42, 12:49, and 14:10) and carries out the Father's works (see Jn 4:34, 5:30, and 6:38–39). This deep and intimate knowledge of the Father is essential in order for Jesus to be the Good Shepherd. The prophecy of Ezekiel is fulfilled in the person of Jesus because through him God is indeed shepherding His people! The knowledge of which Jesus speaks isn't so much conceptual as it is experiential. Jesus knows the Father's joy and sorrow. He knows the Father's hopes and concerns. He knows what pleases the Father and what disappoints the Father. It is this knowledge that allows Jesus to manifest the challenging, comforting, encouraging, and inspiring presence of God. As disciples, we are each entrusted with shepherding roles of one kind or another. Perhaps it is our responsibility for a younger sibling or a subordinate employee. Perhaps it is in our marriage, friendship, or position of civic leadership. In order to be a true shepherd, we must have that same deep communion with the Father from which Jesus lived His life.

How can you come to know more clearly the heart of God?
When have you found yourself influencing others because
you knew it was something God wanted?
How can a faith community help people grow deeper in
their desire and ability to hear the Father's Word and know
the Father's will?

- Second, Jesus is the Good Shepherd because of His relationship with the sheep. Again, this relationship is expressed in terms of personal and intimate knowledge. In John 10 verse 14, Jesus says, "I know mine and mine know me". This is a reference to the mutual sharing of life that exists between Jesus and disciples. Sometimes it can be easy for us to feel anonymous in the world of humanity or to think that God has a generic love for people rather than a specific and personal love for each one of us. This passage stresses that Jesus doesn't care solely about the flock as a whole; rather, the Lord seeks an intimate and personal relationship with each disciple. As disciples, this action of Jesus challenges us in two ways. First, it challenges us to accept and enter into that deep personal relationship with Jesus so that we know the Lord and we allow the Lord to know us. It is that personal and life-changing relationship with God that is the foundation of our Christian identity. Second, as disciples who are called to bring the presence of Christ into the world, this passage challenges us to seek a personal and caring relationship with all those in our care. It can be easy to treat people in a generic way but it can also be de-humanizing to do so. Jesus wants the Christian community to be formed as an extension of His loving relationship with the Father and that relationship is deeply personal.

How have you come to know the personal presence and care
of Jesus in your life?
How do you express intimacy with God in Jesus?

*When are you tempted to treat people in a generic sense
rather than caring for their needs personally?*
*Who is an example of the Good Shepherd who knows His
sheep?*
*Who needs to be dignified by your personal attention and
care today?*

• Third, Jesus is the Good Shepherd because His love will bring
about communion between God and us. This communion
should not be confused with mere social gatherings or organizational unity. Jesus tells us in John 10:16 that there are other
sheep He wants to bring into the fold so that there will be
one flock and one shepherd. Those who are united in this
one flock are those who "hear his voice". The theme of gathering the lost sheep was a central part of Ezekiel 34, but Jesus
re-defines the flock to refer to something more than Ezekiel
had envisioned. For Jesus, the flock isn't just the Jewish people
who were dispersed in exile; rather, the flock refers to all who
hear His voice—even the Gentiles, sinners, and tax collectors.
Our Lord desires that those who respond to His voice calling
them to faith may be welcomed by all others who have come
to Him as well. This is an important instruction on the nature
of our communion and community as a Church. The Church
is not primarily a social gathering of like-minded people and
neither is it primarily an organization of self-defined values
and structure. Instead, the Church is first and foremost those
"called by Christ" who gather in His Spirit and among whom
our Lord dwells. This is a challenging message for us because
it requires us to welcome and love all those whom Christ is
calling into His flock. It also means that we have the responsibility to help others hear, recognize, and respond to the voice
of the Lord calling them to faith. Sometimes it is easy for us to
see the Church like a religious country club or to be selective
of those with whom we will associate. This passage reminds us
that the Church belongs to Jesus and that it is our communion
with God that defines and allows our communion with others.

*When are you tempted to be selective in your associations
with others in the context of the Church?*

How are you challenged by the understanding of the Church as primarily a spiritual reality rather than a social or organizational entity?
Who helped you to hear the voice of the Lord in your life? Who needs your help so they can recognize and respond to the voice of the Lord calling them?
For whom does the Lord want you to be more authentically welcoming as a brother or sister in Christ in your faith community?

- Fourth, Jesus is the Good Shepherd because He provides the model of true love that reveals the Father through our Lord's generous and sacrificial self-giving in the laying down of His life. It should be noted that this passage is the first time in John's Gospel that love has been explicitly given as the reason for the Cross! God's love for the world and for Jesus was already introduced in John's Gospel (see 3:16, 3:35, and 17:24). Verse 17 of this passage indicates that the Father loves the Son because Jesus lives out God's will completely, which is later identified as the laying down of His life for the disciples (see Jn 13:1, 15:13). Jesus will even command His disciples to manifest this same love in their lives (see Jn 13:34). Our Lord's action of laying down His life on the Cross was not an attempt to gain the Father's love, but rather an expression of the loving relationship that already existed. In His sacrifice, Jesus manifested the Father's love and so the Cross becomes the revelation of God, who is Love. This final quality of the Good Shepherd is striking because nowhere in the ancient world or in the Old Testament did divine beings lay down their lives for people. The action of Jesus is singular and shocking. When we think about the Crucifixion of Jesus, we can understand it as a tragedy, an injustice, or an act of hatred. It requires the eyes of faith and the revelation of the Son for us to see the Cross as the ultimate sign of God's love—and then to live that same love in our lives as disciples. Jesus is the model for us to follow.

How does this understanding of the death of Jesus as a manifestation of love change the way you look at a Crucifix?
Who lays down their lives today in witness to God's love?

How can your daily actions be a better witness of the Father's love for others to see?

How does this teaching change the way you understand the commandment of Jesus, "As I have loved you, so you must love one another"?

FIFTH SUNDAY OF EASTER

Our Scripture passage comes from the Gospel of John 15:1–8. This passage contains another one of the famous "I AM" statements of Jesus in which He identifies Himself as the Vine and defines the disciples as the Branches. This image, as well as the actions and relationships associated with it, offers an important instruction for us as disciples.

One of the first images Jesus uses in this passage is that of pruning the vine. Pruning was done for various reasons. First, pruning was a way in which the vine grower could direct the growth of the plant by allowing new sprouts to develop only in certain areas. This image of pruning is especially important in interpreting the movement of the Holy Spirit directing the life of the Early Church. The experience of being pruned or cut back is rarely pleasant but is intended to promote and direct new growth. It is only when the Church in Jerusalem experienced persecution that the apostles were motivated to initiate their great missionary journeys to the larger world—and the Church began to grow in new directions as a result of the pruning that had occurred (see Acts 8:1). Sometimes God wants our lives to develop in new and specific directions, and one of the ways the Lord can motivate that growth within us is by blocking growth in our existing direction. There is a common expression that captures this meaning of pruning that says, "When God closes one door, He opens another one." Branches that are full of life are not deterred in their growth by obstacles or setbacks; rather, living branches are constantly seeking ways to burst forth with new life in new directions. The challenge for a disciple is to seek that new direction in which God wants to direct our efforts for the good of the Gospel.

When have you experienced this pruning that blocked one direction in your life and motivated you to pursue new directions of growth?

Why do some people respond only with frustration, self-pity, or anger when they experience this pruning while others respond with motivation for growth, hope, and creativity? How can we as a Church help people better understand frustrating or painful situations as a motivation for new growth?

How is God pruning the Church today, and what do you think is the new growth the Lord wants to motivate?

Second, additional pruning occurred at two different times. One pruning occurred in late winter (February or March) and involved cutting off the "dead" branches that could not bear fruit. This winter pruning was to ensure the health of the vine and to provide as much space as possible for the living branches to develop. Jesus speaks to this pruning in vs. 2 and 6. In the life of the Early Church, there were some disciples who were in the Christian community but were actually "dead branches". Judas would be such an example because we were told that he belonged to the realm of Satan but was still sitting at table with the disciples (see Jn 13:2). Jesus specifically tells us that such disciples become dead branches because they fail to abide in Him. As disciples, it is important for us to remember that we are the ones who have the responsibility to accept the life of God offered to us or not to accept it. Accepting the gift of God's life means participating in grace-filled opportunities of prayer, the Sacraments, and actions of selfless love for others. When we take advantage of these opportunities, we are abiding in Christ. When we fail to take advantage of these opportunities, we are cutting ourselves off from grace. Our physical presence in the Church does not necessarily mean that we are living members of the Body of Christ. We have to be spiritually united with Jesus in order to be living members of His Body; otherwise, we are just dead branches taking up room and obstructing others in their growth.

How do dead branches damage the overall health of the vine (both in the literal sense of a plant and in the analogous sense of the Church)?

How does this understanding of pruning motivate you to pursue additional sources of grace in your life?

How can we as a faith community revitalize the dead branches to make them alive in Christ?

When have you been a dead branch, and what led you to renew your life-giving relationship with Jesus ("abiding in Him") so as to become a living branch?

Sometimes disciples can allow themselves to become complacent with sinful situations or habits. These parts of their lives become dead branches that occupy time and energy but are not united with Christ. How does this image of pruning speak to these situations?

Third, another pruning took place in the late summer months (usually August). This pruning involved removing the smaller shoots on the vine so that the nutrients could be directed to the main fruit-bearing branches. This focused concentration of nutrients would allow the vine to produce the most abundant fruit. If the smaller shoots were not pruned away then the nutrients would be directed in a variety of different ways that might create more foliage but would not produce more fruit. This is an important lesson for disciples because there is no shortage of ways in which we can spend our time and energy. However, we cannot do everything, and in order to do some things well we must necessarily limit and focus our involvements. To use the image of the Gospel, we need to "prune" away those things that have become distractions in our lives so that we can focus our time and energy in the direction God wants. Jesus' Word helps us accomplish this important pruning of life because the Lord reveals to us the values of the Gospel that can help prioritize and focus our efforts.

What are the principle values and priorities Jesus gives us through His teaching?

When have you had to prune away otherwise good efforts and involvements because they were distracting you from the "main thing" you needed to pursue?

Where might people find themselves if they don't prune away their distractions?

In which ways can we remain fruitless by not accomplishing the "main thing"?

*What keeps people from wanting to prune away distrac-
tions in their lives?*
*How can a faith community help people tell the difference
between what is a priority and what is a distraction?*

Jesus ends this passage with the very important statement of verse
8 when He says, "By this my Father is glorified, that you bear much
fruit, and so prove to be my disciples." Jesus was entrusted with the
mission to glorify the Father (see Jn 12:27–28). Our Lord accomplished this mission by manifesting the love of God on Calvary.
Jesus tells us in this passage that we will continue to glorify the
Father when we bear "fruit". "Fruit", then, refers to the love a disciple
shows in laying down his life for a friend (see Jn 15:13). In doing so,
disciples are fulfilling the command of Jesus to "love one another
as I have loved you" (see Jn 15:9, 12, 17). The love of Jesus that we
receive from our communion with Him must flow through us and
be manifested in our relationships with others. This visible manifestation of God's love in the life of a faithful Christian draws others
into that communion and creates additional disciples. When others
are touched by the love of God through us then we are "bearing
fruit", and the Father is glorified because God, who is love, is being
made manifest in the world. When we become this conduit of God's
love affecting the lives of others then, Jesus says, we prove that we
are His disciples. What a challenging definition of discipleship!
Disciples are not just recipients of God's grace and love; to be a
disciple means that we are active conduits of that grace and love to
others. If we are not bearing fruit, we are not disciples according
to this definition given by Jesus. It is important for us to remember
that this teaching is given in the context of the Last Supper, which
is a Eucharistic setting. The expectation to "bear fruit" and to be
a conduit of God's grace becomes particularly daunting when we
realize the necessity of passing on to others the presence of Jesus
whom we have received in the Eucharist. If we are only receiving
the Lord, but not actively sharing the Lord, then we are not bearing
fruit and we are not disciples.

How does Jesus' definition of discipleship challenge you?
*How does the context of this teaching within the Last Supper
change the way you approach the Eucharist?*

What is the "fruit" you have produced this past week as a result of sharing in the life of Christ in the Eucharist?
Who has become a disciple because of your Christian witness?
What leads a person to think they can be a disciple without bearing fruit?

Sixth Sunday of Easter

O ur Scripture passage comes from the Gospel of John 15:9–17. In this passage Jesus continues His instruction on love as the defining quality of discipleship. In order for disciples to remain in the abiding love, life, and joy of Jesus, they will need to keep His commandments. A disciple can be obedient out of a variety of possible motivations. In this teaching Jesus reminds us that our primary motivation for keeping His commandments should be our relationship with the Lord as friends rather than servants or slaves. The Greek word *doulos* is often translated as either "slave" or "servant". Both translations are valid and each term offers insights into some distinctive aspects of discipleship. It should be noted that many great people of faith in the Old Testament and the New Testament were described as being the *doulos* of God. Some examples include Moses in Deuteronomy 34:5, Joshua in Joshua 24:29, David in Psalm 89:20, Paul in Titus 1:1 and James in James 1:1).

The image of being a slave emphasizes some specific aspects of discipleship. A slave serves in an act of complete obedience to the will of the master. In Mark 10:44 and Matthew 20:27–28 Jesus taught the disciples that they must become the "slave" of all. Jesus even referred to Himself in similar terms. Paul used the term to refer to himself and his obligation to preach the Gospel. Slaves fulfill their duty because of who they are. Christians are called to serve others because of their identity as well. Paul tells us that through our Baptism we owe a "debt" of love to one another (see Rom 13:8–10). In this sense, Christians are called to willingly place their lives in obedience to Christ and unlimited, loving service to others. A slave has no private life of his own; all that he is and all that he has belongs to the master. A slave even surrenders his future to the master's will. This life-long, all-encompassing duty is an obligation and not a choice for disciples. However, the image of being a slave also has some negative aspects to it. Slaves perform their duties mostly out of a desire to avoid punishment. Thus, a slave's obedience to the master's command was often based on fear. Also, a slave simply followed the instructions of the master whether those orders reflected the individual slave's will or not. As disciples, we do owe a debt of love to the other people God has placed in our lives. That debt can never be fully repaid. We also are called to serve the Lord out of duty as part of our Baptismal identity and to even be obedient when God's will takes us where we ourselves would not choose to go. But something can be missing when a person is motivated primarily by a fear of punishment. Sometimes Christians can be motivated in their discipleship for the sole reason of wanting to avoid the wrath of God.

> *Why do you think Paul used the term doulos in a positive way to describe his relationship to God?*
> *Which aspects of the image of a slave can positively inform and inspire your discipleship?*
> *When are you motivated by fear of punishment in your faith life?*
> *What is it about the image of a slave that you do not like?*

The image of being a servant also emphasizes some specific aspects of discipleship. A servant exercises his free will and decides to serve the master. Jesus often used the image of a servant in his parables so as to teach lessons of discipleship. Servants have freedom to come and go on their own terms. Servants can choose the employment they want. Servants can even have their own private lives and make their own decisions for their futures and the futures of their families. The image of a servant focuses on the power of individual autonomy in choosing to serve others. Certainly disciples must choose to place their lives in God's service on a daily basis and so faithfully exercise that same free will and autonomy. As servants, we bear the responsibility of managing our lives and making decisions for the good of others. However, the image of being a servant also has some negative aspects to it. Servants carry out their duties and fulfill the master's will because they desire reward and recompense. Servants can even think that they deserve their just remuneration. Because servants have greater freedom, they can choose when they serve and when they don't. Similarly we are called to be servants who make a free choice each day to place our lives in the service of God and others. Sometimes, like servants, disciples can be tempted to follow the Lord for the sake of reward or to think that God owes them certain blessings and favors. This attitude can be detrimental to the spiritual life and cause frustration and disappointment in disciples. Oftentimes, this attitude is manifested by resentment when difficulties occur and a person feels unjustly treated by God because they "did all the right things" and think they deserve to be preserved from difficult situations. Disciples who are motivated primarily by desire for reward remain self-centered in their attitude. Also, being a disciple is not just something we do forty hours a week like a job; being a disciple requires more commitment than simply being a hired hand for the Lord.

> *Which aspects of the image of a servant can positively inform and inspire your discipleship?*
> *When do you find yourself being motivated in your faith life by a desire for reward or in order to earn God's good favor?*
> *What is it about the image of a servant that you do not like?*
> *Why do you think Jesus used the image of a servant so often in his parables?*

Jesus then tells His disciples that He wants them to be "friends" rather than servants or slaves. This image of discipleship is rich and challenging. Friends care for one another out of love rather than fear of punishment or desire for reward. Friends are friends all day, every day, even when they are not in the presence of one another. Friends want to understand the other person's perspective so they can have a common vision and share a common will. Friends want to spend time together and make such occasions a priority in their schedules. Friends choose to go out of their way for the other person and to help them in any way they can. Friends love one another and know that they are loved by each other. Friends will respond at any hour of the night or day to the other's need. Friends want the other person to be a part of their personal lives. Friends put up with each other's shortcomings and weaknesses while encouraging growth and improvement. Friends know what brings the other happiness and go out of their way to carry out those joy-giving actions as a celebration of their relationship. There are so many great reasons why Jesus chose the image of "friends" to be His lasting definition of discipleship. That's the relationship Jesus wants with us!

> *Which aspect of the image of a friend can positively inform and inspire your discipleship?*
> *When do you find yourself being motivated in your faith life primarily by love for God?*
> *What is most challenging about the image of being a friend of Jesus?*
> *How do you make time to spend with Jesus in the course of your day?*
> *When do you go out of your way to do something simply because you know it brings God joy?*

These various images of discipleship are all given as part of Jesus' commandment to love one another as He has loved us. This is more than a commandment to love. It is also a lasting definition of what love means. The definition of love can vary from one person to the next. It can be easy for us to love others—as long as we get to love them on our terms! Jesus wanted to clarify and establish once and for all what true love looks like and so He defined it for us on the Cross. This definition is meant to prevent any misunderstandings of what Christian love is. While we usually pay attention to the first half of that commandment "Love one another", it is really the second half of the verse that gives the whole verse its meaning: "As I have loved you". The love of Jesus was powerful indeed. He washed the feet of those who denied Him and shared the Last Supper with those who betrayed Him. He forgave those who crucified Him and healed those who were arresting Him. He cared for the needs of others even as He Himself was dying. He loved people regardless of whether they appreciated it, reciprocated it, or even wanted it. He manifested the love of God that is creative, redemptive, sanctifying, and sacrificial. If disciples are His "friends," then disciples will manifest the same love in their lives that Jesus manifested in His life. It's significant to note that Jesus directs the disciples' love to one another rather than to Himself. That's because Jesus will be present in the world through the lives of His disciples. Thus, disciples are to continue their love for Jesus in their relations within the Christian community and in doing so manifest their love of God and Neighbor in one and the same moment. As "Friends of Jesus," we are also called to be friends of all others. That challenge of discipleship requires us to love not only the people with whom we want to share our lives but all those the Lord has placed in our midst—whether we choose them or not. They, too, are Friends of Jesus.

> *How do most people define the meaning of love?*
> *Do you know someone who has demonstrated the same love Jesus showed us through His Life, Death, and Resurrection?*
> *When do you find yourself trying to limit the commandment of love so it refers only to those you choose rather than to those God has placed in your life?*
> *Who most needs to be cared for and loved in our world today because they are Friends of Jesus, and how can we show our love for them?*
> *What are ways in which you lay down your life for others through the menial tasks of each day?*
> *What aspects or qualities of Jesus' love do you find most difficult to witness in your life?*

(A good, personal follow-up to this reflection would be to read various works on the topic of holy friendship from select spiritual authors. A great place to start this follow-up reading would be the treatise written by a Cistercian monk, Aelred of Rievaulx, on Spiritual Friendship in which he wrote, "Here we are, you and I, and I hope a third, Christ, in our midst."[4] Also, Teresa of Avila understood the importance of sanctifying friendships in a disciple's life, and one of the great insights she received in her prayer was this phrase: "I will have you converse now, not with men, but with angels."[5] Teresa's insight teaches us that God perfects and sanctifies our human relationships as we grow in divine friendship with Jesus.)

---

4. St Aelred of Rievaulx, *Spiritual Friendship* (Collegeville, MN: Liturgical Press, 2010), p. 55.
5. St Teresa of Avila, *Life*, Trans. By E. Allison Peers (Garden City: Image, 1960), p. 138.

SOLEMNITY OF THE ASCENSION

Our Gospel passage is taken from Mark 16:15–20. In this passage we hear Jesus' final instruction to the disciples before the Lord ascends. These instructions provide a lasting lesson for the Church and all disciples as we strive to carry out the mission entrusted to us. Let's look at this passage and reflect on some particular aspects of it.

The first thing to note about this passage is the emphasis that Jesus places on the importance of the universal mission: The world's salvation depends on it. The disciples cannot casually dismiss or limit the commission to proclaim the Gospel. Believing the message of Jesus won't just make our lives more peaceful, or more inspired; rather, believing the Gospel and being Baptized will be the source of the world's salvation! That is an awesome responsibility that the disciples now bear, and their failure to effectively carry out that mission will be the basis of their own judgment. If the disciples choose to proclaim the Gospel to one group but not another, they fail to fulfill the Lord's command to be universal in their mission. Thus, they must be careful never to limit or restrain their missionary mandate. Also, it should be remembered that the messenger must be credible in order for the message to be credible. The challenge to proclaim the Gospel, then, requires more than just words; it requires an authentic life and integrity of faith that is conformed to the message. The Gospel isn't fully proclaimed until both the messenger and message are completely and authentically representing the person of Jesus. That is a very powerful challenge for us as disciples who have inherited our Lord's commission through our own Baptism. Jesus continues to send us out "into the whole world" so that we can proclaim the Gospel to "every creature". We can sometimes be tempted to only bring the message of faith into safe or predictable circumstances of success and to avoid those settings about which we are unsure or perceive to be hostile. Sometimes we can even choose to limit our witness so as to avoid those with whom we do not wish to be associated. When we create such limits then we disregard our Lord's command to be universal and comprehensive in our mission. Also, we are challenged to be credible messengers who are radically conformed to the message of the Gospel. Most people have an instinctive ability to detect inauthenticity and insincerity; if we are not authentic messengers of the Gospel then others will not listen to our message.

> *How does the message of the Gospel suffer today because of a lack of credibility in the messengers?*
> *What are ways in which we set limits to our missionary efforts so as to choose some settings to witness the Gospel but exclude others?*
> *Jesus places on the disciple the responsibility of effectively proclaiming the Gospel. With whom do we tend to place blame when others don't believe the Christian message?*
> *In what ways does our faith community do a good job of proclaiming the Gospel "to all the world" and in what areas do we fall short?*

Next, Jesus lists the various signs that will accompany those who believe. These signs have sometimes been understood as extraordinary powers that were promised to the apostles. However, the Biblical text indicates that these signs will be manifested collectively by those who believe—that is a group of believers that transcends time and includes us! These signs are not for the benefit of the individual but are given for the authenticity and credibility of the mission. Many of these signs relate to the ministry of Jesus Himself and the experience of the early Church. Let's look briefly at each of these signs to see what they might mean for us today.

• Drive out demons—On several occasions in Mark's Gospel Jesus is presented as driving out demons (see Mk 1:25–26, 1:34, 3:10–12, 5:8, 9:25–26). Our Lord even commanded His disciples to do the same as part of their sharing in His mission (see Mk 3:14–15, 6:7). For instance, Mary Magdalene, one of the greatest of the early disciples, was someone from whom demons were exorcised (see Mk 16:9). It is important to recall that Jesus came to establish the Kingdom of God, which is necessarily opposed to the power of evil. Christian disciples are called to continue this confrontation with the forces of evil in whatever contexts they exist. For the Church to carry out its authentic and credible mission, we must be disciples who continually strive for holiness by rooting out situations of sin and evil in our own lives and in the lives of others.

How can disciples be tempted to become complacent with sinful situations rather than confront sinful situations in their own lives and in the lives of others?

How can Christians today be deceived into believing that the power of evil does not exist, and what is the danger of such an errant belief?

How does the power of evil attempt to discredit the message by corrupting the messengers?

- Speak new languages—The ability to learn new languages was necessary for the early Church to carry out its universal mission. The disciples lived in one small part of the world with only one cultural experience. In order for the message of the Gospel to be proclaimed to the whole world, it would be necessary for the disciples to go beyond the boundaries of their own familiarity and find ways to effectively communicate the Gospel in different languages, cultures, and life situations. An effort such as this requires creativity, flexibility, and perseverance. As disciples who live in the twenty-first century, we continue to experience this same challenge. For the mission of the Gospel to be authentic and credible, we must learn to make the message of Jesus intelligible and relevant in various cultures and individual life situations. Jesus reached out and effectively communicated with others who were "outside" the Jewish world. For example, His healing of the Syrophoenician woman's daughter in Mark 7:24–30 and the Gerasene Demoniac in Mark 5:1–20. He expects us to go beyond the world of our comfortable familiarity as well.

What are some of the cultures or life situations in our world that present challenging situations when it comes to effectively proclaiming the Gospel?

What are some of the "languages" (ability to relate) we need to develop in order to communicate with others more effectively in our world?

- Pick up serpents and drink deadly things without harm—A similar promise of protection from serpents and poison is also found in Luke 10:19 and Luke 11:11–12. In the Acts of the Apostles we see Paul experiencing this promise as he is preserved from harm despite being bitten by a snake while shipwrecked on the island of Malta (see Acts 28:1–6). Snakes are oftentimes understood to be a symbol of evil, yet the context of this promise suggests a more natural rather than supernatural preservation from danger. (Notice that the promise to be preserved from harm is associated with both the handling of serpents and the ingestion of a deadly thing. Because of this association, it is possible that the "deadly thing" referred to in this passage is actually that of snake venom rather than a different poison.) This sign most likely refers to the promise of protection from all other forces or situations that might oppose the Church or frustrate the mission of the Gospel. In Matthew 16:18 Jesus gives a similar promise to Peter that the powers of Hell shall not prevail against the Church. According to this interpretation, this sign would refer to the ability of believers to persevere despite whatever obstacles, opposition, or danger they may face. That very perseverance in the face of adverse situations adds credibility and authenticity to the Gospel message itself. Throughout history the Church has faced opposition and even poisonous influence from a variety of sources but disciples persevered nonetheless. Not even the forces of death can stop the Christian proclamation of the Gospel. Some historians believe that it was the courageous witness of the martyrs that even converted pagan Rome.

How are you inspired when you see someone persevere in faith despite adverse situations?

What dangers exist for believers today, and how is the message of the Gospel being obstructed or resisted?

What are some of the poisonous attitudes or behaviors that can weaken disciples and diminish the effectiveness of the Gospel message?

How do you see God preserving disciples from harmful situations in very practical ways? Most people experience an instinctive fear when they see a snake and they respond by drawing back. What fearful situations can cause us to draw back from witnessing the Gospel or carrying out the mission of the Church in a particular moment?

• Lay their hands on the sick and they will recover—One of the central ministries of Jesus was that of healing the sick. There are too many occurrences of our Lord's healing action to recount in this space. Jesus makes it clear that authentic disciples will continue His healing work in the world. We see Paul carrying out this work of healing through the laying on of hands in Acts 28:7–8 after he is saved from the serpent's bite. Caring for those in distress, even at risk to one's own personal safety, is a hallmark of selfless love. Christianity is not a private relationship that affects only the believer. Rather, Christian disciples actively allow the love of God to work through them to make a concrete difference in the lives of others. An enduring central ministry for Christians is that of alleviating the suffering of others. Healing is carried out in a variety of ways ranging from personal care to faith-based health care institutions. Healing can occur on physical, emotional, and spiritual levels. Virtually every one we meet, including each of us, is wounded in one way or another. As disciples, we are assured that the Lord will continue His healing ministry through us—if we will only cooperate and be His instrument of personal contact with others.

How do you see the healing ministry of Jesus being carried out in the lives of disciples today?
Why do you think Jesus chose to include healing as one of the four signs of authentic and credible faith?
What are symptoms that someone is experiencing a need for emotional or spiritual healing?
What makes the healing ministry of a disciple different from the healing work of social service agencies or for-profit health care institutions?
What challenges do disciples face today in carrying out the healing ministry of Jesus?

Disciples who believe and are Baptized will continue the very ministry of Jesus in the world. The Lord will give them the tools and the necessary protection to ensure the success of their missionary efforts. With that promise and assurance of divine protection, the disciples were motivated to begin their ministry as fearless and faithful messengers. The same should be true for us as well.

Solemnity of Pentecost

Our Scripture passage comes from the Gospel of John 20:19–23. It is the scene of the Risen Christ sending the Apostles and "breathing" on them. It is an appropriate passage to reflect on as we celebrate the moment when the first disciples were enlivened by the Holy Spirit and filled with enthusiasm to continue the mission of Jesus.

The word "enthusiasm" comes from the two Greek words meaning "God within" (*en theos*). It refers to the experience a person has when they are "filled" with the Spirit of God. In the Greek world it was originally perceived as an arbitrary invasion of God into the psyche that filled the individual with an indomitable energy. This was the way the Greeks explained divine inspiration. In the Christian faith, however, to be enthusiastic is not only to be energetic; it is to be courageous, motivated, and committed. The disciples had that experience and thus began to carry on the mission of Jesus fearlessly as His witnesses even unto death. Because of their enthusiasm, they were able to do the things that Jesus did. The gift of the Spirit transformed their fear into faith. It motivated them from being self-preserving to becoming other-serving, and it changed the mission of the Church from merely a human organization into a holy endeavor. Wow—the Spirit can transform lives and communities!

> *When in your life do you experience "enthusiasm" in the religious sense of being "filled with God"?*
> *What works of faith, as in the Mission of Jesus, have you been led to do as a result of your enthusiasm?*
> *What fears can cause people today to be "paralyzed" in their witness of faith and dampen their enthusiasm?*
> *How can people fulfill their religious observances with a "self-preserving" attitude rather than an "other-serving" attitude?*

In John 19:22 we are told that Jesus "breathed on them." That is an important statement for several reasons. First, it is a direct allusion to the action of God in Genesis 2:7 when the Lord first created humanity with an infusion of Divine Life. This connection to the first creation is reconfirmed in Ezekiel 37:9–10 and Wisdom 15:11 and speaks to the power of the Holy Spirit in the transformation of individual Christians. Jesus' action of breathing on the disciples is a statement that a new creation is taking place in the life and mission of the Church and that humanity is regenerated by the life-giving action of the Holy Spirit. This life-giving spiritual regeneration occurs in the Sacraments through Baptism (see Jn 3:5), through the gift of the Holy Spirit in Confirmation, and in the Eucharistic banquet where Tradition tells us that if we, with faith, eat the Body of Christ, we eat "Fire and Spirit" because it is the Holy Spirit we invoke over the gifts during the consecration.[6]

Second, the gift of the Spirit makes the community of believers, the Church, a fundamentally spiritual reality that carries out the works of God. These are not mere human efforts. When our Lord breathed on the disciples, He gave them the Spirit that could continue to mediate His Divine Presence even in His physical absence. The Church, then, is the Mystical Body of Christ in the world through which Jesus continues His ministry (See 1 Pt 2:5 for a similar understanding of the Church as a "spiritual edifice").

Third, the gift of the Holy Spirit draws the disciples into the communion of life and love, which is the Holy Trinity. This incorporation into the Divine Mystery is manifested by the ability to know the mind of Christ and speak with a prophetic voice in our time (see Joel 3:1 [alt. 2:28], 1 Cor 2:6–16, Jn 15:26–27 and 16:12–15).

How is the prophetic ministry of the Church, that is speaking on God's behalf so as to interpret events from God's perspective, carried out today both in the lives of individual disciples and through the institutional body of the Church? What ministries in your faith community most clearly carry out the work of Christ today?

---

6.   St Ephrem the Syrian, *Sermo IV in Hebdomadam Sanctam*: CSCO 413/Syr. 182, 55, quoted by St John Paul II, *Ecclesia de Eucharistia*, (17 April 2003), 17: *AAS* 95 (2003), pp. 449–450.

*What is a new work Christ wants to accomplish through
your faith community?*
*What prevents people from being able to fully receive and
live the spiritual regeneration of Baptism, Confirmation,
and the Eucharist?*

The Holy Spirit's presence in Acts 2:1–11 was manifested by the
ability of people to hear the message of the Gospel despite "foreign
tongues" (different languages). That means the Holy Spirit is able
to bring about a deep communion of faith that crosses the divisions of language and culture. As Saint Paul teaches us, when one
member of the body suffers, the other members suffer with it; when
one member rejoices, all the members rejoice (see 1 Cor 12:26).
That is a statement of deep communion of life lived on a global
scale. Sometimes, however, we can have narrow vision and become
shortsighted when it comes to understanding and embracing the
universal communion of the Church. When we give in to a narrow
vision, we become selective and limited in our charity and concern.

*When have you experienced your faith as something that
unites you deeply with those whom you have never met?
When do you most tangibly experience the "universal communion" of the Church?
What are some of the attitudes or actions that can cause us
to lose sight of the universal nature of the Church?
How do you express your universal communion with those
whom you have never met?
Jesus sent His disciples to be witnesses to the world, and
that means they were to go beyond the safe confines of their
own community so that others could experience the joy and
peace they themselves had received from the Lord. What
parts of our world most need Christian witnesses today?*

In Assisi, every year on the Feast of Pentecost, Saint Francis of
Assisi used to gather with his followers to pray for the Holy Spirit
to be with them and guide them. Francis believed that the power
of the Holy Spirit could change the world. Through Francis, the
Holy Spirit indeed did change the world. The Holy Spirit is able to
transform fear into courageous faith, anxious concern into peace,

alienation into reconciliation, and disciples into missionaries! That's quite a powerful work!

> *When do you pray to the Holy Spirit?*
> *Through whom is the Holy Spirit working in a particularly powerful way to transform the Church and the world today?*
> *What do you feel prompted to do by the Holy Spirit in your own life of faith?*

In Paul's letter to the Corinthians (1 Cor 12:3b–7, 12–13), he specifies that there are many gifts given by the Holy Spirit to individuals, but that those gifts are for the benefit of everyone and not just the personal benefit of the one who receives the gift. Thus, God equips us and asks us to work together as one body (the Body of Christ) so that the ministry of the Gospel can be accomplished through the Church. Each of us is given some gift that we can use to help carry out that mission. Remember: There are no spare parts on the Body of Christ! If we are not actively engaged in the work of ministry, it is because we haven't found our place and not because there is no place for us.

> *What are some of the gifts, talents, or skills with which you have been entrusted, and how can these be used for the common good and the mission of the Church?*
> *What gifts do we most need in the Church today to better carry out our mission?*
> *What gifts, talents, or skills are you still seeking to use in the service of the Gospel?*

Jesus says to the disciples, "As the Father sent me, so I send you ... Receive the Holy Spirit." The Spirit is given so that we can continue the mission of Jesus in the world. Jesus was sent to make God known, and in order to do that He had to make love known (because God is love). To make love known, He died on the Cross for us in an ultimate witness of self-giving and sacrificial love for others even in the face of hatred, rejection, and persecution. The Holy Spirit empowers us to carry on the mission of making God known in our world through the same demonstration of love. Others come to know God (who is love) through us. That is why Jesus was sent—and that is the purpose for which He sends us.

Who in our time most needs to know the love of God?
How have you come to know about the love of God through
the witness of someone else?
If Jesus appeared to us this Sunday and said, "Receive the
Holy Spirit ... as the Father has sent me so I send you," how
do you think that personal challenge of Jesus would prac-
tically affect your community and its ministries?

Take time this Sunday to pray for the gift of the Holy Spirit and to
be accepting and responsive to that gift when it is given.

> Breathe into me, Holy Spirit, that my thoughts may all be holy.
> Move in me, Holy Spirit that my work, too, may be holy.
> Attract my heart, Holy Spirit, that I may love only what is holy.
> Strengthen me, Holy Spirit, that I may defend all that is holy.
> Protect me, Holy Spirit, that I may always be holy.
>
> Saint Augustine

Solemnity of the Most Holy Trinity

Our Scripture passage comes from the Gospel of Matthew 28:16–20. In this text we read of Jesus' Great Commission to the Church to go forth and make disciples of all nations. Following this Great Commission, Jesus then goes on to specify the two particular ministries that are necessary in order to make disciples: Baptism and teaching. These two ministries are analogous to necessary ingredients of a recipe. Let's look at each of these ministries so as to better understand how we can fulfill our Lord's Great Commission and make disciples in our world today.

The first ministry Jesus commands His disciples to carry out is that of Baptism. Baptism is more than just a religious ceremony or ritual; rather, Baptism is the means by which we become sharers in the Divine Life of God. This gift of Divine Life involves all the Persons of the Holy Trinity. In Baptism, we become adopted children of the Father in the family of God (see Eph 1:5, Gal 4:5–7, Rom 8:14–19, Jn 1:12). Because of that adoption we can call God our "Father" in the Lord's Prayer and refer to one another as brothers and sisters. Baptism also makes us a living Temple of the Holy Spirit (1 Cor 3:16–17) as we are born again of water and the Spirit (Jn 3:5). We also become members of the Body of Jesus Christ on earth (1 Cor 6:15–20, 1 Cor 12:27) and a spiritual edifice dedicated to the honor and glory of God in Jesus (Eph 2:19–22, 1 Pt 2:5). Baptism changes our very identity as we die to our former way of life so as to live the new life of grace. Saint Paul speaks to this change of identity and new life when he tells us that in our Baptism we clothed ourselves with Christ (Gal 3:27) and that in the waters of Baptism we were buried with Christ and rose with Him (Rom 6:4; Col 2:12). Saint Paul develops this thought even further when he says in Gal 2:20 that it is Christ who lives in him. With this fundamental change of identity comes a correlating change in mission and destiny; we are to do the works of God until one day we stand in God's presence.

This Baptismal incorporation into the life of the Father, the Son, and the Holy Spirit has additional effects in us. It heals us from the wound of Original Sin and washes clean all other faults (see Acts 2:38, Acts 22:16, Eph 5:26). It also gives us grace and strength to live the Christian life through the infusion of supernatural grace, gifts, and virtues. Not only does Baptism incorporate us into fellowship with the Holy Trinity but it also brings us into communion with the Church and the People of God. As we celebrate the Solemnity of the Most Holy Trinity, we not only call to mind the mystery of who God is but we also remember that God has invited us to share in His Divine Life through our Baptism. As disciples, it is important for us to remember that each day we are called to live and move and have our being in the Lord (see Acts 17:28). Saint Thomas Aquinas reminded us that our souls are conformed to God by grace so we can assimilate the gift of the Holy Spirit, which is the love given by the Father through the Son.[7] Once God's love is in our hearts, we grow in union with Him and replicate that same unity in all that we do. We, then, become healers of fractures and divisions; in other words, true disciples of Christ. In this way, the communion of persons we find in the Trinity becomes the model for unity in our families, congregations, relationships, and society. These divine actions are known as "Trinitarian Missions" because they reveal the natural internal and external movement of love, which always tries to reach out and repair what is broken. What an awesome gift! Baptism is not a mere religious ceremony; it is the beginning of a Christian's life by which we are drawn to the Father through the Son in the Holy Spirit.

> *How does the above reflection inspire you to learn more about the Holy Trinity?*
> *With which Person of the Holy Trinity do you relate most frequently in your daily life?*
> *About which aspects of Baptism would you like to learn more?*
> *When are you most conscious of the fellowship of the Holy Trinity into which you are invited?*

---

7.   St Thomas Aquinas, *Summa Theologiae*, I, q. 43, art. 5.

> *With which Person of the Holy Trinity are you most unfa-*
> *miliar and how might you learn more?*

The second ministry Jesus instructs His disciples to carry out is that of teaching the newly Baptized to observe everything our Lord commanded. It is significant that Jesus didn't state that the disciples should teach them by making them memorize everything the Lord said. When Jesus commanded that the newly Baptized be taught to observe His commands, He is emphasizing the necessity of living a life conformed to the Gospel. It is one thing to receive the gift of Baptism (see previous reflection) but it is another thing to know how to live it. That is why teaching is so important—it actualizes our new identity in a life conformed to the Gospel. One of the distinctive aspects of Christianity is this necessary integration of belief and practice. Jesus taught His disciples how to love God and Neighbor in a very practical way. He taught them how to care for one another in the community of the Church. He taught them the priority of mercy and forgiveness in their relations with one another. He even taught them to love their enemies, pray for those who persecute them, and give to those who will not repay. Indeed, Jesus taught us to live as children of our heavenly Father (see Mt 5:45). It takes perseverance and encouragement to live well our Baptismal identity by observing in daily practices the way of life Jesus taught. It also requires mentors who are willing to serve as examples and guides to show us how to live our Baptism.

The fellowship of the Most Holy Trinity is the foundation of a solid Christian life. When we learn to live as children of the Father, we become brothers and sisters in Jesus who are united in that love which is the Holy Spirit. Our companionship with Jesus sustains us and gives us encouragement to face challenges. Our identity as children of a loving Father inspires us to please the Father in all that we do. The enthusiasm of the Holy Spirit leads us to seek God's will for our lives in each situation. This ministry of teaching Christians to observe what Jesus has commanded is all encompassing. It is not only for teachers or catechists or parents or priests; we all influence one another in our daily actions and so each of us bears the responsibility of helping others observe what the Christian life calls for in specific situations.

Who taught you what it means to live as a child of God?
In what situations do you find it most difficult to "observe"
Jesus' commands?
How do you see the everyday life of a Christian immersed
in the mystery of the Most Holy Trinity?
Sharing in God's life is not only an emotional feeling or
inspirational sentiment but is meant to have real effects in
how we live each day. What happens when someone tries
to keep their religious beliefs from affecting their daily life?
What happens when someone receives the gift of Baptism
but is not taught to observe Jesus' commands?

Lastly, the final words of Jesus in the Gospel of Matthew are a promise of His lasting presence with the Church when He says, "I am with you always until the end of the world." At the very beginning of Matthew's Gospel, we were told that Jesus would be "Emmanuel", a name that means "God with us" (see Mt 1:22–23). Now, Jesus promises to be "God with us" and thus reveals Himself as Emmanuel in this final verse. We are never alone when we carry out the mission that Jesus entrusted to us. The Lord accompanies disciples who are living out their discipleship and mission. Sometimes it is possible for us to feel forsaken by the Lord in our mission. It is easy to get accustomed to feeling or experiencing God in one way, and when the circumstances of our lives change, our awareness of God tends to fade. In these moments we may face the temptation of walking away from the mission Jesus has given us, and we may even risk our communion with the Lord. Instead of praying, "Lord, why aren't you with me", maybe we should be praying, "Lord, how can I be with you in this moment?" Here the words of Jesus imply both the promise of His fidelity to us and the invitation for us to persevere in Him. He promised us His presence "where two or three are gathered in His name" (see Mt 18:20) and that we would find Him in the hungry, the thirsty, the imprisoned, and the homeless (see Mt 25:35–45). Indeed, the Lord is with us always.

How have you experienced the presence of Jesus in your
practice of discipleship?

When do we tend to doubt the presence of Jesus and how does this understanding of Jesus' promise shed light on those situations of doubt?
How have you experienced Jesus with you in the Sacraments?
How have you experienced the presence of Jesus in the work of ministry?

Eternal God, eternal Trinity, you have made the blood of Christ so precious through his sharing in your divine nature. You are a mystery as deep as the sea; the more I search, the more I find, and the more I find, the more I search for you. But I can never be satisfied; what I receive will ever leave me desiring more. When you fill my soul I have an even greater hunger, and I grow more famished for your light. I desire above all to see you, the true light, as you really are. I have tasted and seen the depth of your mystery and the beauty of your creation with the light of my understanding. I have clothed myself with your likeness and have seen what I shall be. Eternal Father, you have given me a share in your power and the wisdom that Christ claims as His own, and your Holy Spirit has given me the desire to love you. You are my Creator, eternal Trinity, and I am your creature. You have made of me a new creation in the blood of your Son, and I know that you are moved with love at the beauty of your creation, for you have enlightened me. Eternal Trinity, Godhead, mystery deep as the sea, you could give me no greater gift than the gift of yourself. For you are a fire ever burning and never consumed, which itself consumes all the selfish love that fills my being. Yes, you are a fire that takes away the coldness, illuminates the mind with its light and causes me to know your truth. By this light, reflected as it were in a mirror, I recognize that you are the highest good, one we can neither comprehend nor fathom. And I know that you are beauty and wisdom itself. The food of angels, you gave yourself to man in the fire of your love. You are the garment which covers our nakedness, and in our hunger you are a satisfying food, for you are sweetness and in you there is no taste of bitterness, O triune God![8]

Saint Catherine of Siena

---

8. Saint Catherine of Siena, Prayer to the Blessed Trinity from *Reflections on Divine Providence*, Cap. 167, *Gratiarum actio ad Trinitatem*).

Solemnity of the Most Holy Body and Blood of Christ

(CORPUS CHRISTI)

Our Scripture passage comes from the Gospel of Mark 14:12–16 and 22–26. This account of the Last Supper on the Feast of Passover provides the perfect opportunity to reflect on the gift of the Eucharist and to deepen our appreciation of the importance of this Sacrament for disciples. It is through this meal that Jesus establishes the New Covenant with us in His Blood. Through the prophetic instruction of His words and the identification of Himself with the bread and wine, Jesus is teaching us about the meaning of the Eucharist and its intended effect in our lives.

It is significant that the Last Supper takes place in the context of the Passover meal. The Passover meal not only recalled the events of deliverance from Egypt but also allowed the people sharing in the meal to become actual participants in those events of liberation. Jesus redefines the traditional Jewish Passover meal to give it a new significance when He identifies the bread and wine as His Body that will be broken and His Blood that will be poured out. That is a reference to the Cross. The sharing in this meal, then, is a ritual sharing in the sacrificial Crucifixion and Death of Jesus Himself. Saint Paul points to this meaning of the Eucharist when he says, "For as often as you eat this bread and drink the cup, you proclaim the Lord's Death until He comes" (1 Cor 11:26). Our Lord's Death has a saving purpose that perfects the role of the lamb in the traditional Passover meal; namely, the Death of Jesus will bring salvation for much more than one night or deliverance from temporal oppression—the Lord's sacrificial Death will bring salvation for eternity and liberation from the very forces of sin and death. By sharing in this meal, disciples continue to participate directly in the saving effects of Calvary. For this reason the Eucharist has been referred to as the "Unbloody Sacrifice of Calvary." Every time we receive the Eucharist we are accepting in ourselves the salvation won for us in the Death and Resurrection of Jesus. That is the power of the new ritual meal Jesus gave to disciples throughout history so that all Christians could share fully in the grace of our Lord's redeeming Death. To help the priest deepen his devotion during the Eucharistic Prayer, a Crucifix is normally placed on the altar so that as he consecrates the bread and wine to become the Body and Blood of the Lord, he is reminded of the sacrifice of Calvary and the New Passover that he is celebrating. It is important to note that the celebration of the Mass does not repeat the Death of Jesus but allows people of all time to participate in our Lord's one eternal sacrifice.

> *Jesus associated His Crucifixion with the giving of His Body and Blood in the form of bread and wine. How does having a Crucifix near the altar help you focus on the Lord's sacrifice present in the Eucharist?*
> *The Passover was the defining experience of faith for the Hebrew people. In what ways is the Eucharist meant to be the defining experience of faith for Christians?*
> *From what do people today need deliverance and salvation and how can they receive that liberating grace through the Eucharist?*

It is also significant that our Lord defines this meal as a covenant in His Blood. Covenants were important moments in the life of the Jewish people. The first covenant in the Old Testament was made with Noah (see Gen 9:8–17) in which God expressed His divine desire for humanity to flourish. The second covenant was made with Abraham (see Gen 17:1–14) in which God promised that Abraham will be the father of a special nation that will have a divinely appointed future. The third covenant was made with Moses (see Ex 19–24) in which the Ten Commandments are given as a special bond between God and the People who ratify that bond by proclaiming, "all that the Lord has said, we will heed and do". The fourth covenant was made with David (see 2 Samuel 7) in which God promised to raise up a kingdom for his offspring that will be established forever. Finally, the Lord promised a new covenant in Jer 31:31–33 that will be written upon people's hearts.

This new covenant was necessary because of the infidelity of Israel to previous covenants. For hundreds of years the people waited for this "New Covenant" to be realized. When Jesus presides at the Last Supper and announces the New Covenant in His Blood, every disciple around the table would have understood that our Lord was fulfilling the anticipated prophecy of Jeremiah.

Covenants are important in the Old Testament. Covenants were the expression of an enduring relationship with mutual rights and responsibilities. In previous covenants the people were unfaithful to their side of the relationship. In the Last Supper, Jesus represents both God and Man and so He is able to finally fully re-establish our lost relationship with God because He is both human and divine. Jesus, in Himself, is the New Covenant and invites us to participate in that covenant by receiving His Body and Blood. In order to understand the importance of blood in relationship to covenants, we have to remember that all covenants were sealed with a sacrifice that involved the shedding of blood. As the text from Exodus 19–24 indicates, Moses sprinkled the blood of the sacrifice on both the altar and the people thus establishing a sharing of life through the sharing of blood. The shedding of blood was really a way of sealing a person's commitment to a covenant; it was a way in which each party pledged their life blood for the other. It is significant that Jesus calls the Eucharist a covenant rather than a "gift". That is because a covenant has mutual rights and responsibilities whereas a gift is something we only receive. The Covenant of the Eucharist is Jesus' pledge of God's life to us, and it requires the complete pledge of our lives to God in return.

> *How does understanding the Eucharist as a covenant rather than a gift change the way you receive it?*
> *In our lives, what right does God have to our lives because we share in the covenant of the Eucharist?*
> *What daily responsibilities do we incur as part of our covenant relationship with God?*
> *How does Jesus fulfill His part of the covenant with us?*
> *At what point in the Mass do you renew your participation in the New Covenant of Jesus?*

One of the most striking parts of this passage is when Jesus identifies His very Body and Blood with the elements of bread and wine. This would have been a very disturbing statement for the disciples. They could have easily understood Jesus if he were speaking in a symbolic sense, but that is not the case. Jesus makes an explicit identification of His very self with the elements of bread and wine. He didn't say, "This is 'like' my body"; rather He said, "this IS my Body" and "this IS my Blood." The disciples would have been very troubled by this explicit identification with Jesus' Body and Blood because of the law in Lev 17:14 which prohibited the ingestion of flesh with blood. This radical identification of the Eucharistic bread and wine with the very Body and Blood of Jesus led to absurd accusations of cannibalism against Christians in the second century. Of course, the Christians of the Early Church responded by both affirming their belief that Jesus is truly present in the Eucharist but in the form of bread and wine. We see this affirmation in the writings of Saint Paul when he exhorted the early Christians of Corinth to be aware of the awesome reality in which they are participating: "Is not the cup of blessing which we bless a sharing in the blood of Christ? Is not the bread which we break a sharing in the body of Christ?" (see 1 Cor 10:16).

Paul further stresses the importance of reverencing the true presence of Jesus in the Eucharist when he cautions the community to be aware of Who they are receiving (see 1 Cor 11:29, "A man must examine himself, and in so doing he is to eat of the bread and drink of the cup. For he who eats and drinks, eats and drinks judgment to himself if he does not discern the body rightly"). The *Didache*, an early Christian writing from the late first century, affirms the belief that the Eucharist really is the Body and Blood of Jesus when it taught, "Let no one eat or drink of the Eucharist with you except those who have been baptized in the name of the Lord; for it is in reference to this that the Lord said, 'do not give that which is holy to dogs.'"[9] Saint Ignatius of Antioch in the early second century expressed this same belief when he wrote: "I desire the Bread of God, which is the Flesh of Jesus Christ, who was of the seed of David; and for drink I desire His Blood, which is love

---

9.   *Didache*, IX, N. 5.

incorruptible."[10] The metaphysical process by which ordinary bread and wine become the Divine Presence of Jesus' Body and Blood was most famously promoted by the medieval theologian Thomas Aquinas when he articulated the teaching of "transubstantiation" in which the essence of something (its "being" or substantial form) is replaced while the secondary qualities of that reality (its accidental forms of texture, taste, and appearance) remain the same. Following this teaching he also reminded us that this is a matter of faith and in the famous Eucharistic hymn *Pange Lingua* he wrote, "Let faith provide a supplement for the failure of the senses!"[11]

> *How do disciples show respect and reverence for the Divine Presence of Jesus in the Eucharist?*
> *What experiences have awakened within you a realization of the True Presence of Jesus in the Eucharist?*
> *What spiritual graces can we experience when we pray in the presence of the Eucharist that we cannot as readily experience away from that presence?*
> *What can a faith community do to help deepen their awareness of the Real Presence of Jesus in the Eucharist?*
> *How do you respond after receiving our Lord in the Eucharist?*

Lastly, receiving the Eucharist and sharing in the Last Supper has implications for disciples. These implications are not always known in advance as is the case in Mark 14:23–24 where the disciples share in the cup before Jesus explains to them what it means. This is an important teaching for us because we don't always know the implications of discipleship before we commit to the Lord either. Certainly the Christians of Mark's community in first century Rome wondered why they were being persecuted by the empire for choosing to follow Jesus—but they were. It was an unforeseen consequence of their commitment to discipleship. They accepted that consequence nonetheless. To share in the cup of Jesus means that we may be called to share in His cup of suffering, trial, or difficulty as well. We like to know the implications of our commitments before we oblige ourselves, but the life of discipleship calls

---

10. St Ignatius of Antioch, *Epistle to the Romans*, Chap. VII.

11. The Latin text reads, "*Præstet fides suppleméntum Sénsuum deféctui.*"

us to make an irrevocable and complete act of trust without such advance knowledge of where the Lord will lead us. Some other implications for discipleship are articulated in the writings of Saint Paul where he reminds the Christian community of the need to lead a "worthy life" because they share in the Body and Blood of the Lord. In doing so, Paul explicitly connects the reception of the Eucharist with the necessary moral conversion of all who receive it (see 1 Cor 10:14–22). In short, we must become conformed to the presence of Christ we receive.

Additionally, Paul teaches the Christian community that the Eucharist is the source of communion within the Church when he says, "because there is one bread, we, who are many, are one body, for we all share in the one loaf" (see 1 Cor 10:17). We are accustomed to understanding the Eucharist as a great gift, which it is; but this gift has implications for our lives, and it is important that we understand those implications to the best of our ability and strive to faithfully fulfill them (lest we receive the gift but prevent its transforming grace from having the divinely intended effect). The greatest implication of receiving the Eucharist is that we ourselves become a "living tabernacle" carrying Jesus to the world. Saint Paul understood the challenge of living a Eucharistic life and summarized well the obligation of a Christian to be a living tabernacle when he wrote, "We have this treasure in earthen vessels, so that the surpassing greatness of the power will be of God and not from ourselves" (2 Cor 4:7). Ultimately the Eucharist is what should form every aspect of a Christian disciple's life. Saint Paul saw the connection between the Church and the Eucharist because both were revealed to be the Body of Christ (see 1 Cor 12:27). Saint Augustine further explained the formational power of the Eucharist and its relationship to the Church when he taught:

> If you, therefore, are Christ's body and members, it is your own mystery that is placed on the Lord's table! It is your own mystery that you are receiving! You are saying 'Amen' to what you are: your response is a personal signature, affirming your faith. When you hear 'The Body of Christ', you reply 'Amen.'

Be a member of Christ's body, then, so that your 'Amen' may ring true! ... Be what you see; receive what you are.[12]

When have you been asked to make a commitment without knowing the implications and what was that experience like?

What are some of the ways in which receiving the Eucharist should lead to practical moral changes in people's lives today?

In what ways can disciples be tempted to form a communion with one another and share in the New Covenant of the Eucharist that is based on something other than radical commitment to Jesus?

How does the image of being a "living tabernacle" inspire and encourage you in your life throughout the week?

How does the quote from Saint Augustine inspire you?

Paul taught the early Christians that the Eucharist is the source of their communion as a Church. How far do you think the early Christians extended that sense of communion and how did they express it?

---

12. St Augustine, *Sermon 272 on the Nature of the Sacrament of the Eucharist*, pp. 300–301.

Second Sunday in Ordinary Time

Our Scripture passage for this Sunday comes from the Gospel of John 1:35–42. In this reading we hear of the first disciples who follow Jesus. Rather than simply telling us the story of what happened, John shares with us the important dialogue that takes place between Jesus and those two disciples. That dialogue is meant to take place in our lives of discipleship as well. Thus, this passage offers important insights to guide us as we seek to follow Jesus.

One of the very important titles John uses in his testimony about Jesus is that of "Lamb of God". This is a great title of faith and summarizes much of what Jesus will accomplish through His ministry of the Cross. To be the "Lamb of God" means to be the Lamb of Sacrifice (the Passover Lamb). Jesus accomplishes His sacrifice on the Cross of Calvary, and John points to Jesus as the Lamb of God on the Cross by mentioning the hyssop branch (Jn 19:29) and the phrase "break none of His bones" (Jn 19:36)—all references to the Passover Lamb (Ex 12:22; Ex 12:46; Nm 9:12; Ps 34:20). Sacrifices in the Old Testament were a way in which people offered something of God's creation in return to the Lord as an expression of their desire to be in communion with God. There were different purposes for sacrifices. Some sacrifices were offered in Thanksgiving. Some sacrifices were offered so as to establish communion with God and others through the sharing of a sacrificial meal. Still other sacrifices were for the forgiveness of sins. For example, the sacrificial victim paid the price for someone else's sins. Finally, sacrifices were also made to seal a covenant relationship between God and the people with mutual rights and expectations.

Jesus fulfills all of these meanings when He becomes the final and perfect sacrificial Lamb of God. Jesus is our Thanksgiving to God (the word Eucharist means "Thanksgiving") for all the good God has given us in His Son. Jesus is the source of our Communion with God and others as we share in the Lord's Supper where Jesus offers His sacrificial presence in the form of Bread and Wine. Jesus takes our sinful condition on Himself and "pays the price" for our sins by dying on the Cross so as to bring forgiveness and salvation to the world. Finally, Jesus offers us the eternal New Covenant in His Blood at the Last Supper in which we enter into a new and enduring relationship of faith and love with Christ and others every time we share in the Lord's Supper. When the priest raises the Eucharistic Body and Blood of Jesus at Mass and proclaims, "Behold the Lamb of God," he is proclaiming that Jesus is offering all these benefits of His sacrifice to us.

> *Which aspect of Jesus' sacrifice means the most to you*
> *(Thanksgiving, Communion, Expiation, Covenant)?*
> *How does this understanding of Jesus as the "Lamb of God"*
> *change your previous understanding of that term?*
> *What can you do to deepen your appreciation and response*
> *for the sacrifice Jesus has made for you?*
> *For which aspect of Jesus' sacrifice do you need to grow in*
> *greater appreciation and understanding?*
> *How can you pursue this growth?*

When Jesus sees the two disciples following Him, He speaks His first words in the Gospel of John when He asks the question: "What do you seek?" First words are important words. This is the fundamental question of discipleship and it is asked not only of the two former disciples of John the Baptist but it is also a question every disciple must answer. People can seek a lot of things by following Jesus. For some, Jesus is a teacher of wisdom, for others, a remedy for life's problems (miracle worker). Still others can follow Jesus out of habit, curiosity, or family custom. Ultimately, the Gospel of John wants Christians to follow Jesus because He is nothing less than the presence of God who brings salvation to those who are His own. Jesus asks the two disciples to be clear about their expectations and needs, and the Lord asks us to be clear as well.

> *If Jesus asked you the question "What do you seek?", how*
> *would you answer?*
> *What do you tend to pray for more than anything else?*
> *When you come to Mass, what are you seeking?*
> *Why do you think Jesus wanted the two disciples to be clear*
> *and conscious of their motivations and expectations?*

How can the question "What do you seek?" be a good source of reflection to guide you through the many decisions you face each day?

The two disciples do not answer Jesus' question. Rather, they respond with a different question: "Where are you staying?" The Greek word for "staying" is *meno* and can also mean "dwell" or "remain". The Gospel of John uses this term to describe the enduring permanent relationship that Jesus has with the Father and the Spirit. The disciples' question is a search for participation in that relationship because that is eternal life. We all want to be immersed in the life of God to save us from our human weakness, sinfulness, and even death. The disciples wanted to know and understand this profound sharing of God's life, but Jesus did not answer their question. That's because some questions of life and faith can only be known by experience. For that reason, Jesus invites them to "Come and See" so they can experience for themselves what participation in divine life is like. This is a decisive opportunity for the disciples inviting them to be more than just spectators so as to become active participants in the life of grace. In order to follow Jesus, they must leave behind their prior religious pursuits (for example, following John the Baptist) and become obedient to Jesus' Word ("Come and See"). As disciples, we also have to leave behind lesser attachments in order to follow Jesus. Being a disciple doesn't mean that we fit Jesus around our pre-existing schedule. Instead, being a disciple means that we seek the Lord first and foremost as our Savior and that we are obedient to His Word.

What is Jesus asking you to leave behind in order to follow Him more closely?
If you could ask the Lord a question like the two disciples did, what would it be?
Jesus didn't answer the disciples' question but instead invited them into relationship.
When do you feel like Jesus isn't answering your questions, and how could the Lord be inviting you into a new and deeper relationship?

When the disciples received the invitation of Jesus, they had to make a decision to accept it. That decision would change their lives. Certainly they had other plans for that afternoon and the next day but those plans changed in an instant. We are told that all these things happened at the "10th hour" (some translations read "four o'clock in the afternoon"). It is somewhat odd that John includes the actual time when this took place. Scripture scholars are not certain why the time was stated. Some interpret the number ten (10) as meaning a time of perfection or a time of fulfillment.[13] Others, however, understand it as indicating a decisive moment when discipleship begins. According to this second interpretation, discipleship may have many preliminary events that lead us towards a decisive moment when we accept the invitation to "stay" with Jesus Christ on our Lord's terms and no longer on our individual terms. This decisive moment can take many forms and occur in a variety of settings—and is always a moment we never forget. It is the moment when we allow God to take control of our lives in a comprehensive and irrevocable way. It is common to remember the exact place and time when significant events in our lives take place; the same should be true for our faith life. Perhaps we are still in the pre-discipleship stage and watching Jesus from a distance. Or maybe we are still hearing the testimony of others telling us about Jesus. All these moments are meant to lead us to our own decisive personal encounter when we hear Jesus say to us "Come and See," and we accept that invitation in a committed and permanent way. That is discipleship—when we follow the Lord's lead no matter where He goes.

> *As you reflect on these various stages of discipleship, where do you see yourself?*
> *What was the decisive moment when you committed your life to Jesus Christ in a conscious, committed, irrevocable way?*
> *What have been other decisive moments in your life as a disciple when you have deepened your Christian commitment to Christ through specific decisions?*
> *What circumstances or settings can provide the "perfect" environment that allows discipleship to come to fulfillment in a person's life?*

---

13.   For example, see the Pythagorean Tetractys.

Lastly, the story of the first two disciples is not complete until we are told they go out and introduce others to Jesus. We see this movement in the action of Andrew who goes to his brother Peter and brings him to the Lord. The Gospel of John is trying to tell us that discipleship necessarily involves missionary outreach to others inviting them to share in the relationship we have with the Lord. What is striking about this connection between discipleship and missionary action is that Andrew is still a long way from being perfect in his faith. He has acknowledged Jesus as a Rabbi (Teacher) and even as the Messiah (Christ), but Jesus is much more than either of these. Even though Andrew's faith is still developing, he is courageous in telling others about the good news he is already finding in Jesus. That is an important message for our lives as well. Sometimes we can think that we must be more advanced in our faith before we can be missionaries who share it with others. Or we can think that the ministry of sharing faith (evangelization) is a responsibility for clergy or those who have completed advanced studies in theology. We deceive ourselves with such thoughts and we impede our discipleship when we give in to these erroneous perceptions. Every Christian disciple is called to be a missionary who brings others to Christ. In fact, it is an essential part of discipleship itself. If we are not bringing others to Christ then we are not following Jesus in the way our Lord expects.

> *How do you share your faith with others? Who have you brought to Christ?*
>
> *What are some of the erroneous thoughts or perceptions that prevent you from being an active missionary witness of faith for others (evangelist)?*
>
> *Who shared their faith with you and introduced you to Jesus?*
>
> *How can we as a Church help prepare people to be missionaries in everyday life?*
>
> *Andrew first reached out to his brother, Peter. Within your family, who do you think God wants you to communicate an invitation of faith?*

Third Sunday in Ordinary Time

Our Scripture passage for this Sunday comes from the Gospel of Mark 1:14–20. In this text we read of Jesus starting His public ministry and calling His first disciples to follow Him. There are some significant elements in this passage that are worthy of our reflection as we follow the Lord as well.

Jesus began His public ministry by announcing that it was the "time of fulfillment" and that the proper response is to repent and believe the Good News. These are the very first words Jesus speaks in the Gospel of Mark. As such, these words are meant to be the overarching theme for Mark's entire message. When we hear the phrase, "time of fulfillment", it may not mean very much to us. However, if we lived in the time of Jesus we would better understand the hopes that Jesus fulfilled. In particular, the Prophets spoke about a time in the future when God would accomplish great works for the people. Some of these expectations include the following: that God would send a "prophet like Moses" (Dt 18:15–19); that God would establish a new covenant with the people (Jer 31:31–34); that there would be a new Temple (Ez 40–43); and finally that the Messiah would gather the lost tribes of Israel and reconstitute the People of God (see Is 11:11–12, Jer 3:6–18, Hos 1:1–3:5).

When Jesus announced that the time of fulfillment had arrived, He was saying to the people that He Himself is the fulfillment of those hopes! Jesus Himself is the one who speaks God's Word (prophet like Moses); Jesus Himself will establish the new covenant in His blood; Jesus Himself will establish the new Temple in His resurrected body; and Jesus Himself will reconstitute the Twelve Tribes when He gathers the twelve disciples. Jesus is announcing that the hopes and expectations of Israel are fulfilled in Him. All of the Old Testament has been preparing for the moment of His arrival—and here it is. The Good News that Jesus brings isn't a message; it is His very being. He Himself is the Good News we have been waiting for and looking for. That is a very powerful announcement! Now we can understand why the first disciples responded so readily and followed Jesus. Jesus invites us to do the same. We all have deep hopes and yearnings that can ultimately only be fulfilled in God. As Saint Augustine said, "You have made us for yourself, O Lord, and our hearts are restless until they rest in you."

> *What are some of the deep hopes, yearnings, and aspirations we experience that only God can fulfill?*
>
> *How do we try to fill our hopes, yearnings, and aspirations with less than God?*
>
> *As you begin your study of the Gospel of Mark, what is it you want in your faith life during this next year?*
>
> *How can a faith community help people understand that Jesus is the only one who can fulfill their deepest desires?*
>
> *If Jesus stepped into your life today and said to you, "Today I will fulfill your deepest hope," what would be that hope?*
>
> *What happens when we try to fill our deepest hopes with less than God?*
>
> *Some spiritual teachers believe that the deepest human hungers are for love (respect, acceptance, inherent worth); forgiveness (to know we are more than our faults or failures—we have a goodness that is not destroyed by sin); and communion (that we are not alone no matter what we face). How do you identify with these deep hungers and how can Jesus fulfill them for you?*

When we hear the call of the first disciples, it is significant that we are told what each of the two groups left behind in order to follow Jesus. For Peter and Andrew, we are told that they left behind their nets. For James and John, we are told that they left behind their father, Zebedee. These details tell us that following Jesus sometimes requires us to let go of our attachment to material possessions (nets) and relationships (father). The call of discipleship is unique for each person, yet for everyone it will require letting go of anything and anyone that holds us back from following the Lord. In the Early Church, especially during the time of persecution, following Jesus could require great sacrifice. Sometimes people's possessions were confiscated when they were discovered to be Christian. Other times, people were excluded from their families and friendships because of their decision to follow Jesus. If a person was not willing to let go of those attachments, then they would most likely falter in their faith and end up failing in their discipleship. The examples of Peter, Andrew, James, and John are given to us as an encouragement to let nothing hold us back from the Lord.

> *How can a person's faith life (discipleship) cause strain or disruption in personal relationships today (family, marriage, friendships, or professional associations)?*
>
> *Although American Catholics do not live in a time of persecution like that of the Early Church, we are called to the same detachment that marked the lives of the first disciples. When have you felt that God was asking you to be detached from material possessions?*
>
> *If Jesus issued the same call to us today, what are some of the things of which we would have to let go in order to follow Him?*
>
> *In the time of Jesus, families relied on the participation of everyone to accomplish the daily work (fishing). How can the expectations of family or friends prevent someone from following a life of faith?*
>
> *The disciples had very good excuses they could have used to dismiss themselves from the invitation to discipleship. What are some of the excuses we use to explain why we can't follow Jesus in particular moments?*

Peter was a fisherman. That was his skill, talent, profession, and business. Jesus does not tell Peter to walk away from those talents or skills. Rather, Jesus tells Peter that he is to use his professional talents, skills, and abilities for the work of the Gospel: He is to "fish" for men. That is a message of Stewardship for us as well—that we are to use our time and talent for the work of the Gospel. Peter would have to apply the same hard work, perseverance, problem-solving, and teamwork skills that he used to catch fish in order to carry out his ministry in the Early Church. God has gifted all of us with opportunities and abilities that are needed for the work of the Gospel, not just to enrich our personal lives. As disciples, we follow Jesus with our whole life and place our whole being at the Lord's service—including our abilities and opportunities.

What are some of your professional talents, abilities, or skills that you think could be of benefit to the mission of the Gospel, and how might you put them to use as an expression of your discipleship?

When Jesus spoke to Peter, he told him, "You will be a fisher of men," as a way of re-focusing his professional skills. If Jesus spoke to you, what phrase would the Lord use to re-focus your professional life into a mission of discipleship?

Who do you know who serves the Lord through his or her professional life?

As a Baptized member of the Body of Christ, each of us is given a share in Jesus' ministry to the Church and the world. In which ministry of the church do you most enjoy participating and why?

Fourth Sunday in Ordinary Time

Our Scripture passage for this Sunday comes from the Gospel of Mark 1:21–28. This is the inaugural scene of Jesus' public ministry in Mark's Gospel. In this text, we read of Jesus going to the synagogue on the Sabbath and healing the man with the unclean spirit. There are some important lessons for us as disciples as we pray to encounter the Lord each Sunday in our local faith communities.

The first point to note in this passage has been strikingly demonstrated through art. In the Sistine Chapel of the Vatican Museums, there is a side fresco painting of the *Temptation of Christ*. It is a work of Sandro Botticelli, who was not only a master painter but also a master preacher. Pope Sixtus IV was the Holy Father during the time of Botticelli and was greatly affected by this painting every time he entered the chapel. When the painting is carefully examined, one can notice that Satan is dressed as a Franciscan Friar. Sixtus IV was a Franciscan and he did a lot of good things—like building the monastery of San Francesco in Assisi and the original Santo Spirito Hospital to care for the sick in Rome. Botticelli knew the good deeds of the pope—that's why he used the front of Santo Spirito Hospital as his model for the Jerusalem Temple in the scene of Jesus' second temptation. But Botticelli also suspected that Sixtus might have done some things that weren't very good and that he may have supported an assassination attempt on Lorenzo and Giuliano di Medici. Botticelli wanted to remind Sixtus to be careful because a particularly dangerous evil is that which cloaks itself in religious garments and lurks under the superficiality of religious motives. Every time Sixtus celebrated Mass in the Sistine Chapel (which was named after him), he saw the power of evil acting under the guise of religiosity. The Holy Father never had the painting removed or modified. For him it became a source of grace and repentance.

In today's Gospel reading, we see Jesus going into a religious gathering to perform His first miracle. And what does He do? He casts out the evil spirits that are present in that religious gathering. He starts to build the Kingdom of God not by overcoming the evil that is *out there*—in the world of the unfaithful—but by first casting out the evil that is present *in here*—within the lives of those who are trying to be faithful. That's us. There are a variety of ways in which we can learn to cloak the unclean spirits of our lives in the garb of religious justification. Sometimes arrogance is cloaked as excellence; gossip is disguised as wisdom; disregard for the world around us is cloaked as spiritual detachment. Those are some of the unclean spirits from which Jesus wants us to be freed so that we can be disciples who follow the Lord and do His will, and not just disciples who do our own will in the Lord's name.

> *If Jesus came to our church gathering on Sunday morning, what are some of the "unclean" spirits He would want to cast out from our lives—both individually and as a congregation?*
>
> *How are you tempted to pay more attention to the unclean spirits "out there" in other people's lives rather than addressing the unclean spirits in your own life?*
>
> *What are ways in which people use religious facades to cloak sinful intentions?*

Mature disciples are people who willingly ask the Lord to help them identify and root out self-deceptions in their lives. To be a good disciple, we must first allow Jesus to minister to us and heal us of our complacency with sin and weakness. Sometimes it is easier to justify our weaknesses than it is to deal with them. The great Spanish mystic, Saint John of the Cross, taught that even faithful church-attending Christians can succumb to the Seven Deadly Sins if they become complacent in their spiritual diligence.[14] He delineated the following specific ways in which "unclean spirits" can dwell even in the hearts of the faithful and those who are immersed in religious practices every day:

---

14. St John of the Cross, *Dark Night*, Book 1, Chapters 1–7 (Washington DC: ICS Publ., 1991), pp. 360–375.

Pride

This is the attitude by which individuals consider themselves "better than thou" because of their religious practices. In the process, they may even criticize others for not practicing their faith in the same way.

Avarice

Oftentimes, this vice manifests itself as the desire for "excess in religious things"; it is the sense that having more religious items will make a person holier. It can also be the multiplication of spiritual practices in a competitive way or a way that leads a person to only care about their own relationship with God rather than assisting others in their relationship with God as well.

Spiritual Lust

A particularly dangerous tendency is the "desire for spiritual consolation for its own sake." This desire manifests itself when a person prays because they want the consolation of peace or other positive feelings of affirmation. It occurs because a person is seeking the effects of a relationship with God more than the relationship itself. The consoling effects of our prayer can actually become spiritually addictive. Sometimes the Lord withholds His consolation specifically to call us beyond seeking spiritual practices for the sake of their emotional effects.

Anger

This is when a person becomes a "source of contention rather than fostering communion and love." The very purpose of our spiritual life is to help us love God and our neighbor in very real ways. When a person's religious practice or faith life leads them to be filled with anger then something unclean is filling them. This anger can manifest itself as religious judgmentalism, self-righteousness, and condemnatory attitudes towards others. It is the desire to punish rather than to convert and reconcile.

Spiritual Gluttony

This is similar to Spiritual Lust. It is the desire to "strive for spiritual savor rather than spiritual purity". It includes the desire for more and more penances or practices and for the feeling of being respected as a "spiritual person" in the community. It manifests itself when a person pursues one ministry experience after another without a desire for conversion but for participation only.

Spiritual Envy

This occurs when a person actually "feels sad about the spiritual growth of others". It can lead a person to discredit the spiritual lives of others or to actively seek out faults in others. It can cause a person to intentionally not participate in a ministry because of those who are participating in it. It can also lead someone to discredit the benefits offered through that ministry.

Spiritual Sloth

This vice leads us to "give up in prayer because it is difficult" or to "measure God by ourselves and NOT ourselves by God!" Ultimately, it can cause self-deception, making us actually believe that God desires what we already want. It can lead to the temptation of re-creating God in our own image and likeness. It can even lead to spiritual arrogance in which a person prefers to establish their own norms for a faith life rather than accepting the guidelines given by Jesus and handed down in the life of the Church.

> *As you review this list of the Seven Deadly Sins in the spiritual life by Saint John of the Cross, which one strikes you as being most insightful or relevant for your faith life?*
> *How do you see these sins as impeding or obstructing a life of discipleship?*
> *What are some of the virtues that will help people overcome these sins? Some possibilities could be humility, generosity, and courage.*

It is interesting that the man with the unclean spirit speaks up only after Jesus has issued His teaching and that the unclean spirit cries out, "Have you come to destroy us?" When the man heard Jesus proclaiming the message of the Gospel, he realized what the challenge of the Gospel meant and that it would require a change in his life. It is that resistance to change that gave rise to his cry "Have you come to destroy us?" Pope Benedict XVI spoke beautifully about the fear that can arise within us when we hear the challenge of the Gospel addressed to us as well when The Holy Father said:

> Are we not perhaps all afraid in some way? If we let Christ enter fully into our lives, if we open ourselves totally to Him, are we not afraid that He might take something away from us? Are we not perhaps afraid to give up something significant, something unique, something that makes life so beautiful? Do we not then risk ending up diminished and deprived of our freedom? ... No! If we let Christ into our lives, we lose nothing, nothing, absolutely nothing of what makes life free, beautiful and great. No! Only in this friendship are the doors of life opened wide. Only in this friendship is the great potential of human existence truly revealed. Only in this friendship do we experience beauty and liberation. And so, today, with great strength and great conviction, on the basis of long personal experience of life, I say to you, dear young people: Do not be afraid of Christ! He takes nothing away, and He gives you everything. When we give ourselves to Him, we receive a hundredfold in return. Yes, open, open wide the doors to Christ—and you will find true life. Amen.[15]

We have to give the man with the unclean spirit credit for actually listening to Jesus, taking time to understand the meaning of our Lord's message for his life, and realizing the changes that were necessary in order for him to follow God's way. His resistance to conversion gives voice to our resistance as well.

When you hear the message of Jesus, how do you respond? When do you feel like the challenge of faith is asking you to "give up" a part of your life?

---

15. Pope Benedict XVI, *Homily at the Beginning of the Petrine Ministry of the Bishop of Rome* (24 April 2005).

When are you afraid of what following Jesus might ask of you?

What hesitancy causes you to dismiss the personal challenge of the Gospel in your life?

How can our desire for self-preservation cause us to turn away from the risk of faith?

How does the quote from Benedict XVI inspire you to see the challenge of the Gospel in a new and positive way?

FIFTH SUNDAY IN ORDINARY TIME

Our Scripture passage for this Sunday comes from the Gospel of Mark 1:29–39. In this text we read of Jesus going to the home of Simon Peter and healing his mother-in-law. This passage is a wonderful instruction for us as disciples so that we can experience and respond to the Lord's grace in our lives with fidelity and generosity.

It is significant that Jesus heals Simon Peter's mother-in-law by grasping her hand. Mark goes out of his way to tell us about Jesus touching her. That is because it went against the social norms in the time of Jesus for a man to interact in this way with a woman who was not his relative. Jesus is showing us by His action that the Good News He brings to the world will challenge some of our social conventions and that being a Christian may mean going against certain cultural practices. Sometimes our love for God and neighbor calls us to act in unconventional and even shocking ways. This is a common theme in the Gospels. Christian disciples cannot allow their lives to be governed by the expectations of society, culture, or other people. Rather, a Christian disciple must be prepared to do whatever is necessary to manifest the love of God in specific times and places—even if it goes against the expectations of others.

What are some of the social norms or cultural expectations that deter disciples from expressing their faith today?
Who is someone you respect because he or she practices their faith without being restrained by expectations?
When have you avoided compassionate action because you were uncomfortable but through which you could have brought the mercy, acceptance, or healing of God to someone?

There is a striking contrast between the healing of Simon Peter's mother-in-law and the healing of the crowds. It is worth studying this contrast because Mark is intentional in presenting it to us. After her healing, we are told that Simon Peter's mother-in-law began to

serve Jesus and the disciples. This action is significant because it
means she used her gift of healing for the purpose of ministry. It
is further significant as a reminder we all have received gifts from
God's generous mercy, although we don't all respond as faithfully
and generously and she did. Oftentimes, we use our gifts only for
our benefit or to do our will, but she used her gift to serve Jesus and
do His will. Thus, Simon Peter's mother-in-law represents the ideal
disciple when she serves others (see Mk 10:43). Also, this passage
is more than just a story about physical healing. On a deeper level
it is an instruction on how to live our Baptism. This additional
element is introduced when we are told that Jesus "raised" her up.
The word used for "raised" (Greek: *egeiren*) is the same term used
in reference to the Resurrection of Jesus Himself (see 1 Cor 15:4,
Gal 1:1, Rom 4:24, Acts 3:15, 4:10). Thus, we see Jesus sharing His
resurrected life with her by "raising" her and then we are told how
she responds by demonstrating into a relationship of service for
Jesus and those who follow Him (the Church). This deeper understanding of the passage challenges us to share the gift of God's life
with others through works of charity and faithful service for the
mission of the Gospel. According to this interpretation, Jesus and
His first disciples represent the beginnings of the Church, and
Simon Peter's mother-in-law exemplifies an aspect of pastoral
ministry in caring for the members of the Church.

> *How has God blessed you, and how have you used those
> blessings to serve the Lord?*
> *What is the difference between the missionary and the pas-
> toral ministries of the Church, and how can you use your
> gifts to participate in each of those ministries?*
> *What do you think led Simon Peter's mother-in-law to
> serve Jesus and His disciples with the gift she had received?*
> *What can a faith community do to help people become
> more engaged in the pastoral ministries of the Church?*
> *What needs of Christians today are not being adequately
> cared for, and what can you do to help alleviate that need?*

The next scene of Jesus healing the crowds that come to Him ends
quite differently. We are told that the Lord healed all who were ill
and cast out many demons, but we are not told that anyone used

their gift of healing to serve Him in return. Rather, the implication is that they took their gifts of healing and went home. What a stark contrast in response from that of Simon Peter's mother-in-law. The crowds would seek Jesus only when they needed something from Him but not because they wanted to place their lives (which He had restored) in His service. When the disciples report to Jesus that the townspeople are looking for Him, the implication is either that they wanted more miracles or that they wanted to keep the Lord in their town. Jesus refuses to reduce His ministry to that of a local miracle worker who is there to only solve people's physical problems. Rather, His mission is to make disciples—people who will accept the Kingdom of God and follow Him—with lives committed to love of God and neighbor. Such a mission could not be fulfilled for people who were only interested in what God could do for them but not interested in what they could do for God. Jesus left that town to continue His ministry of preaching and healing elsewhere. The crowd's lack of sufficient response challenges us to reflect on the ways in which we have been self-centered or selfish in our response to God's grace in our lives. It also invites us to reflect on why we follow Jesus.

> *What happens to our faith when we think that God exists only to take away our problems?*
>
> *What do you think the crowds thought when Jesus left their town?*
>
> *How have you been tempted to use God's blessings in your life for your own needs rather than in the service of the Gospel?*
>
> *How can we try to control God and keep the Lord as "our own"?*
>
> *In what way do you think the crowds understood the meaning of "discipleship"?*
>
> *What can we do as a faith community to help people move beyond a self-centered or self serving faith and into a Christ-centered discipleship?*
>
> *As you think about this passage in its entirety, what is the enduring lesson you will take from it?*

Sixth Sunday in Ordinary Time

Our Scripture passage for this week comes from the Gospel of Mark 1:40–45. In this text we read of Jesus healing a leper and of the leper's response. On the surface, it looks like a very simple miracle story, but there is a deeper lesson in discipleship being offered as well.

This passage provides us an opportunity to learn something about who the lepers were in the time of Jesus and what their life experience was like. This background will help us understand Jesus' response. Today the term "leprosy" refers specifically to what is known as Hansen's disease. In the time of Jesus, however, the term "leper" referred to people who had a variety of scaly skin ailments. When a person was suspected of suffering such an ailment, their physical distress became worse because they were excluded from the community and forced to live in desolate places away from towns and homes. They were also required to wear torn clothing and to call out "unclean" as people approached (see Lv 13:1–2, 44–46). Thus, they suffered physically, socially, emotionally, and even spiritually (leprosy was believed to be a sign of God's punishment, see Nm 12:10). To be a leper was to live a desperate and miserable life. So far in Mark's Gospel, Jesus has met a lot of people in need as He progressed from healing the man with the unclean spirit in the Synagogue of Capernaum to healing Simon Peter's mother-in-law and now to a leper. This progression shows us that Jesus' ministry will reach out to everyone and that no one is beyond the boundaries of God's mercy. As with the previous healing of Simon Peter's mother-in-law, Jesus is going against certain religious laws and cultural norms in His interaction with the leper. The actions of Jesus in greeting and touching the leper challenge us to demonstrate the same active and courageous mercy in our lives towards those in desperate and miserable circumstances.

Who are the people that suffer the most from being on the margins of society today?

How can people who suffer physically today also experience
emotional, social, and spiritual suffering?
What Grace does the Anointing of the Sick offer so as to help
us overcome the various aspects of our suffering?
How do we insulate ourselves from the suffering of others?
When have you taken a risk (social, physical, or emotional)
to reach out to someone who is marginalized in our world?
Some ancient copies of the Gospel of Mark indicate that
Jesus responded with "anger" when he saw the leper; this
response most likely would have referred to our Lord's reac-
tion to a society that forced lepers to live such a miserable
life. What would Jesus be angry about in our society?
What are some systems that allow or promote human
suffering?

It is interesting that Mark tells us that Jesus was moved with compassion when He saw the leper (some translations use the term
"pity" or "mercy" instead). This is an important message for us
because we tend to understand "compassion" in an emotional sense.
Accordingly, "compassion" refers to the feeling or sentiment we
experience when we see someone else's distress. For Jesus, however,
compassion was not just a feeling or emotion; rather, compassion
was a motivation for action. When our Lord saw other people's
suffering, He was able to identify with them and was willing to
take action to alleviate their suffering. Just as suffering occurs on
various levels (physical, social, emotional, and spiritual), so too does
Jesus' compassionate response occur on various levels. We see this
compassion in how Jesus touches the leper to break the barrier of
isolation. (Note: The healing actually occurs at the Word of Jesus,
so His touch was not necessary. His touch was to render human
contact with a man who was isolated and alone.) In doing so, Jesus
breaks the purity laws and incurs ritual defilement.

Jesus also reaches out to heal the man spiritually by showing
him that God wants his healing, not his suffering, and that illness
is not a sign of God's punishment. Jesus heals the man socially by
allowing him to return to the community and be restored to his
previous relationships. The compassion of Jesus is powerful indeed!
Jesus is not afraid of being made "unclean" or rendered ritually
impure by the situation of other peoples lives; rather, Jesus is the

"strong one" announced by John the Baptist who can make clean what is soiled in our lives and purify what is stained by sin. His holiness has the power to sanctify even the most outcast in our world.

> *As disciples, Jesus wants us to be instruments of His mercy for those who need it. How can the fear of becoming "unclean" (or being perceived as "unclean") prevent us from associating with outcasts in our world?*
>
> *Jesus desired to bring healing to the leper on a variety of levels, not just physically. How can we help heal people who suffer spiritually, emotionally, and socially?*
>
> *Touching the leper was a very risky action that went against the laws of ritual purity. How can our actions of mercy today incur the risk of conflict, division, or other personal liability?*
>
> *What has led us to reduce compassion and mercy to merely emotional or sentimental experiences?*
>
> *Why do you think we have learned to be unresponsive in the face of other people's suffering?*
>
> *What can a faith community do to help people experience compassion as a motivation for action?*

The disobedience of the healed man is another significant aspect of this passage. You see, while Jesus demonstrates His power and control over the forces of illness, disease, and evil spirits, the one thing Jesus does not do is take away our free will and force us to act in a certain manner. Thus, Jesus does not control our human decisions. In this passage, Jesus does what the leper asks, but the healed leper doesn't do what Jesus asks. As disciples, this is a very important and powerful insight for us. Just like the man in the story, Jesus shares manifold blessings with us. Through the Gospel, and in the quiet of our prayer, He asks us to respond to Him in a very specific way. All too often we are like the healed man who is more concerned about getting God to do what we want rather than doing what God is wanting from us. For the healed man, his call to fame was the miraculous healing he received from Jesus. However, as disciples our call to boast should be in how well we fulfill God's will in our lives. In our contemporary secular culture, we value human freedom over all other values; in discipleship, we should value obedience to God's will first and foremost. As God, Jesus knew that the healed man would not follow our Lord's instruction, but He healed him anyway. That, too, is an important lesson for us because it reminds us that we can't control how other people will respond to our good works—but discipleship calls us to show compassion nonetheless. In short, we are responsible for being merciful; other people are responsible for how they respond to that mercy.

> *How much of your prayer is spent asking God for something rather than seeking to listen to what God is asking of you? When do you find it easy to exempt yourself from charitable actions because you don't know how others will respond to your mercy?*
> *The man was separated from the community because of his disease (leprosy), but Jesus ended up being separated from others because of the man's disobedience. How can the disobedience of Christians today end up separating others from the encounter with Jesus?*
> *If you were Jesus, what would you have said to the man after he spoke freely?*

Lastly, this passage teaches us something about the nature of authentic prayer. It is no accident that the leper approaches Jesus with the phrase, "If you will, you can make me clean." First, that prayer is an acknowledgement of God's all-powerful will and of our dependence upon that will. We even see Jesus praying with these same words in the Garden of Gethsemane when he says in Mark 14:36, "Father, if it is possible, let this cup be taken away from me, yet not as I will but as you will." We also see that ultimate desire for God's will to be done in the Lord's Prayer when we say, "Thy will be done." Second, the prayer of the leper shows us that God can do all things, including controlling disease and the forces of the world. Rather than seeing disease and misfortune as a sign of God's punishment, the prayer of the leper invites us to understand it as the opportunity for God's mercy. Third, the leper falls on his knees when he makes his request, which is a sign of adoration and of placing his life humbly before the Lord. In everything the man does, he is praying with the right words, the right attitude, and even the right posture. We should commend and imitate him for his accurate and powerful prayer! When Jesus responds, we see the Lord not only speaking His Word but also performing an action of mercy. Jesus demonstrates the important connection between words and deeds. Not only does He speak a message of consolation to the man but then does something to help him. The man, on the other hand, may have had all his words of faith correct, but his deeds did not correspond to that verbalized faith. For the virtue of faith to be complete and have integrity, there must always be a correlation between what we say and what we do. This two-fold dimension of faith is oftentimes described as *Fides Quae* (faith which is believed) and *Fides Qua* (how I live out what I believe).

> *How does the relationship between* Fides Quae *(faith which is believed) and* Fides Qua *(how I live out what I believe) as demonstrated in this story challenge your own experience of faith as a disciple?*
>
> *What posture helps you enter more deeply into an attitude of prayerful reverence?*
>
> *How does the correlation between the prayer of the leper, the prayer of Jesus in Gethsemane, and the Lord's Prayer affect the way you will approach your prayer?*
>
> *How do you think the man would have responded had Jesus not healed him?*
>
> *Why do you think Mark wanted us to know about a person who had all the right ways to pray but ultimately didn't follow God's will after the prayer was answered?*

SEVENTH SUNDAY IN ORDINARY TIME

Our Scripture passage comes from the Gospel of Mark 2:1–12. The story of the paralytic man who is carried to Jesus by his friends is an excellent opportunity for us to reflect on several aspects of discipleship including our responsibility as Christians to bring others to the Lord, our need to stand firm when facing opposition to the mission of the Gospel, and our need to live out repentance through reparation and ministry.

This passage is not the first time Jesus heals someone in Mark's Gospel, but it is different from previous miraculous accounts. Specifically, this is the first time that Jesus heals someone based on the faith of others. The four men who carried their paralyzed friend to Jesus were determined to overcome every barrier they encountered as they approached Jesus. The first barrier they encountered was that of the crowds. Crowds can play both positive and negative roles in the Gospels. Sometimes the crowds can communicate the message of Jesus to others and lead them to the Lord. But at other times, like in this Gospel passage, the crowds actually become an obstacle to those who would want to meet Jesus. They "prevent" people from being able to see the Lord. This is true today as well. How many people are turned off to religion because of the un-Christian witness of "religious" people? Sometimes people feel turned away from the Church by an unwelcoming comment or gesture made by someone they meet. The list of reasons can go on. We all have a responsibility to reflect upon our actions and identify those ways in which we "help" people meet the Lord in the context of the Church and ways in which we become an obstacle to people who want to meet the Lord. The faith of these four men was not deterred by the crowd. Rather, their faith demonstrated creative initiative in finding an alternate way to meet Jesus: they opened the roof of the house and lowered their friend into the Lord's presence. This is certainly an unconventional method of introducing people to Jesus, and the Lord responds with praise to such creativity.

The faith of these four men is exemplary indeed. They show us what love of neighbor looks like as they bring their friend to meet Jesus. They show us what creativity looks like as they overcome obstacles. It is not difficult to understand why Jesus responded positively when He saw such faith. There are many ways in which we can exemplify the faith of these men and bring to the Lord those whom we know are in need of His healing grace. Sometimes that may mean physically bringing someone with us to Mass or a ministry event (note that the men in this passage brought the paralyzed man to Jesus while our Lord was "preaching the Word"). It may also mean bringing people to the Lord in prayer: part of our expression of Love of Neighbor is to pray for those in need and bring them before the Lord like the men who carry the paralytic in today's Gospel. This is especially true for people who are not able to approach the Lord on their own, people who are "paralyzed" by circumstances that dominate their lives: sin, weakness, addictions, or lack of faith. That can mean everything from self-absorbed behaviors to indifference to others. It is an act of charity to pray for those who cannot or will not pray for themselves. This passage is the first time in Mark's Gospel when Jesus points out someone's faith. He does so to show us what faith "looks like" in action. It is a lesson for us to imitate. The faith of the men was demonstrated in the fact that they were not deterred by the obstacles they faced. That's the faith of good disciples! That's the faith Jesus wants in us as well.

> *Do you know someone who demonstrates a creative and perseverant faith?*
> *Who loved you enough to pray for you when you did not or would not pray for yourself?*
> *For whom do you pray in the same way?*
> *What are examples of things Christians have done that became obstacles to your participation in the life and ministry of the Church?*
> *How have others opened the door for you so as to help you encounter Christ in the Church?*

This passage tells us more than just a story of healing. It is really meant to be a story of discipleship. This additional meaning is communicated through three important elements in the story. First, when Jesus commands the man to "Rise", our Lord uses the Greek verb *egeire*, which is also used to describe the experience of the Resurrection. Thus, Jesus is offering the paralyzed man a sharing in His own resurrected life. We share in the resurrected life of Jesus when we are washed in the waters of Baptism. The life of Jesus is often referred to as "grace" and it has a healing effect in our lives that saves us from sin.

Second, when Jesus speaks to the paralytic, our Lord refers to him as "my son" (Greek *teknon*). There were various words in Greek that were used in different ways when referring to children. If someone wanted to refer to a small child then they used the word *paidon*. By using the term *teknon* Jesus was stressing the filial relationship the man now had with our Lord. The paralytic had become a "Son" to Jesus and a member of God's family in the Church. (For a similar occasion when a term of relationship is used in reference to a disciple, see Mk 5:34). Disciples are people who are called to be in an intimate relationship with Jesus even as a son or daughter is to their parent. This term of affection and relationship is teaching us that the healed man in this passage was not only someone who received the gift of healing but also someone who received the greater gift of relationship. It is the gift of relationship that will change our lives long after the moment of healing is complete. Every time our Lord shares His grace with us it is an invitation into that relationship.

Third, Jesus tells the man to do something as a result of his healing. Specifically, the Lord tells him to "go" and to "pick up his mat". The commandment to "go" (Greek: *upage)* is not so much a dismissal as it is an instruction to be on mission. Our Lord will encounter many people in His ministry and He will issue for each of them the similar commandment to "go". All of these moments culminate in (and derive their force from) the ultimate commission to "go" which is given by the young man to the woman at the tomb in Mark 16:7. That commission is the instruction to become, for others, a witness to the resurrection. The man in this story received a sharing in the resurrected life of Jesus and now he is to go and bring that message to others beginning with those members of his own home.

Fourth, Jesus teaches us something very important about the life of discipleship when He tells the man to "pick up your mat (or pallet)". This may strike us as an odd and even unnecessary instruction. The mat (or pallet) was a symbol of the man's paralysis and as such it serves as a remnant of his former way of life. Jesus does not want disciples who merely walk away from the remnants of their former lives (pre-conversion). Disciples have a responsibility to pick up the pieces as part of their following the Lord. Sometimes people have had difficult experiences of life before their conversion. Those difficulties may have caused damaged relationships, hurt feelings, or destruction to other people's property. Disciples can't simply walk away from these strained situations; rather, disciples have a responsibility to make amends for the wrongs of their past lives and perform works of reparation as part of their repentance and sharing in the life of grace. When Jesus told the healed man to "pick up your mat," our Lord was telling him to make the work of amendment a part of his discipleship.

> *When have you felt yourself sharing in the resurrected life of Jesus?*
>
> *In what moments in your life have you received a momentary grace from God, and how was that grace meant to be an invitation to deeper and lasting relationship with the Lord?*
>
> *To whom in your life are you being sent to "go" and share the message of what Jesus has done for you?*
>
> *Who, especially in your home or family, needs to hear that message?*
>
> *What are some examples of typical amendments or reparations people need to undertake as part of their discipleship?*

This passage represents the first of five scenes in which Jesus enters into controversy with the religious leaders of His time. The particular reason for disharmony in this passage concerns the power of Jesus to forgive sins. Such power is rightly attributed to God alone. Jesus' statements do not take away from God's power, but rather show that God's power is now being exercised on Earth through the Son of Man. This is an important element of the passage and Mark dedicates a significant number of verses to this controversy. The miracle was not only a physical healing but also entailed the forgiveness of sins. People in the ancient world believed that physical disability and illness were the result of sin. Therefore, in order for someone to be healed they had to be forgiven so that the root cause of their ailment could be alleviated. Jesus rightly exercises that authority and power over sin, which He has by virtue of being the Son of God.

However, it is interesting to note that Jesus identifies Himself as the Son of Man rather than the Son of God when He explains the source of His authority. That is because Jesus wants to stress that God will dispense on earth the forgiveness of sins through men. The early Church continued to exercise the forgiveness of sins in Jesus' name.[16] (see James 5:16 Therefore confess your sins to each other and pray for each other so that you may be healed.) Our Lord specifically commissioned His disciples to carry on this work in Matthew 18:18 and John 20:23. Mark wanted Christians of his community to know that the forgiveness of sins is real and offered to them through the ministry of the Church on Earth, which continues the mission of the Son of Man. This ministry of forgiveness is celebrated in the Sacrament of Reconciliation. It was, and still is, considered a blasphemous practice by those who mistakenly believe that priests themselves claim to be authors of forgiveness. That is not true! It is not the priest himself who has the power to forgive, but rather Jesus who forgives through the ministry of the priest. Thus, priests are dispensers of the Sacrament of Forgiveness and not its authors. The power of forgiveness always and only belongs to God; the Sacrament of Reconciliation is how God chooses to minister forgiveness in our world today (see 2 Cor 5:19). As Pope Francis declared, "The Church is commissioned to announce the

---

16. See also: *Didache* 4:14 thou shalt confess thy transgressions in the Church, and shalt not come unto prayer with an evil conscience. This is the path of life. *Didache* 14:1 But on the Lord's day, after that ye have assembled together, break bread and give thanks, having in addition confessed your sins, that your sacrifice may be pure. (http://www.earlychristianwritings.com/text/didache-hoole.html)

mercy of God, the beating heart of the Gospel, which in its own way must penetrate the heart and mind of every person."[17]

Nonetheless, our Lord's Good News of forgiveness was met with opposition and rejection. The spiritual powers that opposed Jesus in Mark 1:24 have found another means by which to resist our Lord: the crowd that complains. Jesus did not listen to the complaints of those who objected to His ministry. Instead, He stated the source of His power and proceeded to make a disciple of the man who was previously paralyzed. Sometimes the Church can face opposition to various ministries of mercy. Whether it is care for the immigrant, the condemned prisoner, the addict, or the notorious sinner, there are always those who will resist such actions and call them blasphemous. This passage should prepare us as disciples to persevere in our efforts to be courageous witnesses of God's mercy in the face of such opposition. It should also encourage us and inspire us to know that the mercy and forgiveness we minister comes from Christ.

> *How are the merciful works of the Church opposed today? This passage is cautioning us that the spiritual battle between the Kingdom of God and the kingdom of evil is waged in human interactions. How do you know whether you are influenced by the Kingdom of God or the kingdom of evil in your daily interactions?*
> *The crowds glorified God when they heard and saw our Lord's actions of healing and Forgiveness. What keeps you from seeking those same graces in your life?*

17.   Pope Francis, *Misericordiae Vultus* (11 April 2015).

Eighth Sunday in Ordinary Time

Our Scripture passage comes from the Gospel of Mark 2:18–22. The challenge of the Pharisees gave Jesus an opportunity to present a lasting teaching on the role, nature, and appropriateness of religious practices. In the context of this teaching, and to demonstrate His point, Jesus used the defining and enduring image of the bridegroom to describe His relationship with the Church. Our study of this passage can help us to be disciples who respond appropriately in our relationship with the Lord.

The Pharisees challenged Jesus to explain why His disciples did not practice fasting like the disciples of John the Baptist. In order to understand their challenge and our Lord's response, it is important to remember the purpose of fasting in the ancient world. Within Judaism, fasting was a deeply rooted religious practice that was sometimes requested by the prophets for various reasons (see Is 58:6, "the fasting I desire..." Jonah to Nineveh, Jon 3:5). Fasting meant abstaining from food or drink for the majority of the day and could be practiced either individually or communally. This practice was oftentimes associated with occasional periods of mourning, prayers of petition for divine favor, or as a sign of repentance. Once a year, the entire Jewish people would fast on the Day of Atonement in a national prayer for forgiveness. Some segments within Judaism (especially the Essenes) practiced fasting in an effort to bring about the Day of the Lord or even the coming of the Messiah. Some documents indicate that observant Pharisees fasted two days a week (Monday and Thursday). Usually the practice of fasting was associated with visible signs such as torn clothing, an unwashed face, or a somber countenance. Little is known about the practice of fasting among the disciples of John the Baptist. The Christian teaching on fasting appears in only a few Gospel verses (see Mt 6:16–18. 15:32. 17:21; Mk 2:18–19. 8:3. 9:29; Lk 2:37).

What can be deduced from our Lord's teaching and these other New Testament passages is that Christians did practice fasting but for a different reason and in a different way than others. The late first century Christian writing known as the Teaching of the Twelve Apostles, or Didache, relates that Christians did fast on Wednesday and Friday (the day on which Jesus died).[18] The Gospel of Matthew makes it clear that fasting is to be a private spiritual practice that expresses the sincere desire for personal conversion. For Christians, fasting is a practice of self-denial and self-control that is intended to free a person from slavery to the appetites. By overcoming the natural attachment to the physical pleasures of this life (symbolized by food and drink), a person became more disciplined and capable of accepting sacrifices and inconveniences for the sake of the Gospel. Sometimes Christians mistakenly think that the practice of fasting is somehow antiquated and irrelevant for contemporary discipleship. Jesus makes it clear that although His disciples did not fast when He was with them, they would fast once He was taken away. Fasting, then, is encouraged as a standard part of a disciple's life. In order for us to follow Jesus in freedom and sacrificial generosity, we must be free of all inordinate attachments to earthly and physical appetites and pleasures.

Fasting, then, is a spiritual discipline that can help us grow in detachment. Fasting can also be an appropriate sign of our contrition and an expression of our desire for conversion of life. Fasting is a way in which disciples can pray with their whole being and can express our longing for God, which is only fulfilled in eternal life. No earthly "food" in this world will ever satisfy our hunger for God and fasting can remind us of our deepest longing. Jesus never criticized the practice of fasting; our Lord did caution that it should be exercised with appropriateness and sincerity.

> *When do you fast and what benefits have you experienced from this spiritual practice?*
> *What attitudes or values of our contemporary culture can discourage the practice of fasting?*
> *What kinds of things do people deny themselves for the sake of worldly accomplishments?*

---

18. *Didache,* Chap. VIII, 1: "Let not your fasts be with the hypocrites, for they fast on Mondays and Thursdays, but do your fast on Wednesdays and Fridays."

How can the practice of regular fasting become an enriching
spiritual practice in your life?
When have you been inspired and encouraged by another
person's practice of self-denial?

In order to explain why His disciples did not fast, Jesus used the image of a wedding feast. This image is important for three reasons. First, the image helps us understand the appropriateness of religious practices. Indeed, it would be difficult to explain why someone should fast while in the midst of a joyful celebration. This teaching on the appropriateness of religious practices is meant as a caution to anyone who would promote a "one-size-fits-all" attitude when it comes to requiring conformity of life among disciples. Rather than being concerned about why Jesus' disciples didn't do the same thing as everyone else, the Pharisees should have respected their decision as a legitimate way of following God.

Second, the image of a wedding feast helps us to understand the spiritual relationship between Jesus and the Church. Other sections of the New Testament expound on this image as well (see Jn 3:29, Mt 25:1–13, Rom 7:4, 2 Cor 11:2–4, Eph 5:22–30, Rev 21:2, 9–10, Rev 22:17). By identifying Himself as the Bridegroom, Jesus is identifying the Church as the Bride. Saint Paul indicates in Ephesians 5:27 that the Bride of Christ will remain faithful and free of serious sin (spotless and glorious). This promise of fidelity is to ensure that Jesus always recognizes His Beloved when He gazes on the Church. It is from this promise of the Lord, and the enduring, irrevocable nature of a marriage sealed with the New Covenant of the Eucharist (the Wedding Feast of the Lamb related in Rev 19:6–9), that the Holy Spirit is given to the Church as an assurance of divine protection. It is from this promise that the Bride may be preserved from every serious infidelity to the Groom (Jesus) that would render her unrecognizable. This preservation from serious infidelity is traditionally understood among Roman Catholics as the gift of Infallibility that prevents the Church from falling into serious errors of faith and morals. Such a gift does not mean that individual members of the Church do not sin or fall into errors of faith but that there will always be a truly and authentically holy and faithful remnant until the end of time, and that official doctrine of the Church will be preserved from serious error in matters of faith or morals. By summarizing His relationship with the Church in terms of marriage, Jesus is also stressing the response He desires from his Bride: complete self-giving in a loving and irrevocable commitment of life.

Third, the image of marriage between Jesus and the Church is established as the pattern for husband and wife in the Sacrament of Marriage as Saint Paul states specifically in Ephesians 5:1–30. Just as Jesus gave Himself completely to the Church, washes her, makes her holy, and nourishes her with His own flesh, so husbands should love their wives. This passage from Ephesians often evokes controversy because it contains the instruction for wives to be submissive to their husbands. This verse needs to always be read in context of the entire passage in order to properly understand it. Paul is not appealing for blind obedience and subservience but for husbands and wives to mirror the love of God for one another. When the distinctive love of Jesus is made present through the marriage of Christian man and woman, the grace of God dwells in their midst.

> *What helps you understand which religious practices are appropriate in particular situations?*
>
> *When should you be concerned because another person is not expressing similar religious practices, and what is the best way to express that concern?*
>
> *How does the marital relationship of Jesus and the Church challenge and inspire you as a disciple?*
>
> *What are practical ways in which husbands and wives live out the distinctive love of Jesus in their marriages? (see Eph 5:1–30).*
>
> *How does your experience of the Mass become more meaningful when you understand it as the Wedding Feast of the Lamb?*
>
> *How is the Lord's gift of the Holy Spirit preserving His Bride, the Church, in spotless glory today?*
>
> *Married people in our society typically wear wedding rings to remind themselves and others of the need to be faithful to their spouse. What can Christian disciples do to have a similar visible reminder that encourages them to be faithful to Jesus?*

As the controversy with the Pharisees drew to a close, Jesus used two examples to illustrate the importance and necessity of adaptability when it comes to growing in our relationship with Him. The first example involved patching an old garment with a piece of new cloth. People in Jesus' time knew that cloth would shrink with repeated washings and that it would not be practical to repair an old cloak with new fabric. The gradual tension of the new patch shrinking would eventually cause it to tear away. The problem was not in the shrinking of the new cloth but in the inability of the old cloth to accommodate the required gradual change.

The second example is that of wineskins. Wineskins were used in the fermentation process, and fresh wineskins would have an elasticity that allowed them to expand with the production of carbon dioxide. However, once wineskins were used for one fermentation process they lost their elasticity and would be incapable of being used for a second process. Instead, they would burst and the wine would be lost because of the wineskins' inability to change. Once again, the problem was not in the fermentation and production of carbon dioxide but in the inability of the old wineskins to accommodate the required gradual change. Each of these examples demonstrates the futility of a person thinking that a dynamic reality (faith) can successfully function in a rigid environment that refuses to change or adapt (a person's pre-existing life). This teaching is important for us as disciples because it challenges us to realize that our relationship with Jesus is going to require an ongoing change in every part of our lives. If we are unwilling to make the needed changes in order to respond to our Lord's movement, the relationship will be ruptured. In order for our faith relationship to endure, God must not only be the center of our lives but we must also be willing and eager for the Lord to change us because of that relationship. Sometimes people try to compartmentalize their relationship with God and to contain the Lord's influence. Such an effort is not only futile but even misdirected. A person who approaches his faith in such a way is setting himself up for the inevitability of failed discipleship.

> *How has the Lord gradually called you to an ongoing conversion in your life and what have been some of the significant milestones of your growth in discipleship?*

*When have you tried to compartmentalize your faith and
what was the result?*

*How do these images help you to understand the emptiness
some people experience when it comes to their relationship
with Jesus?*

*What can a faith community do to help its members desire
the transforming grace of God in their lives and help them
understand what that grace means?*

*What do you think are the root causes of rigidity and refusal
to change in people's lives?*

*How do you know the difference between unhealthy rigidity
and a healthy firmness of conviction?*

NINTH SUNDAY IN ORDINARY TIME

Our reading comes from the Gospel of Mark 2:23–28 and 3:1–6. In these passages we read about two situations in which Jesus encounters controversy over Sabbath observance. These readings provide us an important opportunity to reflect on how disciples are called to respond to the Christian observance of the Lord's Day as a regular part of our weekly cycle of life. This weekly celebration of the Lord's Day on Sunday commemorates the Resurrection of Jesus and challenges us to make it a time of communion with God, communion with others, and communication of the Paschal Mystery.

Any discussion of Jewish Sabbath (Saturday) observance or Christian observance of the Lord's Day (Sunday) needs to be understood in light of our contemporary practices. Our secular culture has little value and offers little support for a day dedicated to God. The frenetic pace of modern life, the demands on young families, the over-programming of personal schedules all impinge on Sunday being a time dedicated to the higher pursuits of faith. For many people, Sunday has become the catch-all day for those things we could not accomplish during the regular week. It has also become the day of preparation for Monday when work projects are finalized for the upcoming business week. All these infringements on the sanctity of the Lord's Day negatively impact the ability of disciples to observe Sunday in a religious way. When the negative influences of consumerism and materialism are added, Sunday becomes little more than an occasion for shopping, secular leisure activities, and dining out.

By engaging in these practices, disciples sometimes require others to work on the Lord's Day so that they can enjoy the pursuits they desire. Christian teaching has always understood that certain work activities are permitted on the Lord's Day when those activities relate to healthcare, emergency services, and needs that cannot be delayed until the regular workweek. However, most activities driven by consumerism and materialism do not meet the previously stated criteria. The patronization of businesses and participation in secular entertainment on the Lord's Day further diminishes both our own individual ability to dedicate that day to God as well as the ability of those who must be employed to satisfy our desires. In light of our contemporary experience of the Lord's Day, this passage offers us a timely opportunity to reflect and redirect our attention and energy so as to experience Sunday as a day of sanctification, communion, and renewal. Let's study this passage to see what Jesus might say to us about His desire for our observance of the Lord's Day.

One of the first things to note is that we are told the disciples were on their way. The use of the term "way" is always important in the Gospels and indicates the path of discipleship rather than just an ordinary, random outing for a non-faith-based purpose. They were on mission with Jesus, and this mission was occurring on the Sabbath. The reality is that disciples oftentimes do have to work on the Lord's Day, just as the priests in the Temple of Jerusalem worked on the Sabbath. Jesus defends the action of disciples who are helping Him carry out His mission even when those efforts occur on the day dedicated to God. In fact, carrying out the Will of God can even be a fulfillment of that day's very purpose. Doing works of ministry is not in contradiction with the commandment to "Keep Holy the Sabbath" (see Ex 20:8–11, Dt 5:12–15). Disciples must take care, however, lest their working on the Lord's Day becomes a distraction for others. We see this distraction occurring in the Pharisees who ask Jesus why "His" disciples were doing what is not permitted on the Sabbath.

The message is this: The actions of disciples reflect either positively or negatively on the Master. People will make judgments about who Jesus Christ is based on how they see Christians act. Each of us has the responsibility to be disciples who praise and honor God in our words and actions so that those who see us will be inspired and grow in deeper respect for Jesus. Sunday is a day of discipleship and mission. As such, it is a day when we come to hear the Word of God in the Scriptures, to be strengthened by the Eucharist, and to be sent on mission to bring God's presence into the world. Anything we do to fulfill that mission is in conformity with God's intention for the Lord's Day; anything we do that is different from that mission is a distraction from God's intention for the Lord's Day for both ourselves and others.

> *The Church calls Sunday, "the Day of New Creation".[19] How can your participation in the Lord's Day help you renew yourself physically, mentally, and spiritually?*
>
> *What areas of your life need to experience "new life" this week?*
>
> *How does this reflection challenge you to reconsider the way you normally spend the Lord's Day?*
>
> *What are works of discipleship or mission that you could start doing on the Lord's Day?*

The Lord's Day is also a day of sacred rest. This rest is the original intention of the Jewish Sabbath as stated in Genesis 2:2. Over the course of time, the Jewish Sabbath also began to include other commemorative meanings such as the liberation from Egypt (Dt 5:14–15) and the Sinai Covenant (Ex 31:12–17). Because the Sabbath grew in meaning, so did the importance of observing it. Texts such as Exodus 31:14 indicate that those who profane the Sabbath shall be put to death (see also Nm 15:32–36). Jesus desires the Sabbath and, conversely, the Day of the Lord to be restored as a day of sacred rest. God's rest in Genesis was not due to exhaustion caused by the work of creation; rather, God's rest was a contemplative rest in which the Lord looked at what He had created and appreciated it with gratitude, healthy pride, and joy. Contemplative rest does the same for us—it allows us to look at our lives and accomplishments with the same gratitude, healthy pride, and joy. We all need to take time so as to understand what our lives and accomplishments mean in the eyes of God. The experience of contemplative rest provides us that opportunity. This contemplative rest requires prayer and reflection in order to bring us deeply into communion with God. It is that communion with God that sanctifies the Lord's Day in a distinctive way as we worship in community and practice private devotions. It is only through our communion with God and the experience of contemplative rest that we can see our lives as God sees them and understand the Lord's will for each of us.

---

19.   Pope St John Paul II, *Dies Domini* (1998).

What obligations most distract you on the Lord's Day?
Which ways are used to avoid the essential obligations in
life?
How can our "Sunday experience" help us reorganize and
improve our life structure?
What do you find appealing about this understanding of
contemplative rest?

When Jesus heals the man with the withered hand we are given another insight into the purpose of the Lord's Day: It is the day on which we celebrate the resurrected life of the Lord. This meaning is communicated when Jesus commands the man to "rise" and uses the same verb used for the Resurrection. Jesus is giving the man a sharing in His own resurrected life that will heal him and strengthen him for the challenges he faces. Each time Christians gather to share in the Eucharist on the Lord's Day they are sharing in the resurrected life of Jesus. In this way, every Friday, Saturday, and Sunday is meant to be honored and experienced according to the events of our Lord's Passion, Death, and Resurrection. Friday is traditionally a day of sacrifice and fasting in commemoration of our Lord's Passion. Saturday is traditionally a day of preparation that may include the Sacrament of Reconciliation. Sunday is the day of celebration when our hopes, fears, trials, and sufferings are joined on the altar to the eternal and unique sacrifice of Jesus who presents us with Himself to God the Father. By observing every Friday, Saturday, and Sunday as a mini-Triduum, the Christian disciple regularly shares in the saving mystery of Christ's love and is called to mirror our Lord's charity and self-giving to others. In this way, the radiant image of the Risen Christ shines forth again in the lives of His faithful disciples who are commissioned at the end of each Mass with the words "Go! You are Sent" (or similar translations). Sunday, then, is meant to be the day on which disciples are commissioned to bring the presence of the Risen Christ into the world. In order to receive such incredible blessings and such an awesome commission, it is important to properly prepare oneself. St John Paul II reminded us:

> Once the assembly disperses, Christ's disciples return to their
> everyday surroundings with the commitment to make their

whole life a gift, a spiritual sacrifice pleasing to God (see Rom 12:1). They feel indebted to their brothers and sisters because of what they have received in the celebration, not unlike the disciples of Emmaus who, once they had recognized the Risen Christ 'in the breaking of the bread' (see Lk 24:30–32), felt the need to return immediately to share with their brothers and sisters the joy of meeting the Lord (see Lk 24:33–35).[20]

A disciple needs to be properly disposed for such a mission—that is the reason for observing Friday as a day of penance and Saturday as a day of preparation.

How does this understanding of honoring the Lord's Passion, Death, and Resurrection each week inspire you?
How would your Sunday experience be different if you prepared for it in this way?
What can a faith community do to help families experience Sunday as the day in which we share in the risen life of the Lord and are sent forth on mission?

Lastly, the Lord's Day is a time during which disciples are called to foster communion with one another. The Pharisees and Herodians in this passage sought to destroy Jesus on the Sabbath. Rather than "save life," they were seeking to harm it. This contrast between the action of Jesus and the actions of the Pharisees and Herodians invites us to consider ways in which we can actively promote communion with others and "save life" on the Lord's Day. It is always lawful in the eyes of God to do good, and the Lord delights when we do His will, especially on The day dedicated to Him. We are first called to foster communion with others, promote life, and do good works among the members of our own family. For this reason, Sunday is typically identified as an important day when families spend time together and seek to relate in peace and good will. It is also a time in the Church when we foster that same communion within the Family of God. Thus, it is appropriate to spend time on Sunday at one's local parish, participating in a faith-enrichment ministry or assisting with events of the local or universal Church. Finally, Sunday is an important day to express our communion with those in need, especially the poor, the ill, the homebound,

20. Pope St John Paul II, *Dies Domini* (30 July 1998).

and all others who may feel marginalized, abandoned, or disadvantaged. Through these works of charity and mercy, disciples carry on the same compassionate works of Jesus and fulfill the Lord's Day according to the will of God.

> *What gets in the way of experiencing Sunday as a day of communion within your family?*
> *What can a faith community do to deepen the communion of the faithful with one another on Sunday?*
> *What charitable works might be done on the Lord's Day as part of our mission as disciples?*

TENTH SUNDAY IN ORDINARY TIME

Our Scripture passage comes from the Gospel of Mark 3:20–35. Due to the various possible dates on which Easter can fall, this Sunday is rarely celebrated in the normal course of a liturgical year and so it is not often that we hear this reading. However, this passage offers some very challenging and insightful messages of faith for us as disciples and reminds us of how easy it is to misunderstand and misidentify the work of God.

The event that triggered the reaction of Jesus' family and the Scribes was the crowd that assembled and filled the house where the Lord and His disciples were staying. This is the same crowd that we heard about a few verses earlier in Mark 3:7–8 and they were composed of both Jews and Gentiles (people from Galilee, Judea, Jerusalem, as well as Idumea, beyond the Jordan, and Tyre and Sidon). The inclusive nature of the crowd explains why they "could not eat" because sharing a meal with Gentiles was a violation of Jewish purity laws (Gal 1:19 and Gal 2:1–14). Our Lord's inclusive mission has begun and not everyone is happy about it. Jesus' family thought that our Lord was out of His mind, (Mk 3:21) which, for them, explained His religiously and culturally offensive action of inclusivity. The Scribes, who were sent from the powerful leaders in Jerusalem, accused Jesus of acting out of evil intent. It is almost always shocking when great people of faith challenge the cultural world of their time. Saint Francis of Assisi was called "Il Pazzo" (Italian meaning "the crazy one") because of his radical commitment to the Gospel and the evangelical vows of poverty, chastity, and obedience. Saint Catherine of Siena was considered a woman of disrepute by some of her contemporaries because of her nighttime missions of mercy to the sick, the suffering, and the condemned. Saint Damian Molokai was defamed by those who were threatened by his radical ministry of mercy and solidarity to the lepers of the Hawaiian Islands. Certainly the list can go on. Sometimes people of profound faith are called to witness God's love and mercy in a way that challenges the comfortable expectations of the world around them. When that happens, there is always a response of rejection, defamation, or accusation. Jesus was willing to withstand such misunderstandings, even by those closest to Him (His own family) for the sake of fidelity to the Father's will.

> *When have you been misunderstood or falsely accused because of a faith-filled action?*
> *How do you process that feeling?*
> *How does the threat of being misunderstood prevent us from acting on inspirations of faith?*
> *Do you think Jesus knew the risks of being misunderstood, and how do you think our Lord overcame the negative response of others?*

It is the accusation of the Scribes that evokes our Lord's most serious response. It is one thing for His own family to think that He was out of his mind, but it is another thing for someone to label His actions as a manifestation of evil. In response to this accusation, Jesus presents a simple parable about what happens when a house is divided against itself; it is destroyed. The power of evil was obviously alive and well so that means it had not been destroyed by division. The people of Jesus' time were all too familiar with stories of how divided households fell. The House of Herod the Great came to an end after his death in 4 BC due to infighting. Even the imperial household was not immune from the fatal effects of internal division as three emperors attempted to reign during the years AD 68–69 following the death of Nero—all of them having met tragic ends due to internal divisions. Our Lord's teaching would have been immediately acknowledged as true. The other point in our Lord's teaching is equally important. Since our Lord has the power to overcome evil without becoming like it, we are left with the conclusion that He is the "stronger one" who can take control. Jesus was first introduced as the "stronger one" by John the Baptist in Mark 1:7 and is demonstrating His greater power over the forces of evil (see Mk 1:21–28).

> *How can a disciple share in the Master's ability to overcome evil?*
> *What barriers are you challenged to overcome and what benefit can that new freedom bring to your life?*

Evil destroys communion and is made evident in division.
What areas of your life keep you from receiving the gift of
communion?

The accusation of the Scribes was particularly dangerous because it basically accused Jesus of practicing magic (demonstrating powerful actions through the authority of evil), which was punishable by death or exile. For this reason, Jesus could not ignore their charge. After our Lord demonstrated why their charge could not be true, Jesus goes on to warn them of the seriousness of their accusation for their own souls: They have committed blasphemy against the Holy Spirit for which there is no forgiveness. This warning has given rise to all sorts of speculation about what exactly constitutes "blasphemy" against the Holy Spirit. This speculation has caused substantial controversy among numerous religious scholars over the ages. In order to properly understand our Lord's warning, we need to remember that Jesus is speaking to the trained religious leaders of His time who were regarded as the authoritative interpreters of tradition. These are people who should have known what the action of God looks like and endorsed it as good (healing the sick, freeing the possessed, and forgiving sins). Instead, they mislabeled as evil what was in reality good. A trained, educated, and influential religious leader and teacher should have known the difference, and so the accusation of the Scribes revealed that they were not open to the action of God (Holy Spirit) in the world. It is that rejection of God's action, which constitutes an unforgivable sin, because one who is closed to divine intervention is also closed to that forgiveness which comes from the Lord. It can be easy for us to sometimes misinterpret the good actions of others by attributing evil motivation. This passage cautions us to interpret good actions with a principle of charity that seeks to give others the benefit of the doubt rather than rashly concluding sinister motives.

Past experiences can give rise to preconceived notions and
prejudices. In dealing with others, how is your objectivity
diminished because of negative presumptions you make
about their motives?
How can charity help you regain clarity and openness about
others' intentions?

For whom do you find it difficult to attribute good and wholesome motives for their actions?

The final part of this passage returns to the topic of Jesus' family who came to see Him. In response to this information, our Lord announces that His new family is composed of those who do the will of God. This qualification is a redefinition of discipleship and a clarification of that quality which allows a person to be "close" to Jesus and to have access to Him. This new definition is not based on blood lineage or any other accidental claim, but on active fidelity to the will of God. In the ancient world of Jesus a person's family was perceived as having a natural claim on an individual's life, and it was expected that a person conform to the values and habits of their household. Jesus was acting in a way that was contrary to the established customs of His family, so they could not readily understand our Lord's actions and intentions. Jesus would allow Himself to be governed only by the will of the Father rather than by any other human affection or earthly connection.

This clarification of discipleship was important for Christians in the early Church because many of them had to leave behind their families in order to follow Jesus. If they complied with the demands of human affections or earthly connections, they might not have been able to persevere in following the Lord when the mission of the Gospel challenged them to go against the expectations and established customs of those around them. It is significant that Mark contrasts those who are inside the house and are close to Jesus (disciples) and those who are outside the house and more distant from Jesus (Scribes and family). This contrast is not only a physical differentiation but also a statement of faith attachment (discipleship) to the Lord. If we want to be close to Jesus then we must go beyond emotional attachments or communal association and commit our lives in active fidelity to the will of God as revealed in the life, ministry, and teachings of our Lord. This is a challenging definition of discipleship! Sometimes people can be tempted to think that the quality of their faith life depends primarily on the feelings they experience in prayer, their involvement in various ministries, the number of religious images they have in their home, or other secondary factors. In this passage, Jesus challenges us to primarily evaluate our faith lives based on how well we do the will of God.

How can people deceive themselves into falsely thinking they are close to Jesus?

Which conditions are typically required in order for you to enjoy prayer and participation in the liturgy?

How can comfort and predictability prevent you from living your faith in a different way?

How does it inspire you to know that you can be part of Jesus' family?

Eleventh Sunday in Ordinary Time

Our Scripture passage comes from the Gospel of Mark 4:26–34. In this text our Lord continues to teach important lessons about discipleship and the Kingdom of God through the use of parables. Let's study each of these teachings to better understand the implications for our lives today.

Jesus uses the parable of the seed and the harvest in order to draw out several points. First, after the seed is planted it seems to grow of its own accord. This growth was a mystery to the people of Jesus' time and indicated God's guidance and control of the process. Second, when it is planted the seed is always relatively small and insignificant compared to the fully mature plant that springs from the Earth. This contrast between the seemingly small and powerless initial appearance and the much larger eventual manifestation describes both the experience of Jesus and the experience of the early Church. Jesus was revealed in Mark's Gospel as the *Stronger One* (Greek: *Ischuroteros* see Mk 1:7) yet our Lord's Passion, Suffering, and Death on Calvary did not reveal His power in that moment; rather, His true power as the *Stronger One* would be manifested in the Resurrection. The early Church experienced a similar small beginning in the midst of persecution, rejection, and resistance yet the disciples were called to trust that mysterious growth was taking place nonetheless. In short, this parable teaches us to trust that the mission of the Gospel is real, effective, and growing even when we only see small results or even seeming failure for our efforts. Growth is taking place in those moments, and God is the one who is in control of it, not us. Third, the seed grows gradually into the fullness of a plant for a purpose and that purpose is to bear an abundant harvest. This process may take time ("first the blade, then the ear, then the full grain in the ear") and we should be careful not to become complacent until the process has reached its mature and intended fulfillment in the harvest. That is an important message because the harvest is the very reason a seed is planted. Imagine how disappointed the farmer would be to have a field full of beautiful, healthy plants that produced no harvest! Sometimes that is how a disciple can be when we are self-centered and self-focused rather than God-centered and other-focused.

This parable reminds us that we have received the gift of faith (seed) for a reason and that reason is so that we will ultimately bear a rich harvest for others and not just care for ourselves. Each of these three points is important for our lives. The growth of faith is, first of all, a work of God while the role of a disciple is to cooperate fully with that work. Human actions, separate from the will of God, may neither hasten nor delay the coming of the kingdom Jesus initiated (planted). There are times when we can feel frustrated by lack of success or seemingly small results in our faith life. This parable gives us confidence that real growth is taking place even in such circumstances and that patience and perseverance are required of Christians. It also challenges us to realize that people may not be impressed with the growth but that they will be impressed with the harvest and that we have a responsibility to continue our growth in discipleship until we are bearing a manifold harvest for God. The Kingdom of God may be overlooked now because it is small and ordinary, but it will grow into a glorious reality. Oftentimes, we are called to accept God's reign in our lives in very small and relatively insignificant ways. By doing so, the kingdom grows within us until we eventually accept God's reign in large ways. If we wait for "greatness" before responding to the challenge of faith, then greatness will never come. By responding to the small moments and relatively insignificant opportunities for faithfulness, we are encouraging the Kingdom of God to grow to maturity.

> *What are some of the small ways in which you can allow faith to grow in your life today?*
> *What are some of the small ways in which you see God's will being done in the world around you?*
> *What are the ways in which people are tempted to search for the great manifestations of the Kingdom of God such that they end up overlooking the small manifestations?*
> *Why do you think Jesus needed to remind the disciples of the importance of seeing the Kingdom of God in small ways*

rather than expecting it to always be manifest in great ways?
What temptations can cause disciples to become compla-cent in their growth before they a harvest is produced?
How have other people seen a harvest take place in your life of faith?

The second parable is that of the mustard seed that becomes a bush. That is a really strange image to describe the Kingdom of God! The mustard bush was a common plant along the Sea of Galilee where it grew to a height of four to six feet tall. It was known as being a hardy plant good for the health that germinated quickly and was capable of taking over a garden.[21] Certainly there are reasons why this plant would be an apt description for the Kingdom of God. Aside from the small beginnings and enormous growth referenced in the first parable, the Mustard Seed was also an image of perseverance (hardy) in adverse situations, good for people (Gospel), spread quickly (missionary), and was difficult to destroy or eradicate (perseverance). It is also important to note that the use of plant imagery to represent powerful kingdoms was common in the ancient world (see Ez 17:22–24 and Dn 4:20–21). That's one of the reasons this parable is so surprising—that Jesus would use the image of a mustard bush to describe the Kingdom of God. You see, kingdoms in the time of Jesus did use the image of trees for self-description, but they always referenced trees that were perceived as symbols of power (like the Cedars of Lebanon, or the mighty Oak). To use the image of a mustard bush to describe a kingdom would have been a joke. That may be precisely the point: what the world considers insignificant and powerless is, in fact, God's work that will grow to greatness.

Lastly, Jesus points out that the mustard bush also bears a certain harvest and that its branches provide shelter for the birds. Sometimes we think of this image as referring to bird nests ele-vated above the ground in the branches. Although this image has been used in Christian iconography as in the apse mosaic of the Crucifix in the Basilica of San Clemente in Rome, the mustard bush actually provided shelter for birds that lived on the ground

---

21. Pliny the Elder, *Natural History* (New York: Penguin Classics, 1991).

and sought protection under low-lying branches. These birds were considered to be more vulnerable than others. This final insight points to the "fruit" the Church bears when it cares for the poor and vulnerable in our world as well. It is the "harvest" of charity that is a necessary sign of authentic faith and mature discipleship. The mustard bush may look great, but it is only of value as it provides protection, security, and benefit for others. Such charity may not mirror the powerful kingdoms of the world but is a manifestation of God's reign.

> *What quality of the mustard seed do you think most motivated Jesus to use it as an image of the Kingdom of God?*
> *How can disciples be tempted to become content with their growth and stop short of Producing a harvest of charity? In what ways do you think the description of a mustard bush by Pliny the Elder most accurately describes the Christian disciple (for example:"hardy","good for health", "spreads quickly", "invasive", and "tenacious")?*
> *In what ways can disciples in the Kingdom of God be tempted to imitate the standards of power and glory as manifested by secular kingdoms in the world?*
> *Most people today are not very familiar with mustard bushes. If Jesus were to use a morecontemporary image to communicate to us the same analogy for the Kingdom of God, what do you think it would be and why?*

TWELFTH SUNDAY IN ORDINARY TIME

Our Scripture reading comes from the Gospel of Mark 4:35–41. This passage seems like a simple story of a difficult journey that highlights the disciples' fear and Jesus' miraculous intervention. However, there are profound lessons of discipleship being taught in this text, and Mark has imbedded these lessons in very subtle ways. Let's look at some of these lessons to see what challenges they offer us.

The reprimand of Jesus to the fearful disciples (see vs. 40, "Why are you afraid? Have you no faith?") is an important key for interpreting this passage: It is a teaching about the need for faith in the face of concern. In the verses that preceded this passage we read about Jesus teaching the crowds on the need for confidence and patience while the seed (Kingdom of God) quietly grows. The disciples heard that teaching and even received private explanation to ensure that they properly understood the message (see Mk 4:34). It is one thing to understand our Lord's teaching, but it is something quite different to be able to live that teaching. This scene of the disciples crossing the sea in the midst of the storm shows how quickly they lose confidence and patience when their faith is tested. To use an image from our current educational system, the disciples may have passed the class but they failed the lab!

For all disciples, our faith must effectively move from the world of theory into the practical experiences of every–day situations. Faith is an act of trust, and faith is demonstrated most in difficult situations when we are tempted to lose confidence and patience. Jesus could command obedience from the wind and the sea. Our Lord could even command obedience from the unclean spirits (see Mk 1:27 and 3:11–12) and physical ailments (see Mk 1:42 and 3:5). However, through the gift of free will it is up to each of us to choose to obey what the Lord says to us. (Note: The Greek word for "obey" is an intensification of the verb "to hear"; Greek: *upakouei*.) This contrast between the disciples who only hear Jesus and the other forces that actually obey Jesus invites us to consider the ways in which we have fallen short of conforming our lives to the message we have received. Jesus could say to the disciples, "Have you no faith?" not because He was challenging their lack of intellectual knowledge but because He was demonstrating their lack of ability to live a life conformed to that knowledge. Proper faith, then, is trusting God with courageous actions even when facing the most distressful situations.

> *What helps you translate your faith from the world of the-*
> *ory into the practical experiences of every day?*
> *What experiences have most tested your faith?*
> *When have you felt like you had no faith?*
> *When have you lost confidence or patience in the midst of*
> *a distressful situation?*
> *How does the connection between "hearing" and "obeying"*
> *help you better understand the challenge of discipleship?*

This Gospel account is carefully crafted to communicate an important message about God's intervention and care for His people. Notice that it is only when the disciples say, "do you not care..." (see vs. 38) that Jesus rises and calms the wind and the storm (the causes of their fear). That phrase, "Lord, do you not care..." is not so much a question as it is an accusation. The disciples interpreted the contrary forces of wind and waves as a sign that God had abandoned them and forgotten about them—that the Lord doesn't care. It is at that moment that Jesus rises and brings great calm where there was previously a great storm. That statement, "Lord, do you not care..." is one of the most dangerous and destructive thoughts that can cross our minds. It is terrible to think that someone doesn't care what happens to us. Human relationships die when we sense that others don't care about us. How much more so when it is the other person who has put us in the very situation of distress that threatens to destroy us. Remember, it was Jesus Himself who instructed the disciples to cross the sea to the other side (see Mk 4:35) and now they think they are about to die because of it. The disciples must have wondered why they were wasting their time fighting for their lives while trying to do what Jesus asked of them if God doesn't care. Jesus knew their thoughts. He knew their individual resolve was being eroded because they felt abandoned and uncared for. Perhaps they even felt used for nothing more than a convenient means of transportation.

And so Jesus rises and manifests Himself to them so they could know that He had not abandoned them; rather, He had been with them all along deep in the hull of the boat. As Christians, we are sent by Jesus and are asked to take the risk of faith and become part of the mission of the Church. Like the disciples, we can sometimes feel overwhelmed by the situations we face. Sometimes we can find ourselves like the disciples, wondering if God cares. In those moments, we need to search for Jesus in the same place the disciples did—they found Jesus in the nave, the hull of the boat, and they went to Him. It is no accident that we refer to the Church as a boat—even in our sacred architecture we call the central hall of a traditional church building the "NAVE" (meaning "boat"). This is our boat and Jesus reposes deep in our hull as well. He is there in the tabernacle awaiting us, reminding us that He is with us, that He cares for us, that He personally knows our distress, and that He does not ask us to go anywhere that He himself has not gone before. The disciples could find the Lord because they knew where He reposed. As disciples, we have a particular responsibility to be witnesses of God's presence and love in the world. Oftentimes that means recognizing when others are being overwhelmed by the challenges of life and faith and being there with them and for them in the midst of their difficulties.

> *When have you felt overwhelmed—and that no one cared—*
> *not even God?*
> *Who was there for you?*
> *How can you be there for someone going through a similar*
> *situation?*
> *When have been comforted and encouraged by spending*
> *time with Jesus in the nave of your church?*

The fear of the disciples and the dire reality of their situation would have meant very much to Christians of the first century. Mark's community was facing the fierce persecutions of the Roman Emperor Nero. Certainly they understood the cry of the disciples who called out, "...we are about to perish". It is no accident that we are also told about the storms that raged as the disciples tried to make their way to the "other side" of the Sea of Galilee. That is because the "other side" was the Gentile side, and the mission of Christianity to the non-Jewish world was filled with obstacles and controversy. Jesus had welcomed the Gentiles as part of the crowds who heard Him teach but that was not enough; Jesus wanted to bring the message of the Gospel into their land. The Acts of the Apostles describes the many controversies that surrounded the efforts of Paul to welcome Gentile converts into the Christian community (see Acts 15).

Sometimes the storms that cause us peril come from outside the Church as in Nero's persecution, and sometimes the storms come from inside the Church through dissention, bickering, scandal. This passage of Scripture teaches us that storms will come from one source or another. These moments are not signs that we are going in the wrong direction. Rather, storms are sometimes the inevitable result of following God's will. There are times when we can feel like we are about to perish from such storms. These situations can happen in families when parents do the right thing but their children do not accept it. The storms can happen in marriages when one spouse is responding to the will of God but the other does not support it. Storms can also oppose us and threaten to tear us apart in our professional, political, and social worlds. Jesus reminds us that no storm will be capable of stopping the mission of the Gospel—as long as we are willing to persevere and call out for God's help in moments of distress.

> *What makes us think that storms mean we are going in the wrong direction?*
> *If storms are sometimes the inevitable result of God's will, what is the Christian understanding of peace and stability?*
> *What personal experiences of distress can actually be the means of our salvation?*

One last peculiar item to note in this passage is found in vs. 36 when we are told that the disciples took Jesus with them "just as he was". In vs. 38 we are told that the disciples addressed Jesus as "Teacher". These clues tell us that the disciples took Jesus with them in the boat with an insufficient understanding of who He was. They had seen the Lord heal people as well and cast out demons so they also considered him a miracle worker, healer, and sage. Perhaps they may have even had the insight to consider Jesus a prophet or anointed by God. By bringing Jesus with them "just as he was", they thought they were bringing a friend, teacher, healer, and wise man—but that was not helpful when they faced life-threatening storms in the midst of the sea. It is in the course of their journey, when they thought that they were on the brink of peril, that they discover who Jesus really is and what the Lord can do in their lives. This discovery happens when they rouse the Lord (literally, "make him rise").

The passage then tells us that when Jesus rose, he commanded the wind and the sea and they obeyed. The use of the term "rose" is intentional and is the same verb used of the Resurrection. Jesus is more than just a friend, teacher, healer, wise man, prophet, or anointed one of God: Jesus is the very Son of God risen from the dead who is Lord of Heaven and Earth. Now HE is someone we all want in our boat especially if we have storms to face. The Risen Lord Jesus Christ has the power to turn even great storms into great calm and to save us from certain peril. There is a catch, however. When the Risen Lord enters our lives, His presence warrants our complete obedience and unwavering trust. As disciples, it is not enough that we allow Jesus into our lives as a friend, teacher, healer, wise man, prophet, or anointed one; we are called to give Him total dominion over every aspect of our lives as the Risen Lord and trust Him in the midst of any storm.

> *What aspect of Jesus' personality attracts you the most and why?*
> *What does it mean to call Jesus 'Lord'?*
> *What part of your life is difficult to surrender to God's healing love and direction?*
> *How can people today misunderstand the presence of Jesus in such a way that it diminishes their ability to trust the Lord?*

THIRTEENTH SUNDAY IN ORDINARY TIME

Our Scripture passage comes from the Gospel of Mark 5:21–43. Although this passage contains two separate healing accounts, these miracle stories are closely related and work together to communicate an important message. Common elements in the two miracle stories include the following: Both healings occur for women, both women were deemed "unclean" according to the Jewish purity laws, both are referred to with the title "daughter", the healing for both is described as a "saving" event, faith is called for in both situations, both involve people falling before Jesus, both involve references to twelve years, touch (human contact with Jesus) is a central element for both accounts, and, finally, what was considered unclean did not contaminate what it touched but was made clean by the power of Jesus. In short, both women are invited into relationship with the Lord. With so many common elements, Mark wants us to see these two healings in relation to each another as complementary manifestations of faith—the faith of those who are healed (saved) and the faith of the community around them.

The first healing takes place in the woman who suffered a hemorrhage for twelve years (Gynecologic bleeding). The Book of Leviticus contains the various purity norms pertaining to such women (see Lev 15:19)—they were deemed "unclean" and anything they touched was unclean. This hemorrhage would have prevented her from having children and could have been grounds for divorce. Indications are that she had no one to care for her because she had to use "her resources" to pay for physicians. She was in a truly desperate situation: physically ill, socially and religiously rejected as "unclean", nearly impoverished, and alone. She has exhausted every hope that the medical arts and religious practices of her time offered—with no relief. Her only hope is this person named Jesus about whom she has heard minimal information. Regardless of how little information she received about Jesus, she acted on it nonetheless! This entire scene leads to her touching Jesus' garment. Such an action violated the purity codes of her time and demonstrated her initiative and courage.

We are then told that she said to herself, "If I but touch the tassel of his cloak I will be saved (healed)." It is at this moment that Jesus seeks her out to speak to her. What the Lord wants to give her is more than just physical healing; Jesus wants to give her a relationship with Him (relationship is indicated by the familiar use of the second person singular pronoun "you"). Jesus wants her to know that her healing was not the result of her own cunning but of His grace and her faithful initiative and courage. Her determination led her to overcome the social and religious barriers that would keep her from the Lord. Jesus broke social customs as well by speaking to her in public. Nothing will stop the Lord from offering the gift of relationship to this woman who approached Him in faith. She did not "take" anything from Jesus; she received grace and the Lord led her to Himself. In Mark 3:31–35 we were told that those who approach Jesus in faith will be members of the family of God. Now Jesus calls this woman "daughter"—a term of faith and relationship as a member of God's family. Her healing may have restored her former life, but Jesus wants to introduce her to new and more abundant life as a disciple.

In response to what has taken place in this woman's life, Jesus can say to her "your faith has saved you". In this scene, Jesus is teaching us something about what it means to be a member of God's family, the Church. In the example of the woman's faith, we are not defined by rules and regulations but by the grace of God and our relationship with Jesus. No one is so unclean that our Lord cannot make them clean. Jesus has nothing to fear from our woundedness—and neither should we as long as we take the initiative to approach Him with determination, honesty, and courage seeking His healing grace. We should also expect that the Lord wants more than simply to be the source of our healing; Jesus wants to enter into a deep relationship with us as He did with this woman. He wants to give us new life and not merely to restore our former life. Every encounter with God's grace is an invitation to this relationship with Jesus.

*What have you heard about Jesus that makes you want
to meet the Lord, and what keeps you from acting on that
desire?*

*The woman had to overcome the social barriers of her time
in order to approach Jesus in public because she was considered "unclean". What are some of the social barriers or
expectations of others that can hinder us from following
our desire to meet the Lord?*

*What does courage and initiative look like today in our
faith lives?*

*How has an experience of God's grace initiated for you a
deep and life-giving relationship with Jesus?*

*What is it about this woman's story that most inspires you
and why?*

*For what situation have you spent years of your life trying to
overcome, and how can that situation become a motivation
leading you to Jesus?*

*In what ways can people seek the gift of God's grace but
then turn away from the invitation to a deep relationship
with the Lord?*

Jairus, the synagogue leader and father of the ill girl, has been with
Jesus the whole time and presumably has seen what took place.
Now he will be called to even greater faith. Messengers arrive to
inform him that his daughter is no longer sick but is now dead. In
response, they encourage him to not "bother" the one they call "the
teacher". Jairus knows that Jesus is much more than a teacher and
he must make a decision—Does he go against the recommendation
of so many people or does he continue to accompany Jesus in an
act of trust and confidence? Jesus calls Jairus to choose faith rather
than fear and so they arrive together at Jairus' home. As a person
of faith, Jairus is asked to enter (with those who believe) into the
house with Jesus. Jesus then removes from the house anyone who
does not have faith—the mourners. At this point, Jairus has chosen
to accept the ridicule and accusations of those closest to him and
to persevere in bringing Jesus to his daughter. He rises above these
obstacles and his faith is not disappointed. Jesus touches the corpse
of the child and in doing so He breaks another purity law (for the
prohibitions of anyone except a family member touching a corpse,

see Lv. 21:1; or even entering the place where the dead person lies, see Num. 19:11–16). However, it is not Jesus' touch that saves the girl; rather it is His Word when He commands her to "rise". That is the same verb used for the Resurrection. She was not only restored to life but she now shares in the resurrected life of Jesus! Like the woman in the first healing, Jesus is giving to Jairus' daughter more than just restoration to a former way of life; Jesus is giving her a new and abundant life in Him. Jairus demonstrated faith and trust even in the midst of seemingly hopeless situations and went against the recommendations and expectations of others.

The passage ends with Jesus giving a peculiar instruction to those in the house: they are to give the girl something to eat. In order to understand this instruction we have to recall some significant elements of the passage: Jairus chose Jesus over his friends, Jairus and those who believe were inside the home with the Lord, and in that context someone who was previously dead received a sharing in Jesus' resurrected life. All those elements point towards this moment as a teaching for the early Church on what being a disciple means: having faith that chooses Jesus in the face of ridicule and rejection, trusting in the Lord's power to address the most hopeless of situations, and welcoming everyone who has been given a share in Jesus' risen life by feeding them. With this understanding, the food that Jesus instructs them to give is His Word and the Eucharist. This girl, who once was dead and the most unclean of all people (corpse), is now to be an equal in the Christian community because Jesus has touched her. Jesus offers a relationship to her through the disciples who will teach her His Word and share with her our Lord's Eucharist. If it were up to the disciples they would never have touched the girl, but Jesus did and now He commands them to help her in developing her faith life. The girl had neither an idea of what preceded Jesus' grace in her life nor what she was supposed to do with that grace—she had to learn a great deal, and the care the disciples give her after she "rises" at Jesus' command will be instrumental in helping her become a mature disciple. This second story challenges us in our discipleship as members of the larger community. Sometimes we can find it difficult to welcome as brothers and sisters all those whom Jesus has touched. Sometimes, too, we can ignore the responsibility we have to give one another "something to eat" that will nourish their relationship with the Lord; rather, we sometimes think it's their responsibility to feed themselves. Jesus wants our cooperation in helping provide nourishment to those who have recently come to know Him so that they can become mature in their faith as well. Being "touched" by Jesus isn't the goal of a Christian life; it's only the beginning.

> *How does the faith of Jairus inspire you?*
>
> *The girl had so much to learn about the Lord after He raised her; In your life who has been touched by the Lord and needs to learn more about Him, and how can you be the one who "gives them something to eat"?*
>
> *How are parents today ridiculed for going against popular expectations and choosing Jesus for their children rather than the recommendations of the world around them?*
>
> *The girl received the saving grace of Christ because of the intervention of her father. Who is an example of such faithful perseverance for you?*
>
> *What are evangelization ministries today that can bring Jesus to us and us to Jesus so the Lord can touch us and we can gain a greater share in His life and grace?*
>
> *What opportunities or ministries in our faith community can feed us to help us mature in faith after we have been touched by Jesus?*

FOURTEENTH SUNDAY IN ORDINARY TIME

Our Scripture passage is from the Gospel of Mark 6:1–6. We read of Jesus returning to His hometown and teaching in the Synagogue. It is a significant moment for Jesus in Mark's Gospel as it marks the last time our Lord enters a Synagogue—a place that previously He had frequented (see Mk 1:21, 1:39, and 3:1–6). The rejection Jesus experiences in this moment has something to teach us as disciples lest we become resistant to the Lord's invitation to conversion in our lives.

One of the reasons Jesus may have encountered difficulty in His hometown is because He acted differently from what people of His time expected of a prophet. It seems that the people were aware of our Lord's "mighty deeds" that had been accomplished up to this point in the Gospel. These mighty deeds would include both His teaching and healing ministry. However, Jesus exercised this ministry in a way that troubled many religious people of His time (see the inclusion of Gentiles, women, and the "unclean" as members in the new family of God). When Jesus came to His hometown, He did so because He wanted those closest to Him to share in the inclusive Kingdom of God that He was establishing. However, many people did not want to be included in that Kingdom when they saw who else was already part of it! Sometimes we can approach our faith life in the same way and condition our association with Jesus on how well the Lord fulfills our agenda and expectations. However, that is not how the relationship of faith works. Jesus did not come to Earth so that He could be like us—but so that we could become like Him! Sometimes we want our Lord's presence and attention (like the people of His hometown), but we don't want to accept the changes of life and attitude that He asks us to undertake in order to remain in a committed relationship with Him.

How can people today have such strong expectations of Jesus that they end up turning away from Him when He doesn't fulfill those expectations?

When do you find it tempting to decide your participation in a parish ministry based on the other people who are involved?

How does the phrase, "Jesus did not come to earth so that He could be like us—but so that we could become like Him" challenge you?

The other reason Jesus encountered resistance among the people of His hometown was because of His ordinariness. They not only knew Jesus and were familiar with Him but they knew Him to be from an unexceptional background (son of a carpenter and a member of an ordinary family). He was not part of the educated class who had the freedom and skills to dedicate Himself to the study of the Law. The Gospel of Luke relates that Herod actually hoped Jesus would perform some amazing miracles, demonstrations of power, or other extraordinary feats—but the Lord didn't do that (see Lk 23:8). Nor was Jesus someone who was regarded as outstanding during His years as a child. It is precisely the ordinariness of Jesus that made it difficult for His hometown to accept that He was capable of great deeds. Great people in the ancient world were somehow known to be outstanding even from the moment of their births. The Scriptures tell us very little about Jesus' life as a child. (It is true that the second century texts, *The Infancy Gospel of Thomas* and the *Protoevangelium of James,* provided non-biblical stories about the childhood of Jesus. These narrations tried to satisfy the curiosity of early Christians who wanted to hear more about the deeds of Christ as a child. The Christian leaders of the early church easily disregarded these stories as an attempt to present Jesus more as a Greek hero rather than as the Eternal Word living among us.) Sometimes we expect God to act only in very extraordinary ways in our lives, yet the Lord is most often present in amazingly ordinary ways. The people of Jesus' hometown wanted the Lord to prove to them that He was "special", but He didn't do that. He asked them to accept that God is present in the ordinary and to choose to respond to that presence. Jesus did not force people to accept Him or convince them of His divine nature. Sometimes we can find it easy to overlook the presence of God in the ordinary events and moments of daily life because we are looking for the extraordinary instead. This passage is a challenge for us to look at familiar things in a new way. Sometimes, too, people can experience similar difficulties of faith when the Church and individual disciples act in ordinary ways. This difficulty of faith is especially true when mistakes are made or situations of human weakness show forth on an institutional level.

> *When has a person of ordinary background and training shocked you with an extraordinary ability and what was your reaction?*
> *How can we be tempted to dismiss excellent ministry opportunities because we are looking for something "better" or "more special"?*
> *What qualities or virtues do you think the people of Jesus' hometown needed in order to accept the Lord?*
> *How do you experience the presence of God in ordinary ways?*
> *Some people say, "Seeing is believing", but this passage invites us to reconsider the process such that "Believing is seeing". If you knew that God would manifest Himself to you today in ten ordinary ways, how might that change the way you approach the ordinary situations you will face?*

These difficulties caused the people to be "scandalized" by Jesus. Literally, they were "tripped up" in their ability to accept the Lord. This difficulty accepting Jesus seems to have included those closest to Him as our Lord indicates that a prophet is not without honor except "...among his own relatives". Mark has already introduced us to the challenge of faith posed to those closest to Jesus in Mark 3:20–21 and 31–35. This inclusion of Jesus' closest relatives in those who must make a decision about Him reminds us that discipleship is a personal conviction and that each person must make the choice to accept God in Jesus on our Lord's terms. If Jesus' family are to be His disciples, and they will be, then it will be because they have made that decision just as we must make that decision.

The passage then goes on to tell us that Jesus was unable to do any mighty deeds aside from curing a few sick people. It is not that Jesus needed people's faith in order for Him to be capable of mighty deeds; rather, mighty deeds had a purpose, and where there was no openness to receive God on God's terms, or where the very display of mighty deeds would become a further difficulty in accepting Jesus, then the Lord chose not to work those deeds. Mighty deeds are always meant to be an invitation to discipleship and not a cause of difficulty or scandal in our discipleship! Jesus never performed deeds to prove Himself or force people's acceptance and belief. When the people of His hometown closed their hearts to Jesus, they also closed themselves to the action of God. Some people, however, were open to accepting Jesus, and for them He did perform mighty deeds of healing (see Mk 6:5).

> *Who is someone you think is close to Jesus today, and how can you learn more about their decision of faith in the Lord?*
> *What do you think would have been the result if Jesus had performed mighty deeds for the people of His hometown?*
> *When has a mighty deed of God led you to deeper faith?*

One final comment should be made about this passage because it contains the phrase regarding the brothers (James, Joses, Judas, and Simon) and the sisters of Jesus. There is a good deal written on this topic in both Catholic and non-Catholic Scripture commentaries. The question is not whether Jesus had brothers and sisters but what the term "brothers and sisters" means and whether those brothers and sisters were also children of Mary. Catholics believe that Mary maintained perpetual virginity throughout her life and so they interpret the "brothers and sisters" of Jesus to be either half-brothers and half-sisters or cousins. Evidence in the early Church does provide basis for such an interpretation. First, the belief in Mary's perpetual virginity can be traced to the earliest times of Christianity. Second, Mark 6:17 uses the term "brother" to refer to the half-brothers (Herod and Philip) who were Herod's children from two different mothers. Third, the use of the terms "brother" and "sister" for other relatives in the Jewish context was also explained by the first century historian Flavius Josephus.[22] Fourth, if Mary did have other children, there should have been no reason for Jesus to entrust her to the care of the Beloved Dis-

---

22. Flavius Josephus, *Antiquitates Judaicae*, Book 20, chap. 9.

ciple at the foot of the Cross (see Jn 19:27). These factors may not definitively settle the question but do demonstrate that the Catholic doctrine of Mary's perpetual virginity is both reasonable and historically founded. One of the reasons Joseph is usually depicted in Christian art as older than Mary is due to an ancient tradition that Joseph had other children from a previous marriage, and that accounts for the mention of the brothers and sisters of Jesus in this passage. It should be remembered that this Gospel passage mentions the family of Jesus, not to generate biblical debates, but to demonstrate how ordinary and well-known Jesus was to the people of His hometown.

When we allow ourselves to become sidelined in our faith by relatively minor issues then we are distracted from paying attention to the most important things. It's important not to let such a distraction deter us in our lives as disciples. The topic of Jesus' family is only one example of the many ways in which we can allow issues that are peripheral to the person of Jesus to distract us from focusing intently on the Lord.

> *What issues or topics in Church life or Scripture can distract people from focusing intently on following Jesus today?*
> *If you had to identify the three most important teachings of faith for a Christian disciple to focus on, what would be those teachings?*
> *What are methods you can use to keep your conversations of faith focused when they become distracted?*

Fifteenth Sunday in Ordinary Time

Our Scripture passage comes from the Gospel of Mark 6:7–13. In this text we read of how Jesus sent the Twelve on mission to do the same works our Lord was doing: proclaim the Kingdom of God, deliver people from the forces of evil, and heal their suffering. These ministries remain part of the Church's fundamental mission even today. Let's study this passage so that we can better understand how it challenges us to grow in discipleship and mission.

It is interesting that Jesus sent the disciples on mission while they were still being formed by the Lord. We might think that the disciples needed much more training and education before they could be sent to do the works of Jesus. After all, at this point in the Gospel the Twelve had been with Jesus for only a few weeks or so. We like to be fully prepared and credentialed before we are sent out on our own to accomplish a great work. That was true in much of the ancient world as well (remember that Aristotle spent twenty years learning from Plato before he founded his own school). In light of such lengthy times of preparation the Twelve must have felt very ill-equipped for the mission entrusted to them. However, Jesus knew that being a disciple is different from being a philosopher. Disciples can only grow as they practice and share what they themselves are in the process of receiving. Discipleship is not a program of study from which we graduate and are somehow certified for ministry; rather, discipleship can only move to a deeper level when we have learned to minister to others even as Jesus has ministered to us. Jesus called the disciples to Himself in Mark 3:13–14 for the explicit purpose that He could send them forth on mission. Now after hearing His teaching and watching His mighty works they were sent in fulfillment of the purpose for which they were first called. This passage is telling us that all disciples are, in fact, missionaries. Sometimes we can find ourselves wondering why we are not able to go deeper in our own discipleship, and this passage asks us to reflect on how well we have shared with others what we have already received. If we are keeping our experiences of faith enrichment and spiritual insights to ourselves then we are not fulfilling our missionary role as disciples.

> *How have you experienced Jesus' teaching enlightening you, and what are your opportunities to share that enlightenment with others?*
> *How have you experienced the Lord liberating you from evil influences, and who might need to experience that liberation through you?*
> *What healing has Jesus effected in your life (physical, emotional, psychological, or spiritual) and what are your opportunities to assist others in their healing process?*
> *When have you experienced growth in your discipleship because you willingly shared with others what you yourself were receiving from the Lord?*

Jesus then instructs the Twelve and prepares them for their journey. The word for "journey" is most accurately translated as "way" and indicates the original name for disciples of the Lord: they were known as "Followers of the Way" (see Acts 22:4, 9:2). The use of that word means that Jesus is not just giving an instruction for a temporary missionary journey but that the Lord is giving a lasting teaching on how disciples are to always carry out their ministry. The purpose of the walking stick was for support and protection as well as being a symbol of power and authority (see the staff Moses and Aaron carried). The commandment to bring no bread, no beggar's bag, and no money in their belt was to remind them of their need to rely on divine providence. The beggar's bag in particular was prohibited so as to distinguish the Twelve from other travelling philosophers and miracle workers (healers) who charged for their services and profited from their ministry. Jesus did not want His disciples to be people who sought personal gain from the ministry of the Gospel.

They were also to not wear two tunics, which may seem strange to us, and we need to remember that a tunic was an expression of who a person was (clothes were symbols of identity). The prohibition against bringing two tunics may very well have been an effort to prevent the Twelve from portraying multiple, confused, or even conflicting identities in their discipleship. It can be easy for us to have multiple aspects to our own identities based on nationality, religious confession, race, profession, family roles, civic involvements, and sports interests. This prohibition against bringing "two tunics" may be a challenge for us to define ourselves first and foremost as disciples of Jesus in every situation. Every other aspect of our identity is of lesser priority and should never confuse that primary identity.

Lastly, they were to wear sandals, which is a direct connection to how the Israelites were instructed to eat the Passover meal in preparation for their exodus from Egypt. This final command to wear sandals, in conjunction with the command to carry a staff (walking stick), implies that the Twelve were being sent by Jesus to announce a new exodus from slavery to freedom in the Christian way of life. This new exodus was the beginning of the new People of God (the Church) formed by the Twelve (representing and reconstituting the Twelve Tribes of Israel) in response to the rejection Jesus experienced in his hometown (see Mk 6:1–6).

> *How does the Church today continue the ministry of leading us in a new exodus from slavery to freedom?*
>
> *How does the image of carrying the staff (walking stick) help you to understand, interpret, and appreciate the ministry of the local bishop who carries a staff (crosier) as a symbol of his office?*
>
> *In what ways are we tempted to rely on our own strength rather than God's providence for the success of our ministry and of the Church?*
>
> *How are you reminded in practical ways that God is in control of your life?*
>
> *How can the desire for personal gain by those entrusted with leadership responsibility diminish the credibility of the Gospel and effectiveness of ministry today?*
>
> *In what ways can our discipleship be compromised when other identities are allowed to be of equal or greater importance than being a disciple of Jesus (Particularly, when we try to wear "two tunics")?*

Jesus ends His commission to the Twelve by instructing them on how to deal with both success and failure in their mission. When their message is received, they are to remain in that place and continue their ministry. It is only when their mission is unfruitful that they are to move on so that the proclamation of the Kingdom of God can continue. The reality is that the Twelve will experience both success and failure. Jesus does not want them to be surprised by that reality but to be prepared for it and to anticipate their response to it. The action of "shaking the dust from your feet" was practiced in Acts 13:51 as a warning to the people of Pisidian Antioch. This instruction acknowledges that even with the best efforts of the Twelve there will always be some people who freely choose to reject the message of the Gospel. Such rejection is not necessarily a sign of failure on the part of missionaries but of human freedom and hardness of heart. When confronted with such situations, the Twelve are encouraged to seek out other groups that will be receptive to their message rather than wasting additional time and resource trying to convert unwelcoming or unreceptive communities. This is an important message for us. We need to remember that not all of our missionary efforts will be effective or successful. Failure and rejection will be a part of the Church's experience today just as it was the experience of Jesus and the Twelve. Rather than focusing our efforts, attention, and resources in ministries that are not working, this passage encourages us to re-focus our efforts in new ways that may be more effective. It can be safe and predictable to keep doing the same old thing, but when the same old thing isn't working, it is time to change and grow. The Church has a responsibility to be creative and persevering in its efforts to bring the Gospel to all people. We cannot accomplish that mission if we are intent on continuing unsuccessful or unfruitful efforts.

> *How do you know when it is time to "move on" in your efforts to share the Gospel with others?*
> *What ministries of the Church are most successful in proclaiming the Kingdom of God?*
> *What ministries of the Church need to be re-focused so they can become more effective in accomplishing the goal of evangelization?*

*How do you know when your best efforts have been put
forth in a particular mission effort?*

*Who are the "other communities" around you that are wait-
ing to hear the Gospel through you?*

Lastly, this passage is an important opportunity to reflect on the
ministry of the Twelve when they "anointed many sick people with
oil". This practice is also described in James 5:14–15 as part of the
healing ministry of the early Church. Today we celebrate the Sacrament of the Sick by anointing with oil as well. Oil is the visible sign
of the invisible healing grace of Christ. Oil (primarily olive oil) has
natural properties that can assist in the healing process (see Lk 10:34
where oil was used to heal the wounds of the injured man in the
Parable of the Good Samaritan). When people suffer a debilitating
illness (physical, emotional, psychological, or spiritual) then they
experience loss of freedom, vulnerability, fear, isolation, and even
abandonment. The practice of ritual anointing, and the prayer of
the Church, gives strength, encouragement, healing, and spiritual
grace to assist the person in their distress. It also assures them that
the community of faith is standing by them in their illness and supporting them with their prayers. This prayerful support of the faith
community is an important aid in helping a sick person experience
weakness in a faithful way so as to grow in trusting dependence on
God and others. The grace received in the Anointing of the Sick
offers salvation and healing on a variety of levels.

*How have you experienced the grace of the Anointing of
the Sick?*

*What fears or temptations have you experienced when you
suffered serious illness or weakness?*

*How can the prayer of the Church and this Sacrament help
us overcome our fears and temptations?*

*This passage tells us that the Twelve both anointed people
and healed them which implies two actions (one liturgical
and one physical). Why do you think Mark wanted us to
distinguish between the Sacramental act of anointing and
the physical act of healing people?*

SIXTEENTH SUNDAY IN ORDINARY TIME

Our Scripture passage comes from the Gospel of Mark 6:30–34. In this reading we hear of Jesus calling the apostles to rest with Him. The crowds follow, and eventually Jesus responds by teaching them and feeding them like a shepherd caring for His sheep. This simple scene in the Gospel of Mark offers some important insights for us as we carry out our Lord's ministry as well.

The word "apostle" means someone who is "sent out" and in Mark 6:7 we read about Jesus sending the Twelve on mission to proclaim the Kingdom of God in word and action. Now the Twelve (the "sent ones") return to Jesus to report on their efforts. Jesus responds by inviting them to rest in a deserted place. The biblical notion of rest is founded in the Book of Genesis where God "rested" on the seventh day establishing the experience of rest as a gift to humanity (see Gn 2:2–3). This gift of rest is not primarily to alleviate exhaustion but to foster a contemplative appreciation for having shared in God's creative and redemptive work. This spiritual rest is meant to foster and deepen our intimate relationship with the Lord so that our efforts of ministry are not just "working for God" but a "participation in God's work". There is a big difference between those two approaches to ministry. It is the experience of regular spiritual rest and appreciative contemplation with God that allows us to know the mind of Christ and to do God's will with eagerness, generosity, and freedom. Jesus wanted the twelve apostles to have this experience of spiritual rest so they could better understand how their efforts participated in God's divine will for the world. The passage then goes to tell us that the crowds kept coming in large numbers and so they sought to go away by themselves in a boat. The continuous needs of the crowds remind us that there is always more work to be done and that a disciple must balance the need for contemplative rest in Christ with the need for ministry to others. One dimension of discipleship is not possible without the other. If we only work tirelessly to serve the needs of others then we run the risk of becoming detached from the life-giving relationship with Christ that is the foundation of our identity as disciples. If we only seek to be withdrawn in contemplative rest with Christ then we can fail to accomplish the ministry of Jesus entrusted to us, which the world so desperately needs. It is important for disciples to balance these two important dimensions of their faith lives so they can be effective and responsive instruments of God.

> *What time do you set aside in your schedule for regular, contemplative, appreciative rest with God?*
> *How are you tempted to cut short your spiritual rest in order to carry out the overwhelming duties and responsibilities of discipleship?*
> *What opportunities exist for you to spend extended time with the Lord, and what holds You back from accepting those opportunities?*

The crowd was perceived as an inconvenient burden by the apostles. We are told that they were not even able to eat because of the people who came to them in large numbers. The disciples responded by trying to evade the crowds so as to care for their own needs. Jesus perceives the crowds in a different way, however. Rather than being a problem, Jesus sees the crowds as a blessed opportunity that allowed the Lord to carry out His ministry. These two differing perceptions challenge us to be careful in how we perceive and respond to circumstances as well. Sometimes it can be easy for disciples to feel burdened by the questions or needs of others. Sometimes another person's desire to explore faith can even become inconvenient and problematic for us because of the time and preparation it takes to respond. Jesus sees such moments as open possibilities for bringing the Gospel into people's lives. The Lord is showing us in this passage that we should be eager and thankful when we have the opportunity to affect and influence people with the gift of faith.

> *When have the demands of a successful ministry experience felt problematic or burdensome to you?*

When have you experienced surprising success in a minis-
try that presented a ripe opportunity for you to bring the
Gospel into people's lives, and what personal sacrifices did
you have to make in order to accomplish that ministry?
Jesus understood that the presence of the crowds was a ripe
moment that needed to be responded to lest it become a lost
opportunity. What are ripe moments in the Church today
that need urgent response and what are lost opportunities
we are experiencing?
When have you experienced the attitude of the apostles—
the perception that ministry opportunities are a problem-
atic burden—and what has been the effect of that attitude?
Why do you think Jesus chose to teach the crowds rather
than try to retreat once more with the disciples?

We are told that Jesus had compassion on the crowds because they
were like sheep without a shepherd. Motivated by compassion,
our Lord began to teach them many things. The image of God as
a shepherd for Israel is deeply rooted in the Old Testament and
features prominently in the first reading for this Sunday's liturgy
(Jer 23:1–6). Shepherds had four primary responsibilities: to gather
the sheep, to guide the sheep, to protect the sheep, and to care for
the sheep. Jesus presents Himself in this passage as the shepherd
who fulfills all of these roles. The Lord gathered the crowds to Himself rather than sending them away and scattering them (see Mk
6:35). Jesus also teaches them in an action of loving direction and
guidance for their lives (see Mk 6:34). The Lord cares for them by
feeding them not only with His Word (teaching) but also with the
Bread of the Eucharist (see Mk 6:37–44). Finally, the Lord protects
them by confronting the efforts of those who would seek to dismiss
them (see Mk 6:36–37) as well as through the ongoing ministry of
healing and deliverance accomplished through the apostles.

How does Jesus continue to fulfill the responsibilities of
being our shepherd today?
In what specific ways do you need the protective, collective,
caring, and guiding ministry of Jesus in your life?
How can you make yourself open and receptive to Jesus as
your shepherd?

What can prevent people from wanting to be a member of God's flock?

Lastly, it is interesting to note that the crowds followed Jesus for some time and over significant distances without being prepared for the journey. That is why they arrived at the end of the day with no planned provisions (see Mk 6:35–36). Obviously the crowds heard about Jesus and responded immediately to the possibility of meeting the Lord for themselves. It is rare that we would respond with such immediate initiative and lack of planning. The action of the crowd is not a statement of their irresponsibility but of the readiness of their discipleship. They were willing to drop everything in order to seek the Lord and spend time with Him. We too can be urgently motivated to respond immediately to all sorts of situations and opportunities but when it comes to disciples, we can be hesitant and even procrastinate in our response.

What urgent opportunity motivates you to drop everything and respond immediately?

When do you find yourself responding so slowly to faith opportunities that the occasion passes before you can participate?

How does the power of evil use the temptation of procrastination to rob people of valuable encounters with God?

What can a faith community do to help people respond with urgency to faith opportunities?

SEVENTEENTH SUNDAY IN ORDINARY TIME

Our Scripture passage comes from the Gospel of John 6:1–15. This text relates the story of the multiplication of the loaves and fishes and initiates the Eucharistic teaching of Jesus known as the "Bread of Life Discourse". The miracle of the loaves and the fishes was deeply rooted and revered in the memory of first century Christians and is the only miracle of Jesus that appears in all four Gospels (Jn 6:1–15, Mt 14:13–21, Mk 6:32–34, and Lk 9:10–17). As the inaugural event for the Bread of Life discourse, this passage contains several important lessons for us as disciples and introduces themes to help us better appreciate our experience of seeking the Lord every time we share in the Eucharist.

The first lesson for discipleship is expressed by Jesus' desire to lead us to deeper faith. The passage begins by telling us that a multitude followed Jesus because they saw the signs He performed. This indicates that they were following Jesus more as spectators than as believers. They may have seen the signs, but they did not understand what those signs meant. The word that is used to describe the crowd's sight (Greek: *Eoron*) refers to an experience of superficial observance. Jesus, on the other hand, "sees" (Greek: *Theasamenos*) the multitude and is able to look deeply into their hearts and understand their need for growth in faith. The verb used to describe Jesus' sight really means to have insight and not just superficial observance. In vs. 3 we are told that Jesus sat down, and in doing so, assumed the position of a teacher in the ancient world. This chapter, then, is about the instruction Jesus wishes to offer the crowds so that they can move from being mere superficial spectators, who watch Jesus do things, to committed disciples, who understand the meaning and purpose behind Jesus' actions. If the crowds do not develop this deepened insight, they will misunderstand Jesus' identity and try to make the Lord fit their own expectations. We see this mistaken response to Jesus in vs. 14 and 15 where the crowds acclaim Jesus as a prophet and a king.

Those who do receive Jesus' teaching, and develop deepened insight into our Lord's actions and person, are able to correctly profess the faith of a disciple who follows the Lord, not because of what Jesus does but because of who Jesus is (see Peter's confession of faith in Jn 6:68–69). Jesus wants us to move from being spectators to becoming committed disciples as well. In order for that growth in faith to happen, we must come to understand the deeper meaning in our Lord's actions. If our faith is only a matter of rote prayers, religious rituals, and memorized creeds, this passage invites us to let Jesus become our teacher so He can lead us to understand the relationship offered to us in prayer, the reality of grace being presented to us in religious ritual, and the intimate self-communication of God shared with us in creeds. Those who accepted the revelation and insight of Jesus grew closer to Him; those who did not accept that deepened faith ended up walking away from the Lord (see Jn 6:66–68). The quality of our discipleship will depend upon the insight we gain from Jesus as our teacher so that we can look beyond the signs that fill our lives and see the reality of God's presence in our midst.

> *How can a person today be a superficial spectator when it comes to his or her experience of faith and Church?*
> *What ministries or opportunities can help members of our faith community understand the meaning and purpose behind their practices of faith, ritual actions of worship, or forms of prayer?*
> *How has the growth from superficial awareness to deepened insight occurred in your faith life?*
> *When Jesus "sees" your faith community, in what way do you think the Lord most wants to lead you so that you can be more committed disciples?*
> *How can people today, who misunderstand Jesus' action in the world, remain superficial spectators of faith?*
> *Into what errors can a superficial faith lead them?*

The second lesson of discipleship occurs when we are told that Jesus posed a question to "test" Philip. Jesus asked Philip, "How are we to buy bread, so that these people may eat?". Jesus was really more interested in hearing what Philip had to say than the solution Philip offered. We are then told that the Lord already knew what He was going to do (note—many Scripture scholars believe that this phrase is the central point of this entire passage and sets the stage for Jesus to deliver His greatest gift to the disciples). Philip responded by stating the impossibility of addressing the need with human resources. In doing so, Philip was revealing his temptation to trust only in his own ability and self-sufficiency to resolve the problem. Jesus wants the disciples to acknowledge their inability so that they might be able to realize the Lord's power to do what they cannot accomplish on their own. Along with Philip's response of what cannot be done, Andrew offers an answer of what can be done: He presents a child who has five barley loaves and two fish. Jesus accepts this meager and insufficient offering of the disciples and transforms it into an abundant and new reality. The lesson of discipleship is this: God can do infinitely more with our lives than we can accomplish on our own.

Like Philip, we can be overwhelmed with the needs of the world around us. Sometimes we wonder if our efforts really make a difference. In those moments, it is important to remember that one of the greatest temptations is to do nothing because we can only do a little. Mother Teresa is quoted as saying, "Not all of us can do great things. But we can do small things with great love." Nothing done with love is ever small because God is love, and what we do with love we do with God, and God is never small. In this Scripture passage, we are reminded that discipleship is about God and not us. God can do great things with what we offer Him; the problem is that we often don't offer the Lord very much with which to work. Our challenge is to offer Christ the gifts of our lives with love and confidence so that God can do great things with those gifts. If Andrew had tried to feed the crowd himself with those gifts of five loaves and two fish then only a few people would have been fed. Because Andrew offered them to Jesus, the Lord was able to feed thousands. Sometimes Jesus tests us to see if we are trusting in ourselves or in Him. . How we address daily situations and whether or not we offer the Lord our meager gifts provide the answer to that test.

*When are you tempted to "Do nothing because you can only
do a little", and how does this passage help you overcome
that temptation?*
*Who for you is an example of faith, like Andrew, who offers
to the Lord with love and generosity the insufficient gifts
of their lives?*
*How does God test you to see if you put your faith in your
own self-sufficiency or in God's grace?*
*What are small things that you can do with great love in
your everyday life?*
*The offertory time at Mass is meant to be a prayerful experi-
ence of spiritually offering our lives to the Lord. Our lives are
to be used by Him, transforming us to become His presence
in the world, even as the bread and wine are transformed
to become His Body and Blood. How does the offering of
Andrew affect the way you will prayerfully enter into the
offertory at Mass?*

The third lesson of discipleship occurs when we are told that this
event took place at the Feast of Passover. This is a very important
element of the passage and it is meant to connect with other events
that occur in John's Gospel on the Feast of Passover: The gift of new
wine at Cana (see Jn 2:13) and the celebration of the Last Supper
(see Jn 13:1) are two such events. It is no accident that these three
events are connected by the Feast of Passover (Wine, Bread, and the
Last Supper). They are all Eucharistic moments. The Gospel of John
presents the gift of the Eucharist as something that occurs during
the daily life and ministry of Jesus and not simply something that
took place once at the Last Supper. This presentation is meant to
encourage disciples to understand the importance and significance
of receiving the Eucharist as part of our regular daily lives as well.
The Eucharistic significance of this passage is indicated in two ways.
Notice how Jesus Takes, Gives Thanks (literally, "*Eucharistizes*"),
Breaks, and Gives the five loaves and two fish to the crowds, and
it becomes more than enough for them.

We need to remember that these four verbs are very significant
and are only used in this combination in the context of Eucharistic
scenes (see Mk 14:22–23, Lk 22:19, 24:30, 1 Cor 11:23–24). Anytime
Jesus uses these four verbs the reader automatically knows that our

Lord is celebrating the Eucharist. This insight should inform the way we read this passage. John wants us to learn something essential about the Eucharist so he included a very important additional detail: There is symbolism in the fact that there are five loaves and that the name of Jesus appears five times in this literary unit (see vs. 3, 5, 10, 11, 15). This numeric connection between the name of Jesus and the number of loaves points to an identification of Jesus with the bread. Thus, when Jesus gave the five loaves He was giving Himself to the crowds!

> *How does the Real Presence of Jesus in the Eucharist affect the way you prepare for Mass?*
> *How has the Eucharist become an important part of your regular Christian life and discipleship?*
> *What are symbols we use today that help us understand the Real Presence of Jesus in the Eucharist (like the frequency of the name of Jesus equating with the five loaves)?*
> *How do you think Jesus wants to change our faith community at every Mass?*

The fourth lesson of discipleship is communicated when are finally told that the people were "satisfied" (see Jn 6:11). This is the only time in John's Gospel that we are ever informed of people's satisfaction. This phrase echoes the instruction to first century Christians known as the Didache which relates that disciples shared in the Eucharist until they "had their fill".[23] John is speaking about more than just the physical satisfaction of hunger; John is referring to that deep longing of our hearts that only God can satisfy. Jesus, and only Jesus, was able to satisfy that hunger in the multiplication of the loaves and fishes through the gift of the Eucharist. This singular ability of God to satisfy our deepest longings and yearnings was expressed beautifully by Saint Augustine when he said, "You have formed us for Yourself, O Lord, and our hearts are restless until they rest in You."[24] Our hearts are made for God and we become frustrated and dissatisfied when we try to fill them with other things.

---

23. *Didache*, Chap. X, 1.
24. St Augustine, *Confessions*, I, 1.

This passage teaches us, as disciples, that Jesus wants to satisfy us just as He satisfied the crowds that day so long ago. The Lord wants to lead us to deep insights of faith so that we can know His presence with us and His action in our world. He invites us to share our life with Him when we make a spiritual offering of ourselves so that He can share His life with us in the Eucharist. When we seek to fill our deepest hungers with accomplishments, entertainment, human relationships, positions, possessions, or the pursuit of pleasure then we inevitably remain unsatisfied and empty. This Gospel passage is good news for disciples who have been hungering for more—that hunger is an invitation by God to deeper relationship with Himself.

> *From what false sources do people seek satisfaction for the deep longings of their hearts today and what is typically the result?*
> *When have you experienced lasting spiritual satisfaction from your relationship with God in Jesus, and how did you foster that satisfying relationship?*
> *What helps make the Mass a satisfying experience for you, and what is it that detracts from the Mass making it less than a satisfying experience?*
> *How have you realized the truth of Saint Augustine's quote?*

The fifth lesson of discipleship is presented through the command of Jesus to the disciples when He said, "Gather up the fragments left over, that nothing may be lost." In response to our Lord's instruction the disciples gathered twelve baskets of fragments. There are two important messages for us in this act of gathering. First, the word used for "fragments" (Greek: *Klasmata*) is the same word used in other first century Christian writings to refer to the fragments (remnants) of the Eucharist. Today, we gather the "fragments", or remaining pieces of the Eucharist, and place them in the tabernacle. Like the Early Church, we treasure the gift of the Eucharist as an enduring gift of Jesus. We reserve the Eucharist in the Tabernacle for purposes of personal prayer and for the distribution of Communion to the sick and homebound. In all of these actions, we are fulfilling the Lord's command and showing our respect for Jesus in the Eucharist. In addition to the reservation of the remaining

Eucharist in the tabernacle, we also show our reverence for any fragments by placing special cloths on the altar (called "corporals") to preserve any possible pieces of the Host or drops of the Precious Blood that may accidentally fall.

Second, the twelve baskets would be immediately understood as a symbol for the restoration of the Twelve Tribes of Israel. The act of gathering that took place was not only to ensure reverence for the gift of the Eucharist but also to demonstrate that, through the Eucharist, the New People of God are being constituted and the Church is being formed. The word Jesus used when He commanded the disciples to "gather" (Greek: *Synagein)* is the same word used by the early Christians in the first and second century to describe the "gathering" of the community of the Church.[25] It should be noted that this term is only used in John's account of the multiplication of the loaves and fishes and indicates the author's clear intention to connect the act of gathering with the formation of the Church. The people in this story first started to gather to Jesus because they saw the signs the Lord was performing.

Jesus wants us to be gathered to Him for a deeper reason of faith. Our Lord will ultimately gather all people to Himself when He is exalted on the Cross (see Jn 12:32), and that spiritual gathering continues by our participation in the mystery of Jesus' Death and Resurrection that is celebrated in the Eucharist. In order to be drawn to Jesus, disciples must develop the insight of faith that allows them see in the bread and wine the very reality and presence of Jesus' Flesh and Blood (see Jn 6:53–57). When disciples share in the Eucharist with informed awareness and reverence, we are gathered to Jesus just as the fragments were gathered in baskets—and the Church is formed. The formative power of the Eucharist in constituting the Church as the Mystical Body of Christ was also taught by Saint Augustine who said, "Be what you can see and receive what you are".[26]

> *What signs of respect and reverence for the Eucharist have inspired your faith?*

---

25. This description can be seen in the *Didache*, 1 Clement, and Ignatius.
26. St Augustine, *Sermon 272 on the Nature of the Sacrament of the Eucharis in Sermons*, pp. 300–301.

How do you show reverence for the Eucharistic presence of Jesus in the Tabernacle?

When has the presence of Jesus in the Tabernacle been a focus of your prayer?

Have you ever been distracted by someone's lack of reverence for the Eucharist or for the presence of Jesus in the tabernacle and how was that lack of reverence demonstrated?

How does Saint Augustine's quote about the relationship between the Eucharist and the Church inspire you?

How can a faith community help people understand the necessary and formative relationship between the Eucharist and the Church?

What prevents the Church from fully experiencing the gathering Jesus desires through the gift of the Eucharist?

EIGHTEENTH SUNDAY IN ORDINARY TIME

Our Scripture passage comes from the Gospel of John 6:24–35. In this text we read about the crowd's challenge for Jesus to produce a sign superior to that of Moses who gave Manna in the desert. We also hear of our Lord's identification of Himself as the "true bread" that came down from heaven. The dialogue between Jesus and the crowd reveals that they do not understand who He is. Their misunderstanding is revealed by the fact that they greet Him with the title "Rabbi". In this passage, Jesus reveals to them and us His identity. This revelation is meant to inform our discipleship so that we can seek the food that never perishes.

The first instruction that Jesus gives to the crowds who follow Him is that they should work for the food that endures for eternal life as opposed to the food that perishes. Jesus can provide this food because He bears the "seal" of the Father. Seals in the ancient world were a sign of authority, verification of authenticity, and endorsement of mission. Jesus bears the seal of the Father and so Jesus can be the agent of God who reveals the Father to the world. In order for the crowds to understand and accept Jesus as the one upon whom the Father has set His seal, they will have to know the Lord as more than just a Rabbi; they must acknowledge Jesus as the Eternal Word that has come down from heaven. The crowds that followed Jesus were seeking momentary satisfaction for their hunger. Jesus wanted to offer them something that would satisfy their hunger for eternity; namely, a life-giving relationship with God.

Rather than seeking fleeting pleasures and momentary curiosities, Jesus wants to offer us the same life-giving eternal relationship that He wished to give the crowds. Our world is full of wonderful, created goods that offer enjoyment, entertainment, and comfort. In the midst of these goods, we need to remember that no created thing, not even human relationships or professional pursuits, can satisfy us for eternity. We were created to know, love, and serve the Lord in this life and to be with God in eternal life. While we enjoy the goods of creation, as disciples we must be able to always look beyond them to discover the goodness of the Creator and be drawn into relationship with God in Jesus through our adoration, praise, and thanksgiving. It is important that we understand the necessity of relating to God in the person of Jesus. Jesus points to this necessity when He responds to the crowds who were seeking to do the works of God. Our Lord instructs them that the greatest work of God they can do is to believe in the one whom God has sent. Jesus reveals the fullness of God's will in His very person (see Jn 14:9). Thus, the only food that endures for eternal life and is worthy of all our time and energy in this life is the relationship revealed to us by the Father in the Son.

> *What are some of the temporary hungers or curiosities than can draw people to seek the Lord for momentary satisfaction today?*
> *How can a faith community better help people realize that their momentary hungers and curiosities are really an invitation to a profound and lasting relationship with Jesus Christ?*
> *What has helped you look beyond the temporal goods of creation so as to enter into relationship with the Creator? How can moments of dissatisfaction and frustration become opportunities for deeper faith?*
> *When has the Lord drawn you to Himself and awakened within you the gift of faith by feeding a momentary hunger in your life?*

In response to our Lord's instruction and invitation to believe in Him, the crowds demand a sign to validate His claim. If Jesus is the one upon whom the Father has placed His seal, He is greater than Moses, and the crowds expect Him to demonstrate a sign greater than anything Moses did. The specification of the sign of Manna has particular significance. We must remember that the gift of Manna had a purpose, which was to keep the Hebrews moving forward in the desert so they would not want to return to Egypt (a place of slavery). Manna, then, was food for the journey that sustained the people as they progressed towards the Promised Land. Jesus fed the five thousand people in John 6:1–15 but the crowds did not understand that sign, and so they failed to grasp the significance of the food that was provided to them as their fathers also did in the desert (see Nm 21:5). In this week's Gospel passage, Jesus is now leading the crowds to a deeper understanding of the bread that He gave in last week's reading. Like the crowds, sometimes Jesus has to first feed us so He can lead us. The problem is that we can forget the purpose of the Lord's food and can become complacent in our faith life. This complacency happens when we choose to stop growing in our discipleship because we think we have gone far enough or because we don't want to embrace the faithful sacrifices that are required in order to continue growing closer to the Lord. The crowds were seeking Jesus so that they could have the next piece of bread and not because they wanted to commit their lives to Him. The same thing can happen to us when we come to church because we want to feel better about the way we are rather than to become the persons God wants us to be. The food that Jesus gives in the Eucharist and in our relationship with Him is meant to transform us and motivate us to move forward in our discipleship until we reach the promised land of heaven.

> *What tempts you to become complacent in your journey of discipleship?*
> *What happens when a person tries to progress in their life of faith without seeking food for the journey?*
> *How does the Word of God in Scripture provide food for the journey?*
> *How does the Eucharist provide food for the journey?*
> *What happens when we want to be fed but are not willing to be led?*
> *What is the next step God wants you to take in your journey of discipleship to the promised land of heaven?*

The Gospel passage for this Sunday ends with Jesus identifying Himself as the "Bread of Life". Several interpretative keys needed to correctly unlock the meaning of this self-revelation are contained in the passage itself. For example, when Jesus says that the bread of God is that which comes down from heaven, we need to remember that in the beginning of John's Gospel we were told that the Word was with God, was God, and the Word became flesh and dwelt among us (see Jn 1:1,14). Also, the comparison between Moses, as the one through whom the Law was given, and Jesus, as the one through whom grace and truth are received, was previously introduced in the prologue of John's Gospel (see Jn 1:17). This section of chapter 6 of John's Gospel builds upon these insights previously given. The reference to Manna (previously discussed) was also understood as an image for the Law of Moses from which the people would "feed" their hunger for God's Word. Only in Jesus can the hunger for God's Word be fully and completely satisfied, and for this reason our Lord says, "whoever comes to me will never hunger, and whoever believes in me will never thirst" (Jn 6:35). The image of people being fed with God's Word (self-revelation) was deeply rooted in the writings of the Old Testament. This image is especially true in the Wisdom literature. For example, Sirach 24:21 states about wisdom, "Those who eat of me will hunger still, those who drink of me will thirst for more." The verse of Proverbs 9:5 expresses the famous invitation of personified Lady Wisdom when it says, "Come, eat of my food, and drink of the wine I have mixed!" These references are not about being fed with physical food but about being fed on the Word of God. The text of Isaiah 55:10–11 contains the most important verses for properly interpreting Jesus' reference in this passage of John's Gospel when the prophet states:

> Yet just as from the heavens the rain and snow come down and do not return there till they have watered the earth, making it fertile and fruitful, giving seed to the one who sows and **bread to the one who eats**, so shall **my word** be that goes forth from my mouth; it shall not return to me empty but shall do what pleases me, achieving the end for which I sent it.

It is in light of this background that most Scripture scholars interpret Jesus' statement in this passage to mean that He is the self-revelation of God (Word) who alone can feed our deepest hungers and bring us into eternal life. The Law was revealed through Moses and was symbolized by Manna, but those who were fed by that gift continued to hunger. Those who feed on the revelation of God in Jesus, the Eternal Word, will receive life and never hunger. The Eternal Word of God continues to be present for us when the Word is proclaimed, especially when the Scriptures are read at every Mass. Jesus offers to feed our souls by revealing to us the Father in His very person and by teaching us through life, ministry, Death, and Resurrection the life we are called to live as faithful disciples. For this reason, the proclamation of the Gospel receives special attention and reverence since those texts show us most clearly the person of Jesus as the revelation of the Father. After all, we cannot enter into the Christian mystery until we know the Christian story, and for this reason Saint Jerome taught that "Ignorance of Scripture is ignorance of Christ".

> *When has the Word of God in Scripture been food for your soul?*
> *How does the phrase, "We cannot enter into the Christian mystery until we know the Christian story," challenge you to read Scripture?*
> *How have the Scriptures fed your relationship with Jesus?*
> *What can a faith community do to help people hear Jesus speaking to them in the Scriptures?*

Nineteenth Sunday in Ordinary Time

Our Scripture passage comes from the Gospel of John 6:41–51. This reading is a continuation of the Bread of Life discourse and introduces the response of the crowd to Jesus' identification of Himself as the bread that came down from heaven. This passage offers several challenging teachings for us as disciples.

The passage begins by telling us that people "murmured" in response to Jesus' teaching. This action is sometimes translated as "grumbled" and means that they both disagreed with and disliked what Jesus was revealing to them. This chapter began with our Lord recognizing the crowd's need for deeper insight and that is why Jesus sat down to teach them (see Jn 6:2–3). He wanted people to follow Him as disciples because they understood and accepted who He was rather than to follow Him as spectators who were drawn by entertaining signs (like the multiplication of loaves and fishes). When Jesus revealed His identity as the bread that came down from heaven, the people reacted negatively to that insight. They were prepared to follow Jesus on their own terms but not on our Lord's terms. However, when the people wanted to follow Jesus on their own terms they misunderstood our Lord's mission and tried to make Him a symbol of earthly power as their king (see Jn 6:15). Now that Jesus is revealing to them His true identity they find Him offensive and refuse to accept that revelation. The action of murmuring was nothing new in the Scriptures. In fact, we are told in the Old Testament that the people murmured against Moses because they did not like the experience of being led in the desert and the hardships it entailed (see Ex 15:24, 16:2, 8). In both the Book of Exodus and in this passage we see a connection between the people who received bread from heaven (Manna and Jesus) and who murmured against the Lord in response.

This passage invites us to consider ways in which we can disagree or dislike what Jesus is revealing to us about His identity or our responsibility as disciples. It is always easier to follow the Lord on our own terms rather than on His terms, but when we do we run the risk of remaking Jesus in our own likeness instead of being formed into His likeness. Even today people can take offense when they hear the claim that Jesus is the only Son of God. They may find it easy to accept Him as a philosopher, teacher, miracle worker, or holy man but reject Him as the sole revealer of the will of God and heavenly mysteries. Also, it can be easy today for people to object to the demands of discipleship as Jesus identifies Himself with the poor, the lame, the blind, and the crippled, and our Lord asks us to serve Him in the least of our brothers and sisters. Lastly, we can even find ourselves murmuring against the Lord when the values of the Gospel go against our political, national, or economic ideologies, opinions or values.

> *The basic question the crowds had to answer and that we must answer is this: Do we follow Jesus because He says and does what we want, or do we follow Him so that we can say and do what He wants?*
> *What teachings of the Church or message of the Gospel can cause people to murmur in disagreement or disapproval today?*
> *How can people try to cast Jesus into mistaken roles today because they misunderstand His identity?*
> *What are ways in which people try to remake Jesus into their likeness rather than being formed into our Lord's likeness?*

Another interesting point about this passage is that it contains so many references to the heavenly descent of Jesus (see Jn 6:41, 42, 46, 50, and 51). This is a theme that began in John 3:13 and reaches its culmination in this chapter. The crowds rejected Jesus' revelation of His heavenly origin because they thought they already knew Him based on His human origins. By rejecting Jesus' revelation, the crowds were revealing their desire to remain in disbelief rather than acknowledge the truth of Jesus' claim. Our Lord does not address the cause of their grumbling but does teach that faith is the gift of God that draws people to Him. Those who do come to Him will be raised on the last day. Jesus is identifying for the people that those who reject Him are really rejecting God (see Ex 16:8 for a similar accusation of Moses to the Israelites). Jesus came to lead us into heavenly realities and no one is more capable of doing that than He, who came down from heaven. Jesus teaches us heavenly mysteries so that we will hunger and thirst for more. By sharing with us this heavenly bread that is the teaching of God, Jesus is nourishing our souls with the gift of faith. For this reason the Lord can say that no one can come to Him unless the Father draws him. He can also say, "They shall all be taught by God" (see Is 54:13), because He Himself is the Word of God who speaks what He knows to be true (see Jn 3:34–35). Because Jesus is the Eternal Word of God, the Lord can lead us to Himself by sharing with us the gift of Himself. That statement is true in two important ways.

First, the Lord can lead us to Himself through the gift of His revelation. This revelation is present wherever the Word of God is found: Scripture, Tradition, and the living faith experience of the Church. Second, the Lord leads us to Himself by Himself through the gift of the Eucharist that is His very presence. In both of these situations Jesus is both our destination and the one who sustains us. It is because of our Lord's heavenly origin that He can lead us to Himself by the gift of Himself in Word and Sacrament. In each of these moments, we encounter Jesus as "heaven on earth" and are drawn to be with Him. When we reject the true heavenly origin of these two manifestations of Jesus then we are also rejecting the heavenly destination to which our Lord is drawing us. Sometimes people can be tempted to reduce the Word of God to mere human reasoning or pious thoughts. The reality is that Jesus teaches us so that we can know Him, recognize Him and respond to Him in this life and be with Him in eternal life. The Lord feeds us with His Body and Blood not to satisfy our hunger here but to make us hunger for Him until we are with Him forever in heaven. This eternal dissatisfaction in the human spirit is alleviated in the Eucharist in which we all receive a foretaste of the Heavenly Banquet. Many saints and Christian authors including Baldwin of Ford and Teresa of Avila have described this longing as "an affliction that is health". In other words, our natural hunger and thirst for the presence of

God, as it is satisfied in the Eucharist, brings both relief and an increase in our desire for the joys of heaven.

> *When have you experienced something of "heaven on earth" and how has that experience made you hunger and thirst for more?*
> *How does this understanding of Jesus, leading us to Himself with the gift of Himself, help you understand the Lord's presence in Word and Sacrament?*
> *When we only think of Jesus in terms of human (physical) origin, how do we diminish our ability to receive the grace offered by our Lord's presence?*
> *How do people describe the Word of God when they only understand it in its literal origin?*
> *How do people describe the Eucharist when they only understand it in its physical origin?*

This passage ends with Jesus making an even greater and more startling revelation of His identity. He not only repeats His claim that He is the living bread that came down from heaven but now He goes on to say that the bread which He shall give for the life of the world is His flesh. With this revelation we now have two distinct and complementary meanings for the expression "bread of life": Jesus' teaching (Word) and Jesus' flesh (Sacrament). These two interpretations have an obvious relationship to the Mass and comprise the Liturgy of the Word and the Liturgy of the Eucharist. Jesus Himself interprets these symbols for us when He emphasizes the teaching dimension of the bread of life in the first part of the discourse (vv 25–50) and the sacramental dimension in the second part of the discourse (vv 51–59). These two manifestations of our Lord's presence are intricately connected. The beginning of John's Gospel told us that the eternal Word of God became flesh and dwelt among us (see Jn 1:1, 14). Now Jesus tells us He gives that same flesh for the life of the world. The flesh of Jesus is the incarnate Son of God dwelling in our midst. This gift of Jesus in Word and Sacrament is the way in which our Lord fulfills the mission entrusted to Him by the Father.

In John 3:16 we were told that God so loved the world that He gave His only Son. Now in chapter 6 we are being informed of how the Father gives His Son: through the revelation of His teaching (Word) and in the gift of His very flesh (Eucharist). The passage of John 3:17 goes on and tells us that God sent His Son so that we might believe and have eternal life. Now in chapter 6 Jesus is telling us in what we are to believe—and how we are to receive that eternal life. The action of the Father in sending and giving occurs throughout the life of the Son. The first great action of sending and giving occurred in the incarnation when the eternal Son of God became flesh and dwelt among us so that we could know the Father and through that knowledge and relationship have life. The second great action of sending and giving occurred on the Cross of Calvary when Jesus fully revealed God in His self-giving love unto death. The third great action of sending and giving occurs in every Mass when Jesus continues to reveal the Father through His teaching (especially in the Scriptures) and to give Himself to us in the Eucharist (flesh and blood) with the same sacrificial love He manifested on Calvary. All of these actions of sending and giving are accomplished so that the world might have life (see Jn 3:16 and Jn 6:51). These actions of sending and giving are intended to continue in and through the lives of faithful disciples so that others can receive the gift of Jesus through us.

> *How does the understanding of Jesus as the Eternal Word who reveals the Father (see Jn 6:44–47) change the way you will listen to the Scriptures and homily (Liturgy of the Word) at Mass?*
>
> *Why do you think Jesus wanted us to be fed with both His Word and flesh?*
>
> *In what way does the Liturgy of the Word and the Liturgy of the Eucharist communicate the central themes of faith and love in John's Gospel?*
>
> *This chapter has been a point of discussion among Catholic and non-Catholic scholars; what happens if we only emphasize the revealing and teaching presence of Jesus and what happens if we only emphasize the sacramental presence of Jesus?*

Twentieth Sunday in Ordinary Time

Our Scripture passage comes from the Gospel of John 6:51–58. This reading warrants special attention because it contains our Lord's very challenging teaching on the gift of the Eucharist. Let's study some of the distinctive aspects of Jesus' instruction in the Gospel of John in order to understand how this great gift of our Lord is meant to affect our lives as disciples.

One of the first things to notice about this reading is the language Jesus used when He instructed them to "eat" His "flesh". This language is striking because of the graphic realism portrayed by such terms. When Jesus speaks of "eating" He uses the Greek verb *trogein* that usually describes the action of animals who munch, gnaw, or crunch their food. The more common and socially respectable verb would have been *phagein*. By using the verb *trogein*, Jesus is emphasizing the reality of physically consuming and digesting the Bread He will give (this verb is highly concentrated in this passage and appears four times in vs. 54, 56, 57, and 58). This physical emphasis was most likely used so as to eliminate any possible attempt to interpret His words symbolically or allegorically. When Jesus spoke of His "flesh" He used the Greek word *sarx* that could mean nothing other than the physical corporeal reality of His very body (the use of the term *soma*, meaning "body", could be interpreted symbolically [as was done by the Docetists] but *sarx* had only a literal and no symbolic meaning).

It is this realism of Jesus' teaching that shocked the crowds even more than our Lord's identification of Himself as the revelation of God (see reflections of previous weeks). Jesus knew of their difficulty in understanding and accepting His teaching. Rather than softening His instruction to make it more palatable to the crowds, our Lord actually intensified His instruction. We see this intensification as He moves from using *phragein* in vs. 51 to using *trogein* in the rest of the passage even after they object to his statements in vs. 52. Jesus was challenging them to accept God on God's terms and not to make the Lord's teaching conform to their preferences, sensibilities, or limited ability to understand and accept His instruction. This passage clearly identifies the flesh (and blood) of Jesus as real food (and drink). The stress on the realism of the Eucharist as the true presence of Jesus' Body and Blood was meant to prevent interpretations that could reduce people's understanding of the Eucharist to a merely symbolic reality. This stress on realism was also meant to correct those who believed that faith was only a matter of knowledge a belief held by the Gnostics rather than a practical experience of living each day in deep physical communion with God in Jesus.

> *How do people interpret the reality of the Eucharist in a merely symbolic way today?*
>
> *The Docetists were an early sect that denied that the Eternal Word of God really became flesh and dwelt among us (Incarnation); they believed that Jesus was a purely a spiritual being and that we could experience Him in a spiritual (but not physical) way. How does the Docetist perspective express itself today?*
>
> *The Gnostics believed that being a person of faith meant possessing certain secret knowledge, and they emphasized the role of knowledge as being more important than living out principles of faith in every day actions. How does the Gnostic perspective express itself today?*
>
> *Jesus did not soften His teaching in response to the crowd's disbelief, but rather intensified it so as to stress the realism of His Flesh and Blood. How does our Lord's teaching on the reality of the Eucharist challenge you to approach the Mass differently?*

Jesus also teaches the crowds about the effect the Eucharist is meant to have in transforming the one who receives it. He says that those who eat His Flesh and drink His Blood have eternal life. No other food can change us like the Eucharist can! Well, actually there was a food mentioned in the Scriptures that changed humanity but not for the better—it was the fruit of the Tree of Knowledge that introduced sin and death into the world (see Gn 3:3). The food that Jesus now gives in His Flesh and Blood has the power to overcome the death of sin and make us sharers in the life of Grace. We have a common expression that says, "You are what you eat"; with reception of the Eucharist as a believing Christian, we truly can become members of Christ's body who share in eternal life and participate in the love of the Father, Son and Holy Spirit. Because of this effect of the Eucharist we are actually "divinized" by our physical communion with Jesus. It is important to note that Jesus so closely identifies His very self with the reality of food and drink that He can say in vs. 57, "He who eats me will live because of me." The gift of the Eucharist is the gift of the very person of Jesus. He offers more to us than His teaching, example, or personal friendship—He offers His very self! This is a powerful insight into John's theology of the Eucharist. Namely, the Eucharist brings us into a physical participation with the life of Jesus and that participation is an abiding relationship (see vs. 56) that allows us access to the life-giving love between the Father and the Son. Jesus doesn't just tell us about this relationship with the Father; He offers to share it with us in Himself.

> *How do sin and spiritual death surround your life each week?*
>
> *How can your sharing in the Eucharist help you overcome the toxic environments you face?*
>
> *Most food we eat is transformed into us. How does this teaching on the power of the Eucharist help to transform us (divinize) and increase our desire for more frequent reception of our Lord's Flesh and Blood?*
>
> *Jesus stresses the necessity of receiving Him as the Bread of Life and He identifies that Bread in two ways: as His Revelation (Word) and as His Flesh (Eucharist). What happens when someone receives His Word but not His Flesh?*
>
> *What happens when someone receives His Flesh but not His Word?*
>
> *Why do you think Jesus stressed the importance of both actions of reception in order for disciples to participate fully in His gift of eternal life?*

Our Lord uses an important phrase when He addresses the misunderstanding of the crowd. He says "Amen, Amen." This is the same word that we use when we receive the Eucharist and the Body and Blood of the Lord is presented to us. The word "amen" is an ancient term that comes from either Hebrew or Aramaic. It is difficult to translate which is why we continue to use it rather than an English expression in our prayer today. The word "amen" has meanings that include, but are not limited to, the following: "It is true", "I believe", "It is firm", "It is certain", "It is trustworthy", "It is validated", "It is dependable", and "I am in agreement". Sometimes people can be tempted to use an English expression instead of this ancient term, but any attempt to translate it inevitably reduces and limits its meaning. Jesus reaffirmed the truth of what He was saying because the crowd would not accept His teaching. Their difficulty is understandable in light of the many Old Testament's teachings against consuming blood (see Gn 9:2–4, Lev 17:10–14, Dt 12:16). That prohibition was based on the belief that blood was the principle of life and belonged to God alone.

    In the gift of the Eucharist, Jesus specifically wants us to share in His divine life and so our Lord changes the prohibition to an invitation and even a commandment. The Body and Blood of Jesus is the source of our communion with God and not the cause of our alienation. Jesus reaffirms that this teaching is true, dependable, and must be accepted and lived by the Christian disciple. When we come forward to receive the Eucharist we respond by saying "Amen." In doing so, we are making a complete and irrevocable gift of our lives to God who is giving His life to us in the Flesh and Blood of His Son. We are not only professing our belief in what the Eucharist is (the reality of Jesus' presence), we are also confirming our desire and openness to be transformed by that reality so that we no longer live for ourselves, but it is Christ who lives in us (see Gal 2:20). We are also saying that there is no other reality in our lives that will define us or shape our values more than the person of Jesus Christ. Ultimately we are saying that the one belief on which we are willing to base our lives, no matter what happens, is the belief that Jesus Christ is present to us in the Eucharist.

How does this understanding of the term "Amen" inform, inspire, and challenge you as you come forward to receive the Eucharist?

The teaching of Jesus went against the social and religious sensibilities of the crowd. How does our Lord's teaching challenge your sensibilities?

Jesus has the power to turn the cause of our alienation into the source of our Communion. What alienates you from God and how can that part of your life became an occasion of grace instead?

When we say "Amen," we are stating our agreement to every- thing Jesus intends in the Eucharist, not only to that which we can understand.

In what way is our "Amen" an open-ended statement of faith that develops and matures as we grow in discipleship?

This passage begins and ends with a reference to Jesus being the bread that came down from heaven. This divine descent of God's presence into the world began in the first chapter of John's Gospel when we were told that the Eternal Word of God became flesh and dwelt among us (see Jn 1:1,14). The descent continues when we are told in John 3:16 and 3:18 that God gave and sent His Son so that the world might be saved and have life. Now in John 6:51–58 we are informed of how we share in that life promised earlier in the Gospel. At this point we need to remember the fragments (*klas- mata*) that were taken up following the multiplication of the loaves and the fishes in John 6:12–13. These fragments have been in the background throughout the entire sixth chapter of John. Jesus, the eternal Word of God incarnate, will continue to give Himself for us on the Cross of Calvary in the separation of His flesh and blood. This sacrifice will be made present for us to participate in when our Lord gives Himself to us in the Eucharist. Jesus dwelt among us (literally, "tabernacle" Jn 1:14) so that we could become a living tabernacle of His presence when we receive Him in the Eucharist.

This passage tells us that Jesus "will give" this bread to us, and the use of the future tense of the verb is meant to signify that the Eucharistic sacrifice will be fulfilled in our Lord's suffering and death. This sacrifice is then made present to us in the Eucharist throughout time as we continue to receive from the twelve baskets of fragments collected from the feeding of the multitudes. It requires the eyes of faith to encounter God in the broken flesh and poured-out blood of Jesus on the Cross. Our decision to accept that moment as the ultimate revelation of God's love is the faith that grants us access to God's life in Baptism and the Eucharist (symbol of water and blood flowing from the side of Jesus in Jn 19:34). Our participation in that love takes place through our eating and drinking of the Lord's Flesh and Blood in the Eucharist. In doing so, we become a living tabernacle of Jesus in the world. The Eternal Word who became Flesh now offers His Flesh as Bread so that we can become that bread for others. Thus, God continues to give the Son from the Incarnation, through the Cross of Calvary, through the Eucharist, and through us to the world. The fact that Jesus is the source of life has been emphasized throughout the first six chapters of John's Gospel. Now in this passage we are taught how we are to share in the gift of Jesus' life.

> *What responsibility do you assume every time you receive the Eucharist?*
>
> *How does the Eucharist, as a manifestation of God's love, challenge you to love more selflessly and sacrificially in your life?*
>
> *How does the connection between the Cross of Calvary and the Flesh and Blood of Jesus in the Eucharist challenge you to receive the Eucharist with greater awareness and reverence?*
>
> *How can the image of being a "living tabernacle" inspire you as you go forth from church each Sunday?*

TWENTY-FIRST SUNDAY IN ORDINARY TIME

Our Scripture passage comes from the Gospel of John 6:60–69. This text contains the response of Jesus' own disciples to His discourse on the Bread of Life. This teaching is a decisive point for all disciples who must choose to accept or reject what our Lord is revealing in this passage. This passage represents the various possible responses to Jesus' teaching: Murmuring (vs. 61), Disbelief (vs. 64), Betrayal (vs. 64), Rejection (vs. 66) and finally Peter's Confession of faith (vs. 68). Our acceptance or rejection of this teaching occurs on both conceptual and practical levels. Certainly, Jesus intended that the Eucharist would be the source of unity and communion for all believers, but this Gospel passage reminds us that it can be an unintended source of division. Let's study this important passage carefully to see what insights it can offer us for our lives as disciples.

One of the most striking features of this passage is that Jesus does not soften His teaching in any way or attempt to diminish the powerful message He has communicated. Rather, the Lord continues to reiterate the absolute necessity of accepting Him as the Revealer of God's Word and His crucified flesh and poured-out blood given for us in the Eucharist as the reality of God's love. We need to remember that it was our Lord's own disciples who objected to this teaching and not unbelievers. If Jesus had meant anything other than the reality of His own flesh and blood becoming real food and drink in the Eucharist, He would have taken this opportunity to clarify and explain the misunderstanding to the disciples who were questioning the teaching. This would have been the perfect time for the Lord to give His teaching a symbolic understanding or to explain to the disciples that they could still follow Him without accepting this challenging revelation.

However, the Lord did not offer any symbolic interpretation or any exemption for discipleship. When the disciples object to His

teaching, they call it "hard". This is a word that means "unaccept-
able" or "offensive". Indeed, throughout history there have been
people who have considered the message of our Lord's presence
in the Eucharist to be offensive or difficult and who have tried to
explain it in more palatable ways or in a manner that is easier to
understand. On the one hand, the early Church Fathers (especially Ignatius of Antioch, Irenaeus of Lyon, John Chrysostom,
and Augustine) all defended the real presence of Christ in the
Eucharist and focused their teaching on the effects that reception
of the Sacrament should have in the lives of Christians. Pascasio
Radberto (c. 785–860) was one of the first medieval theologians
to confront a developing symbolic interpretation of the Eucharist
by emphasizing the realism of Jesus' presence. On the other hand,
Berengar of Tours (c. 1000–1088) represented a school of thought
that began to promote a position of ultra symbolism, which emphasized a moral emphasis to the Eucharist. In response to ongoing
medieval controversies, Thomas Aquinas (1225–1274) promoted
the metaphysical principle of transubstantiation to explain the real
presence of Jesus in the form of bread and wine. Martin Luther,
Ulrich Zwingli, John Calvin, and The Anglican Bill of Thirty-Nine
Articles (especially Articles 28 and 29) all had difficulty with the
explicit teaching of the enduring Real Presence of Jesus' Flesh and
Blood in the Eucharist and sought to explain it in terms based on
the faith experience of the congregation or other aspects.

In response to these attempts to render the teaching on the
Eucharist more acceptable and understandable, the Council of
Trent reaffirmed the reality of our Lord's true and enduring presence in the Eucharist. This historical summary simply shows that
religious people of serious intent have historically struggled, with
more or less success, in an effort to accept, understand, and express
the teaching on the Eucharist. What is consistent in this historical
survey is clear: Any attempt to reduce the Eucharist to a merely
symbolic presence has been repeatedly and consistently rejected
by the Church under the guidance of the Holy Spirit. Our Lord's
words remain as challenging today as they were nearly two thousand years ago. His teaching is not ours to change but to accept.
Jesus did not alter His teaching according to the capacity of the

disciples to understand, but rather challenged them to accept His Word as it was presented to them.

> *How is practical disbelief in the Real Presence of Jesus in the Eucharist expressed today in people's actions at Mass? When have you been challenged to deepen your belief in the Eucharist and change the way you receive our Lord in Communion?*
>
> *If you were in Jesus' situation and disciples were leaving you because of what you had said, what would you have done?*
>
> *The Eucharist is meant to be the source of our communion but can sometimes become the cause of our division; what does this statement mean to you and how does our Lord's experience in this Gospel passage challenge you to work for greater Christian union?*
>
> *If you were asked to explain the real presence of Jesus in the Eucharist to someone who was not a disciple, how would you do it?*
>
> *How do you express your belief in the real presence of Jesus in the Eucharist?*

Our Lord then goes on to address the disciples' disbelief by identifying the source of their doubt: They are attempting to understand the mysteries of God with limited human knowledge and experience. Jesus specifically says, "The flesh is of no avail." The Gospel of John uses the word "flesh" (Greek *sarx*) thirteen times to refer both to the flesh of Jesus and the flesh of human beings. The flesh of Jesus manifests the Divine Presence, makes the love of God known to the world, and is the source of our life (because Jesus is the Eternal Word of God who became Flesh and dwelt among us; as God, He can give us His Flesh as Bread in the Eucharist). The flesh of human beings, however, is limited in understanding and only sees what is "below", a term that means the things of this world. As such, the flesh of human beings only perceives on a superficial or physical level and is not able to grasp the divine presence operative in the world.

By pointing out the danger of using superficial human experience as the basis for faith, Jesus is cautioning the doubtful disciples to let go of their human expectations and to accept His divine revelation. It is through this divine revelation in the Word of Jesus that the Spirit is offered to disciples. The response of the doubtful disciples is explicitly identified as "murmuring" or "grumbling". This term indicates that they are now responding to Jesus in the same was as non-believers did in the preceding verses and that they were following the Lord for earthly reasons rather than divine reasons (that is, they perceived Jesus as a great prophet, messiah, or teacher rather than as the presence of God incarnate). Jesus recognized that their inability to accept His teaching stemmed from their erroneous faith, and so the Lord challenges them with the interesting phrase, "What if you were to see the Son of Man ascending to where he was before?" The presumption is that the disciples would then understand Jesus' divine nature and would accept His instruction and authority. This passage is teaching us that our ability to accept Jesus' teaching in an uncompromising way must be based on our firm belief in His divine nature. If we believe Jesus to be anything less than the Son of God incarnate, who represents completely and authentically the Father, then we will reduce our Lord's teaching to mere opinion rather than the revelation of that truth necessary for salvation. That is what the doubtful disciples were doing: reducing Jesus to what they could understand, and because of their lack of faith in who He was, they ended up rejecting what He taught.

We need to remember that these disciples are the very ones who received privileged insights, special revelation, and prolonged association with the Lord. Despite these tremendous advantages they now walk away. This is an important caution for us as disciples lest we unintentionally follow their erroneous ways. Sometimes we can feel privileged because we have been given great experiences of faith, opportunities for ministry involvement, or special theological insights. This passage cautions us that discipleship is not based on information, association, or involvement but on our acceptance of Jesus' Word as people who are filled with the Holy Spirit and drawn by the Father. If we are rejecting any word of Jesus then we are resisting the Holy Spirit and the invitation of the Father. Jesus' Word is as challenging for us today as it was for the disciples two thousand years ago. In order for us to remain faithful to the Word of Jesus speaks, it is necessary to believe in His divine nature as God and to accept what He reveals, especially when we cannot understand it. It is that act of faith in the person of Jesus and utter trust in His Word that will allow us to remain faithful during difficult and challenging moments.

> *How are people today tempted to reduce faith to only what they can understand?*
>
> *What could attract a person to Christianity today other than a firm belief in the divinity of Jesus, and what is the danger of that attraction becoming the basis of someone's faith?*
>
> *How can our faith community help disciples move from a superficial human-flesh perception of reality to a faith-based, Jesus-flesh revelation of reality?*
>
> *What experiences have made you feel privileged in your discipleship, and how can those experiences become the basis of false confidence when it comes to remaining faithful to Jesus?*
>
> *What teachings of the Gospel and the Church do people reject today; what reasons do they give for rejecting those teachings; what does this passage identify as the underlying reasons for their rejection?*
>
> *The reality is that few people overtly or vocally reject Jesus but they do so by intentionally not following the Lord's will in their practical lives, and by doing so they are no longer "following" Him. What are ways in which we unconsciously reject the Lord by choosing to live contrary to the values of the Gospel?*

Not all the disciples reject Jesus and His teaching. Peter expresses correct faith in this passage when he says, "Master, to whom shall we go? You have the Words of eternal life. We have come to know and are convinced that you are the Holy One of God." Peter's confession shows that the Father is, indeed, drawing disciples to Jesus who can acknowledge in Him the presence of God. Peter's statement of faith also demonstrates the utter obedience to Jesus that is a hallmark of authentic discipleship in the Gospel of John (see the Mother of Jesus in Jn 2:5, John the Baptist in Jn 3:29, The Samaritan Villagers in Jn 4:42, and the Royal official in Jn 4:50 for other examples of such faith). What is distinctive about Peter's confession of faith as opposed to these previous examples is that Peter clearly identifies Jesus as being the agent of God. Peter also acknowledges that Jesus does more than simply teach a message.

Rather, Peter is expressing his faith that the Lord reveals the will of God and communicates the Spirit. Peter expresses this confidence through the use of the Greek word *rhemata* rather than *logos* when he speaks about the "Words" of Jesus. The term *rhemata* means more than simply "words"; it refers to the very thing being communicated. Thus, when Peter says that Jesus has the *rhemata* of eternal life, Peter is stating the following: What Jesus is offering (Revelation and Eucharist) is itself eternal life. This confession of faith is a profound insight and expresses the correct response for disciples. The reality is that each of us must also answer the question of Jesus when He asked, "Do you also want to leave?" If we have found our life in the things (*rhemata*) of Jesus then we will not leave Him, but if our life is rooted in realities apart from Jesus then our enduring discipleship remains uncertain.

> *What are the things that most give your life meaning?*
> *What part of your life is "of God"?*
> *What are some of the things Jesus has accomplished in your life for which you are eternally grateful?*
> *Peter's acknowledgement of faith went beyond his understanding and expressed his total open acceptance to all that Jesus wants to reveal. What makes it difficult for you to express an open-ended commitment of faith to Jesus?*
> *Peter also says, "Lord, to whom shall we go ..." Sometimes we like to maintain alternative sources of security in case we need "somewhere to go" in times of trial or distress. To what places do you go when you need security or reassurance in your life?*

Twenty-Second Sunday in Ordinary Time

Our Scripture passage comes from the Gospel of Mark 7:1–8, 14–15 and 21–23. This text contains an important teaching regarding the role of religious practices and defilement. Although the immediate controversy involved the ritual purity regulations of the Scribes and Pharisees, this instruction is an enduring teaching for all Christian disciples. Let's study this text to see what lessons we can learn for our discipleship.

The first lesson Jesus teaches is an instruction on the nature of religious laws and regulations. It is important to remember that Jesus does not discard the Law of Moses, but rather establishes a certain prioritization within it. Laws and regulations have the purpose of safeguarding and protecting what is good for us. Some rules promote the good by requiring certain actions while other rules protect the good by restricting certain actions. In order to understand how to properly interpret and apply various regulated practices, it is always necessary to remember the ultimate good being promoted or protected by those practices. Laws and regulations are meant to serve as external checks and balances that indicate a proper interior disposition. When a person is in violation of a law or regulation, they should question whether their actions are still promoting or protecting what is good. In this passage, the purity laws were meant to foster holiness that promoted communion with God and neighbor. However, when those practices became absolutes in themselves, they no longer served their intended purpose. Rather than becoming a source of communion, those same regulations became a cause of division. Christianity has regulations for its life and discipleship as well.

The Great Commission for the Church is to communicate the living gift of faith through history. This divine gift of the living faith reality is known as Tradition (Note capital "T")—a word that means "that which is handed down". The great Tradition of faith is articulated and fostered by various traditions (note the small "t" used to indicate expressions and practices) that promote and protect the living gift of faith itself (Tradition). These individual practices (traditions) may change somewhat in their external forms, yet continue to communicate the same essential reality (Tradition). For this reason the Church states that, "The Sacred Tradition and Sacred Scripture of both the Old and New Testaments are like a mirror in which the pilgrim Church on Earth looks at God, from whom she has received everything, until she is brought finally to see Him as He is, face to face."[27] Sacraments such as the celebration of Mass and Confession, have been an essential part of the Christian faith since the time of Jesus, yet the actual way in which those sacraments have been celebrated (that is, particular vestments or other ritual regulations) has varied at different times. When regulations become emphasized more than the essence of faith, we are in danger of falling into rigid legalism. When regulations are discarded without consideration for their formative value, we are in danger of losing important safeguards and encouragements for Christian discipleship. In order to develop into mature discipleship, it is important to know both the essence and the expression of religious laws and practices. Only then can they fulfill the purpose for which they were given: greater communion with God and neighbor.

> *How can rigid legalism undermine authentic discipleship?*
> *How can the casual discarding of religious regulations (libertarianism) obstruct growth in authentic discipleship?*
> *What helps you understand the difference between the essential nature of faith (Tradition) and the particular expression of faithful practices (traditions)?*
> *How do these two understandings complement each other?*
> *What happens when someone tries to conserve the Tradition without traditions?*
> *What happens when someone tries to conserve the traditions without a love for the Tradition?*

The second lesson Jesus teaches concerns the danger of mistaken priorities. Our Lord makes this caution by quoting the Prophet Isaiah when he says, "In vain do they worship me teaching as doc-

---

27.   See 1 Jn 3:2; Vatican II, *Dei Verbum*, 817–836.

trines human precepts (see Is 29:13)." Jesus does not criticize human precepts in themselves but only when divine status is given to them. When that happens, it can be easy for disciples to substitute daily practices for true and authentic devotion to God. It can also become tempting to esteem certain practices in such a way that we actually look down on others who do not follow those same practices. Finally, when we confuse human precepts with divinely revealed doctrines we are in danger of disregarding the priorities God has given us in favor of the priorities we want, which are always of lesser value. The Scripture verses not included as part of this Sunday's Gospel reading indicate a particular example by which the Pharisees and Scribes allowed exceptions to the divine mandate to honor one's father and mother in favor of created human exemptions. In this action, the Scribes and Pharisees are accused of not only violating God's will but of actually disregarding it. It is important for us as disciples to know the difference between what is divinely inspired and what is humanly expressed or legislated. Such knowledge is never a license to disregard what is humanly expressed or legislated, but rather an encouragement to properly interpret and apply it in particular circumstances. When rules and practices become a weapon with which we attack or condemn others, we have violated the greatest Law God gave us: to Love God and our Neighbor.

> *What religious reasons can people use to exempt themselves from the great commandment to care for God or neighbor today?*
> *When have you seen someone use religious rules or practices as a weapon with which to demean others?*
> *How can you develop and maintain a clear sense of relative priorities between divine doctrines and mere human precepts?*

In the third lesson Jesus teaches the true nature of purity. In the religious and cultural world of our Lord, people believed that impurity was based on external factors such as the food consumed, associations with other people, or the geographical area in which a person lived. Jesus redefines purity laws based on internal factors instead. Our Lord presents a list of twelve vices which cause impurity and are distinctive in that they affect our relationship with other people. In order to understand the meaning of this list, it is important to remember that "blasphemy" was primarily an action of slander or false accusation whereby the name of God was invoked in an attempt to falsely authenticate statements about another person. It is significant that Jesus identified sins that are interpersonal in nature rather than religious (against God). Our Lord is not denying the significance of religious sins, but rather stressing the particularly damaging effect of interpersonal sins. It is these harmful actions towards other people that cause us to be impure in the eyes of God. This is an important lesson for disciples. We need to remember when we approach God in prayer that the Lord is aware of how we have approached others throughout our day.

The Letter of James from this Sunday's second reading makes explicit that authentic religion is expressed in our relationship with others (see Jas 1:27). James is not dismissing Christians in the first century of their religious obligation to God, but rather reminding them that their obligation to the Lord cannot be fulfilled when they disregard their duty to one another. Sometimes disciples can delude themselves into thinking that their spirituality or faith is distinct from their real-life interaction with others. This Gospel passage serves as a timeless reminder of the interconnectedness between love of God and love of neighbor and that impurity in one relationship inevitably brings impurity into the other. It is not our association with external factors that renders us impure in the eyes of God; it is our decisions of injustice, indifference, and selfishness that render us impure.

> *What happens when disciples disassociate their relationship with God from their relationship with neighbor?*
> *Why do you think Jesus didn't include any religious sins in the list of vices he presented?*
> *Which of those vices do you think is particularly damaging today for marriages, friendships, families, or professional interactions?*
> *If you were to compose a list of virtues that would promote purity in the eyes of God, what would those virtues be?*

Finally, this reading is an important opportunity for us to consider some additional ways in which this Gospel passage should challenge us. In order to understand the meaning Mark intended, we should be aware that the text of vs. 2 actually says that the Pharisees and Scribes, "...observed that some of his disciples ate their *bread* with unclean, that is, unwashed hands". Mark has mentioned bread several times in his Gospel so far (see 6, 36, 38, 41, 44, and 52) and it has often had a Eucharistic connection. This passage could be a continuation of that double meaning in Mark's use of the term. With this insight in mind, we can now pay attention to some other curious details. For example, Mark tells us that the Pharisees and Scribes noticed that "some" of the disciples acted in this way. The implication is that others did not act this way. Mark is pointing out the potential danger of diverse practices within the worshipping Christian community. It is important to recognize the value of practical unity in our religious celebrations lest division result because some do not act in the same way as others. Also, Mark gives specific examples of ritual washings that he then proceeds to explain.

The implication of the explanation is that Mark's audience would not have known the meaning behind these practices if they were not informed. This, too, is an important lesson for us as disciples. If we do not know the reasons behind our religious actions, we can hardly expect those actions to have much meaning for us or for God. These two examples indicate that Mark wanted the Christian community to be unified and conscientious of their worship experience. Mark wanted them to be sincere and authentic in their prayer and prioritized in their faith. He neither wanted the Church to preserve practices without reflecting on them nor to discard practices without understanding them. Basically, Mark wants us as a Church to know what we do, why we do it, how to do it, and for whom we do it when it concerns our lives of faith. Most of all, Mark wants our celebration of the Eucharist to be our source of communion with God and neighbor and never the cause of our division. By reflecting on the lessons presented by our Lord in this passage, we can better experience the Eucharist in the way Mark wanted it and Jesus intended it.

What are prayer gestures that you make at every Mass but whose meaning and purpose you do not fully understand?

*How can you learn more about the various parts of the
Mass and the significance and meaning being expressed
in the liturgy?*

*How can someone be distracted by others at Mass in such a
way that the celebration ends up being a cause of division
rather than a source of communion?*

*What are examples of diverse practices within the wor-
shipping community that can foster division or become
distractive because some are acting differently from others?
How do you know when diverse gestures are enriching and
warranted?*

TWENTY-THIRD SUNDAY IN ORDINARY TIME

Our Scripture passage comes from the Gospel of Mark 7:31–37. In this passage we read the story of Jesus healing the deaf man who could barely speak. It is a significant moment of healing and contains several indications that it is also meant to be an instruction in discipleship. Let's study this passage to see what it has to offer us for our lives of faith.

One of the more interesting things to note about this passage is that it contains the word *ephphatha* that is preserved from the Aramaic language of Jesus. One of the only other times in Mark's Gospel that we have an Aramaic phrase is when Jesus heals Jairus' daughter with the expression *talitha koum* (Mk 5:41). Both of these scenes are important moments of discipleship and may have preserved actual words of Jesus due to their possible use in the early Church Baptismal rites. This interpretive key will now help us unlock this passage as an instructive moment with sacramental and discipleship significance. The first thing to note about discipleship is that Jesus takes the man away from the crowd by himself. This demonstrates the Lord's desire for us to spend time with Him in a privileged environment of communion, friendship, and formation in the Christian way of life. The distractions of ordinary daily life and the noise of the crowds can prevent us from being able to focus our attention on the Lord and to foster a relationship with Him. It can be intimidating and threatening to leave the comfortable world of our everyday social, professional, and familiar environment. However, Jesus can form us in faith, hope, and love most effectively when we enter into His world on His terms and leave behind the security and control of our own world. Such an experience of spending time with Jesus is the intended purpose of faith-based retreats, conferences, and pilgrimages. Sometimes it is much easier to stay in our own world rather than to accept the invitation to enter into the world of Jesus and possibly be changed by Him.

The second thing to note is that Jesus opens the man's ears so that he is able to both hear and speak clearly. On a level of discipleship, this two-fold healing has significant implications. The ability to articulate and profess faith is entirely dependent on how well we have heard the message of faith. We cannot communicate what we have not received and understood. This man is an image of all disciples who are not able to express clearly and readily their faith in Jesus. The source of this inability is usually due to their lack of knowledge. Disciples are responsible for seeking out opportunities to grow in their faith so that they can hear and understand the Word of God in its fullness. Only then can a disciple communicate to others that which they themselves have received. This hearing occurs through personal study, participation in the faith community, adult faith enrichment, and the prayerful study of Scripture. The final lesson of discipleship is the personal connection Jesus establishes with the man by placing His finger in his ear and touching his tongue. These gestures tell us that discipleship is not possible without a personal connection to Jesus Himself. The crowds may have heard about Jesus and even this man might have been told about Jesus, but he must be personally connected to the Lord in order to understand the Word of God (hearing) and to proclaim His faith (speaking). This important lesson reminds us that no matter how much we study or witness our faith, if we are not personally connected to Jesus, our efforts can become empty and meaningless. Faith is first and foremost a relationship of trust in the Living God. What we learn may inform us about the Lord who is touching our lives, but it cannot replace that relationship or be a substitute for it. As disciples, it is important that we remain connected to Jesus each day so that we can hear His voice and proclaim His faith.

What are privileged environments of friendship, communion, and formation where you can experience Jesus in a focused and intense way?

How do disciples keep their ears open and attuned to the voice of Christ?

How do you know when you are becoming deaf to the voice of Christ?

What areas of your faith do you not understand well?

When do you find yourself unable to express your beliefs
in discussions of faith with others?
How do you know when you are personally connected to
Jesus, and what can you do to foster that personal connec-
tion more regularly?

As was mentioned in the previous reflection, some Scripture scholars believe that this passage contains elements of the early Church's
Baptismal practices. It is interesting to note that the blessing of the
ears and the mouth of a newly Baptized infant are still a part of
our Baptismal rite today. The actual prayer says, *"The Lord Jesus*
made the deaf hear and the dumb speak. May he soon touch your
ears to receive his word, and your mouth to proclaim his faith, to
the praise and glory of God the Father."[28] This action of Jesus, then,
has important sacramental significance for us. Sometimes parents
perceive Baptism as an obligation to be completed in a half hour
rather than a responsibility that takes a lifetime to be fulfilled.

Baptism isn't the completion of a disciple's journey of faith;
rather, Baptism is the first step of that journey. The opening of the
ears and the mouth are important symbols for what a life of full
and mature discipleship will look like. The ears are symbols of how
we receive the gift of faith. As Saint Paul tells us, "How then will
they call on Him in whom they have not believed? How will they
believe in Him whom they have not heard? And how will they hear
without a preacher?" (Rom 10:14) Hearing, then, is a symbol of our
ability to receive the gift of faith. The reality is that there are many
obstacles that can prevent us from receiving and understanding the
gift of faith. Some obstacles are internal while others are external.
Internal obstacles include distractions, false beliefs, sinful practices, and prejudices. External obstacles include lack of religious
formation, the absence of authentic Christian witnesses, inactivity
of the family in the life of the Church, and a secular culture that
promotes values that are hostile to faith.

When the ears of the newly Baptized are blessed, we are asking God to remove every obstacle, both internal and external,
that would prevent the person from authentically and completely
receiving the gift of faith. We are praying that their life will be

28. *Rite for the Baptism of One Child* (1970 Missal).

"open" to receive Jesus in every possible way. This action of reception is somewhat passive, however, and is only half of what mature
discipleship requires.

The other half of mature discipleship is that of active witness.
The mouth is the vehicle of speech and as such is a means by which
we actively profess and express our faith. The blessing of the mouth,
then, asks the Lord to remove any obstacle that can prevent us
from authentically and completely witnessing the faith we have
received. Such obstacles can be internal or external. Internal obstacles include fear of rejection or persecution, unfamiliarity with the
language of faith, or trained passivity in the face of opportunity.
External obstacles can include a hostile culture in the home, office,
or larger society. When we are open to profess our faith, we will
do so with competence, courage, and creativity. A mature disciple
receives and professes completely and authentically a living relationship with Jesus Christ.

> *What are some of the internal and external obstacles that
> you have experienced in your desire to hear the message
> of faith?*
> *What are some of the internal and external obstacles that
> you have experienced in your ability to express the message
> of faith?*
> *What can a faith community do to help people become
> mature disciples who both hear and profess the gift of faith?*

Another interesting thing to note about this passage is that of the
actual healing. While there are various gestures and other actions
associated with the experience of healing, it is quite clear that Jesus'
Word is what caused the miraculous event. Scripture scholars note
that actions such as the touching of ears, use of spittle, touching of
the tongue, and groaning were used in parts of the ancient Gentile
world by various healers. These elements may have been awkward
for the early Church to explain and may account for the omission
of these details in the Gospels Matthew and Luke. However, Jesus
may have been trying to teach us something by the use of these
gestures and actions. The Lord knew the cultural world of those
whom He served and so He may have used these gestures and
symbols as a means of inculturation. That means Jesus found a way

to make the Gospel relevant to foreign cultures while preserving the power of His Word.

In doing so, Jesus used the same gestures employed by pagan healers so that people could understand His healing work, but then Jesus revealed that it was not those gestures that accomplished the healing, but rather His command. The cultural symbols served to engage our attention and lead us to an acceptance of the Lord's Word. Our world has cultures that are foreign to the world of Jesus as well. In order to present the Gospel in an intelligible way we must sometimes learn to carefully use the symbols and expressions of our contemporary cultures to lead people to better understand the work Jesus is trying to accomplish in their lives. However, the challenge is to use those symbols to express carefully and distinctly the unquestionable power of Jesus' Word. Not all symbols and expressions of contemporary culture are compatible with Christianity, but those that are compatible may be used to appropriately facilitate the proclamation of the Gospel. The Church is constantly called to proclaim the message of the Gospel in a relevant and effective way. The example of Jesus in this passage challenges us to be creative, courageous, and discerning in how that proclamation takes place today.

> For what cultures today does the message of faith need to become more relevant?
> How can inculturation sometimes end up distracting and distorting the message of faith?
> What principles should guide authentic, faithful and effective inculturation of the Gospel?
> How do you know when a message has become focused more on the culture than the Gospel?

The passage ends with Jesus instructing the crowd not to tell anyone about the healing. However, they then go out and proclaim the event. The implication is that the man shared in the action of the crowd. It is ironic that Jesus opened the man's ears so that he could hear clearly but then the man does not obey what he hears our Lord telling him. Jesus has power to control the forces of nature, disease, and evil spirits, but the Lord respects our free will and does not force us to do His will. Rather, the Lord opens our ears to hear Him and asks us to willingly cooperate with His will, especially when it conflicts with our own desires. Disciples are called to be obedient to God's will and to do what God wants rather than what they want. It is in our obedience that the gift of faith reaches perfection and we use the gifts God has given us according to the Lord's intention.

> *How does this teaching invite you to reconsider your use of the Lord's blessings in yourlife?*
> *In what area of life do we tend to be most resistant to following God's will by doing our own will instead?*
> *How do you dispose yourself to know God's will?*

Lastly, it is worth noting that this entire healing takes place because the crowds brought the deaf man to Jesus and asked the Lord to lay His hand on him. This man was fortunate to have a community that cared enough to bring him to Jesus as the Lord drew near. The man himself may have had no idea who Jesus was or the change that Jesus could effect in his life. The crowds did know those things and so they took initiative in facilitating this encounter with the Lord. There are many people today who do not know Jesus, their need for Jesus, or the effect the Lord can have in their lives. This passage encourages us to be part of the faithful crowd that brings others to the Lord so the Lord can make them His own and share with them the power of His Word. This initiative requires that we are open and hospitable as a faith community and that we are inviting towards those who are not currently active members of our church. It also means that we look around at the people we encounter every day and consider how Jesus desires to touch their lives. They may never meet the Lord if we do not invite them to come with us when we go meet the Lord. Remember: The man in this story would have never come to Jesus had it not been for the crowd. Jesus wants us to use our gift of speech to invite others so they can share in what we are already experiencing. The gift of faith and discipleship is deeply personal but never intended to be kept private.

> *What are opportunities or ministries to which you can invite people so they can become familiar with the Lord?*
> *What does an open and hospitable faith community look like?*

What does a closed and inhospitable faith community look like?

Who has been placed in your life and needs to meet the Lord, but they aren't aware of their need or don't know how to meet Him?

Who introduced you to Jesus?

TWENTY-FOURTH SUNDAY IN ORDINARY TIME

Our Scripture passage comes from the Gospel of Mark 8:27–35. In this reading we hear of Peter's famous confession of faith. This confession is also recorded in the other Gospels of Matthew and Luke. More information and insights regarding this scene can be found by consulting the reflections on those texts (see Mt 16:13–28 and Lk 9:18–22). Let's study Mark's account to see what it offers us in our lives as disciples.

Jesus poses the most fundamental question to disciples when He asks, "Who do you say that I am?" In fact, the question of Jesus' identity and authority is one of the most important themes of Mark's entire Gospel and was first expressed in our Lord's first miracle (Mk 1:21–28). Various people in Mark's Gospel have tried to answer that question but their answers always fall short of capturing Jesus' full identity. For some Jesus is a wonder worker and for others a teacher. Still others see him as a prophet. In this passage we read about Peter identifying Jesus as the Messiah and our Lord using the term "Son of Man" to speak of Himself. These titles give us insights not only into who Jesus is but also how we are to respond as His disciples. Who we believe Jesus is will determine how far we will go in following Him and what sacrifices we will be willing to make for the sake of discipleship. After all, who is willing to give up his life for a miracle worker? Or who would willingly accept crucifixion for a prophet? Jesus can make a radical claim on our lives only because He is the Son of God. When we reduce the Lord to anything less than God incarnate, we also diminish our necessary response as His disciples. Bishop Robert Barron has often commented that we must consider Jesus either as Lord, liar, or lunatic. The English scholar C. S. Lewis previously popularized this three-fold option when he wrote:

> I am trying here to prevent anyone saying the really foolish thing that people often say about Him: I'm ready to accept

Jesus as a great moral teacher, but I don't accept His claim
to be God. That is the one thing we must not say. A man
who was merely a man and said the sort of things Jesus said
would not be a great moral teacher. He would either be a
lunatic—on the level with the man who says he is a poached
egg—or else he would be the Devil of Hell. You must make
your choice. Either this man was, and is, the Son of God, or
else a madman or something worse. You can shut him up for
a fool, you can spit at him and kill him as a demon or you
can fall at his feet and call him Lord and God, but let us not
come with any patronising nonsense about his being a great
human teacher. He has not left that open to us. He did not
intend to. ... Now it seems to me obvious that He was neither
a lunatic nor a fiend: and consequently, however strange or
terrifying or unlikely it may seem, I have to accept the view
that He was and is God.[29]

Jesus claims to be the Son of God and that claim has implications
for our lives. If Jesus is not who He claims to be, there are only two
options: Either He is a liar and attempting to deceive us, or He is
a lunatic and delusional in His thinking. This is a serious question
that every disciple must answer. Who we believe Jesus to be will
have real implications for how we follow Him. Obviously we would
not follow someone we believe to be a liar or a lunatic. If we are
following someone we truly believe to be the Lord, we need to
understand and accept the implications of that belief. Namely, as
Lord, Jesus has total claim to every part of our lives. He is Lord of
our homes and our families. He is Lord of our marriages and of
our businesses. He is Lord of our finances, sexuality, and politics.
He is Lord of our leisure, our habits, and our friendships. Jesus
asks each of us to answer this question as a fundamental act of our
discipleship and subsequently to live out the consequences of that
response. If we want to know what we really believe about Jesus,
we only have to look at our lives and see how we are currently
allowing Him, or not allowing Him, to affect us. This statement
echoes the oracle of the Prophet Malachi in the Old Testament
when he summoned the priests of Israel with these words, "A son

---

29. C. S. Lewis, *Mere Christianity* (London: Collins, 1952), pp. 54–56.
   (In all editions, this is Bk. II, Ch. 3, "The Shocking Alternative.")

honors his father and servants their master. If then I am a father, where is the respect due me? And if I am a master, where is the respect due me?" (Mal 1:6) Today's Gospel also challenges each of us to answer the question of Jesus and to conform our life to that answer: "Who do you say that I am?"

> *What excuses do we give for acknowledging Jesus as the Messiah and Son of God and then disregarding what the Lord teaches?*
> *What parts of your life have you not yet submitted to the Lordship of Jesus?*
> *What parts of your life do you most easily submit to the Lordship of Jesus?*

Peter responds to Jesus' question by confessing Him to be the Messiah (Christ). The term Messiah comes from Hebrew and means "The Anointed One"; the term Christ comes from Greek and means the same thing. Such people as priests, prophets, and kings were anointed in the Old Testament and were recognized as people who were given a divinely appointed task in the world. This idea of divine election (or appointment) was for the purpose of accomplishing God's will. Thus, many people could have been anointed in this way and the term could have referred to any person who was acting on God's behalf. One form of Judaism during the time of Jesus did hope for a unique "anointed one" who would restore the Davidic kingship and the wellbeing of the Jewish people. This expectation would have been a natural threat to the established civic and religious authorities. It appears that Peter understood Jesus in this way and that explains why Jesus immediately cautioned the disciples in Mark 8:30 not to tell anyone what they had heard. Still, Peter's confession actually falls short of confessing Jesus' truest identity.

Yes, He is the Anointed one of God, but He is much more than that. Peter fails to grasp that Jesus is actually the Son of God. We live in a culture that esteems certain people for their fame, wealth, and success. In a real way they are the ones we consider anointed by God. Perhaps they are athletes who are paid large salaries or musicians who make it to the top of the pop music charts. Any time we think someone is chosen in a special way, which warrants our attention, esteem, and admiration, we are responding to them as an "anointed one". Sometimes we will even find ourselves "following" such a person by wearing t-shirts bearing their identification or pursuing information about them in the media. Sometimes, too, these people can be consulted for their political, economic, and moral opinions as though they were authorities whose teachings should guide our beliefs. Whenever any person occupies such a role in our lives other than Jesus, we have chosen a secular messiah instead of the Lord.

> *To whose opinions (political, economic, or moral) does the media appeal as a "chosen one" in an effort to guide your beliefs?*
>
> *For whom would you reduce your prayer life in order to spend time with that person?*
>
> *How do you know when you have made someone into a false messiah?*
>
> *How do you know when someone is really anointed by God for a special task in the world? What is the task God has anointed you to do in His name?*

The passage then relates the mutual rebuke of Peter and Jesus. The term "rebuke" is strong and was used in previous situations of demonic possession. It is important to remember that the Gospels present the ministry of Jesus as a struggle between the Kingdom of God and that of Evil. To rebuke someone is to identify them as being on the side of evil. Following Peter's confession of Jesus as the Messiah, our Lord taught the necessity of His Suffering, Death, and Resurrection. Peter did not believe this reality to be part of God's plan and so Peter attempts to rebuke Jesus because he thinks that our Lord is actually expressing an evil statement and is on the wrong side of the struggle. In return, Jesus rebukes Peter and identifies him as "Satan" while instructing Peter to "get behind me". This rebuke is most instructive.

For Peter, it means that he has unwittingly become the voice of Satan who is tempting the Lord to reject the necessity of suffering as a result of faithful witness to the Father's will. Peter could not accept that the Messiah should suffer and die. Perhaps Peter did not want to follow such a Messiah because it could mean his own personal suffering. Whatever the reason, Peter clearly tries to deter Jesus from pursuing what our Lord knows to be His divinely appointed mission. In response to this temptation, Jesus instructs Peter to "get behind me". This command is not a banishment, but rather an instruction in discipleship. Peter can only be a disciple when he follows the Lord and not when he tries to lead the Lord (Mk 1:16–18). Jesus is identifying the problem by which Peter has ended up on the wrong side of the struggle between the Kingdom of God and Evil: Peter tried to lead without first following. This is a very important lesson for us as disciples. Sometimes we find ourselves in situations of leadership, and it can be easy to forget that we are first and foremost disciples. We can lead as only we follow. Before anyone can be an apostle who leads others, that person must first be a disciple who is constantly following Jesus. When we try to become a leader of others without following the Lord, we risk seeking our own will rather than the will of God. That erroneous pursuit of self-will means that we can end up on the wrong side of the struggle between the Kingdom of God and Evil.

Following Jesus means that we are willing to go wherever the Lord leads. That willingness requires following the Lord even when it means persecution and suffering as a result of witnessing our faith. An old story is told about Peter fleeing the city of Rome to avoid martyrdom at the hands of civil leaders. On his way out of the city, he encounters the Risen Lord and Peter asks him, "*Quo vadis?*" (Where are you going?), to which the Lord replied, "*Romam eo iterum crucifigit*" (I am going to Rome to be crucified again). After hearing this, the story says that Peter gained courage, turned around, and returned to the city where he was eventually crucified upside down.[30] In this gospel passage we see that Peter did not want Jesus to accept suffering and death because Peter did not want to embrace those things in his life. The cross is the inevitable consequence of faithful witness. It is our natural aversion to suffering, rejection, and persecution that tempts us to not follow Jesus when discipleship begins to require sacrifice.

> *What part of my life am I afraid to lose if I make a radical commitment to follow Jesus?*

---

30. See [Apocryphal] Acts of Peter, *Vercelli Acts*, XXXV.

What am I holding onto with such attachment that I am
not free to follow where the Lord leads?
What sacrifice am I prepared to make for the sake of fol-
lowing Jesus?
How do I try to find alternative methods of resolving situ-
ations so I do not have to face persecution or rejection as a
result of Christian witness?
Is there a cross in my life that I need to bear today?
When are you tempted to interpret an experience of suffer-
ing as something that is necessarily evil?

Twenty-Fifth Sunday in Ordinary Time

O ur Scripture passage comes from the Gospel of Mark 9:30–37. This text contains a very specific and important teaching on the source of greatness in the Kingdom of God. It also contains an enduring caution on the destructive effects of competition and self-seeking in the life of the Church. Let's study this passage in greater detail to understand how it can help us better live our lives as disciples who seek to be great in the eyes of God.

The passage begins with Jesus instructing the disciples on His Passion, Death and Resurrection that will take place in Jerusalem. In response to our Lord's teaching we are told that the disciples failed to understand and were afraid to ask him anything. That is an intriguing response to our Lord's teaching and worthy of our study. The failure to understand is probably not in regards to what Jesus will experience, as this is the second time that our Lord has informed them of His pending Suffering, Death, and Resurrection. Rather, the failure to understand most likely refers to the disciples' inability to comprehend the practical implications of our Lord's Passion for their own lives. The Passion of Jesus is not meant to be something our Lord experiences as everyone else watches. The Passion of Jesus is something we are meant to live out as we follow Him in His sacrificial and selfless love for others. The disciples did not understand how they might be called to follow in that way, and so we see their incomprehension manifesting itself in bickering and competing against each other.

The other interesting element we are told is that the disciples were afraid to ask Jesus anything. Their fear takes on new meaning in light of their incomprehension and indicates that the disciples did not even want to know what the suffering of Jesus had to do with them. That is intentional ignorance. Jesus offered them privileged insights into discipleship, and they chose to not understand or apply those insights to their lives. Because of their failure to conform themselves to our Lord's death and resurrection, they may not be able to accept the challenges of faith that will come their way as Jesus enters Jerusalem and ascends the Cross of Calvary. Their intentional failure to seek understanding is offered to us as a negative example of discipleship. Such willful ignorance has actually caused them to become distanced from Jesus even as they accompany Him on the way to Jerusalem. The "way" is more than a geographical journey; it is actually the spiritual journey of each disciple.

This passage challenges us to consider how human weakness, fear of sacrifice, and complacency of faith can cause us to fail to understand the meaning of Jesus' passion for our lives as well. Disciples are people who constantly seek to understand the events of their lives through the mystery of the Death and Resurrection of Jesus so as to faithfully interpret and respond to those events. Oftentimes, however, we can fail to understand how the Death and Resurrection of Jesus has any meaning for the situations we face. In such moments, we are like the disciples. We can also find ourselves avoiding opportunities for faith enrichment, the Sacrament of Confession, and discipleship formation because we don't want to even know how those experiences might affect us or challenge us.

> *What event or experience most gives meaning to your life?*
> *When is the message of Jesus difficult for you to understand?*
> *Of the three most difficult situations you are now facing, how can the mystery of Jesus'*
> *Passion, Death, and Resurrection give you understanding, direction, and encouragement?*
> *What ministry experiences (or Sacraments) do you avoid because you are uncomfortable or "afraid" of them?*
> *In what area of your life do you find it most convenient not to ask questions of faith or seek better understanding of moral principles?*
> *How can fear keep us from experiencing the consolation and friendship of Jesus?*

When Jesus and the disciples arrived at the house in Capernaum, our Lord asked them what they were arguing about on the way. We are then told that they were silent because their discussion was about who was the greatest. The use of the term "argue" indicates a hostile interaction rather than a respectful discussion. There are two important lessons Mark wants us to gain from this moment in the story. The first lesson concerns the way in which Jesus' suffering is perpetuated in the life of the Church. The Body of Christ, the Church, continues to suffer when its members argue and compete against one another in destructive pursuits for honor, privilege, and power. The fact that the disciples were now in the "house" at Capernaum connects their discussion with issues related to the house or Church experience of the first century (known as *domus ecclesiae)*. Indeed, the Spirit of Christ always suffers when unhealthy dissentions and divisions arise in the Church and cause disharmony, alienation, humiliation, and hurt.

The second lesson concerns that envy which gives rise to competitions for greatness. According to the values of the world, great people are those who have power, wealth, influence, and the respect of others. When we allow these values to govern our lives as disciples, we end up comparing ourselves to those around us in order to see who is "greater". This concern with other people's accomplishments and status can lead us to put others down in an effort to make ourselves look better. It can also evoke sadness in us when we see another's success or good fortune. This attitude of envy is destructive to the individual Christian soul and to the Christian community as a whole. As disciples, our true dignity is found primarily in our relationship with Jesus Christ. What we own, what we do, and who we know should be relatively unimportant when compared with being a friend of Jesus. In moments of doubt or insecurity we tend to grasp for false assurances of our worth. Envy was disintegrating the disciples both in terms of their collective communion and their individual integrity.

As Christians who want to be faithful disciples of Jesus, we need to learn from the experience of these early followers of the Lord so as to overcome the mistakes they made. When members of the Church (the Body of Christ) argue and compete in destructive ways, we end up hurting the Spirit of Christ in our midst. Also, when disciples begin to base their security on anything other than their relationship with Jesus, we become susceptible to the erosive envy that focuses on other people's lives rather than the life to which Jesus calls us to live. It is natural to desire greatness rather than lowliness or powerlessness. Certainly this message had particular meaning for Mark's community as they were undergoing the first persecution of the Christian Church in Rome. Undoubtedly they wanted to be "great" in a way that would allow them to avoid suffering and death rather than be vulnerable and faithful. It was tempting for Christians of the first century to seek false security when their faith was tested. It's certainly true for us today as well.

> *How does the Body of Christ, the Church, suffer today because of arguing and competing among its members?*
> *Who in the world suffers most because some people desire to be better than everyone else?*
> *How does the competition for greatness among members hurt a faith community?*
> *For which false assurances of worth and security do people tend to grasp today?*
> *How has your experience of envy been destructive to your personal happiness and your ability to rejoice in another's good fortune?*

In response to the disciples' errant topic of conversation, Jesus offers an authoritative teaching on the true nature of greatness within the Christian community. We know this message is offered as an authoritative instruction for the Church because our Lord "sits down" and assumes the formal role of a Teacher. Our Lord's teaching has two aspects to it. The first aspect concerns a redefinition of greatness. Our Lord replaces the secular criteria of greatness (stated above) with that of humble service. Great people in the time of Jesus were served by others and given the first places of honor at gatherings. Jesus tells the disciples that the Christian community is to value and esteem those who serve rather than those who are served and to honor those who assume the last place rather than those who seek the first place. This message is as challenging today as it was for the people of Jesus' time. Our secular culture tells us that greatness is found in our positions, possessions, and persons with whom we associate. Such secular pursuits are to be specifically identified and intentionally rejected when they infiltrate and infect the life of the Church. We must consciously seek to esteem and honor those who assume positions of service and humility.

The second aspect of greatness concerns the ability to receive one who is like a child in the name of Jesus. This aspect of greatness requires some explanation in order to fully understand the challenge it presents to us as disciples. When Jesus placed a child in the center of the group and embraced the child, our Lord was demonstrating that a simple and powerless individual (a child) is worthy of acceptance, respect, and love. Association with children in the time of Jesus could not contribute anything towards an individual's worldly greatness. Children were powerless and had little social standing in the adult world. For this reason, ancient Roman authors provided little information about children prior to adolescence. Jesus is teaching the disciples that real greatness is in the ability to receive Him when they receive one such as a child (powerless and insignificant in terms of social status).

Christian servants can minister and serve others because they have the eyes of faith that allow them to see the presence of Christ in the least of His brothers and sisters. That ability to see Christ in others, especially the powerless, vulnerable, and those lacking social status, is a hallmark of a truly great disciple. It is this faithful recognition of Jesus in others that distinguishes a Christian disciple from a mere social worker.

> *Who do you think is an example of Christian greatness according to the teaching of Jesus in this passage?*
> *How can a faith community recognize and esteem people who serve others?*
> *How can secular values of greatness hurt the Church today?*
> *Who are the simple and powerless ones in your midst in whom you can serve the presence of Jesus?*
> *When is it difficult for you to recognize the presence of Jesus in another person?*
> *What can help you develop the eyes of faith that recognize the presence of Christ in others?*

Finally, let us take a moment to reflect on these words by St Thomas Aquinas:

There is in man something great, which he possesses through
the gift of God; and something defective, which accrues to
him through the weakness of nature. Accordingly magnanimity makes a man deem himself worthy of great things in
consideration of the gifts he holds from God: thus if his soul
is endowed with great virtue, magnanimity makes him tend
to perfect works of virtue; and the same is to be said of the
use of any other good, such as science or external fortune. On
the other hand, humility makes a man think little of himself
in consideration of his own deficiency.[31]

---

31. St Thomas Aquinas, *Summa Theologiae*, II-II, q. 129, a. 3, ad 4.

TWENTY-SIXTH SUNDAY IN ORDINARY TIME

Our Scripture passage comes from the Gospel of Mark 9:38–43, 45, and 47–48. In this reading Jesus continues to address His disciples' destructive and mistaken pursuits of worldly greatness while at the same time offering a challenging instruction on the necessity of sacrifice and the purpose of faith. These instructions have a great deal to offer us as disciples as well.

The disciples bring to Jesus what they falsely believe to be a problem: Other people, who were not among the inner group of followers, were healing in the name of Jesus. Jesus explains to them that this situation is a blessing and not a problem. The problem was not in the healing but in the disciple's possessiveness and defensiveness of their ministry. The disciples were exemplifying the unhealthy thirst for power and control that would stifle and thwart the good works of others if those works challenged their authority or encroached on their mission. Their objection raises the question as to why they themselves were not trying to heal the possessed man in the first place. Perhaps they were envious that someone else was doing what they should have been doing.

It is interesting, too, that the disciples objected to the actions of the healer because "he did not follow us." They seem to demonstrate little concern for the one who needed healing while they were overly concerned and possessive about their own status as leaders. Their objection makes us wonder what their ultimate priority was—that people follow Jesus or that people follow them. These attitudes can be destructive in the life of the Church today as much as they were destructive in the lives of the disciples nearly two thousand years ago. Sometimes people involved in parish ministries can be very possessive about their authority and field of responsibility which might lead them to be resentful and antagonistic towards others who offer to assist with those efforts.

Also, the feelings of jealously and the pursuit of exclusive power and control can lead to envy when others succeed in their ministry efforts. Such feelings can even cause those involved in ministry to undermine and sabotage the noble efforts of others who desire to promote the Gospel. The battle for power and control can be fought with rules and regulations, budgeting, facility allocation, slander, malicious comments, and appeal to false loyalty. The spirit of possessiveness and defensiveness is recognizable any time we feel threatened by another's success or resentful when God's will is accomplished through another's ministry. As disciples, it is important to realize that such feelings reveal a need for conversion and repentance so that we can promote the work of the Holy Spirit wherever, whenever, and through whomever God wants. Such an attitude will lead us to care for those in need rather than seek a mistaken greatness based on the ability to control rather than the willingness to cooperate.

> *The disciples were upset that some people did not follow them, while Jesus reminds them that being a disciple means first and foremost following Him. How can we be tempted to want people to "follow us" today instead of rejoicing when they follow the Lord?*
>
> *How can the desire for power and control give rise to envy and subversive actions in your home, marriage, and even within a faith community?*
>
> *In what ways can self-concern lead those in authority to ignore the needs of the suffering (the "little ones")?*
>
> *What are the weapons people use to wage their battles for power and control?*
>
> *How do you know when you are giving in to the same temptation for self-preservation or self-promotion, power, and control that was manifested by the disciples, and what can you do to seek conversion and repentance for these destructive and divisive desires?*
>
> *How can the power of evil use the human desires for power and control to thwart the work of God and lead disciples astray?*

Jesus then gives the Church an important governing principle in its relationship with the larger world: Those who are not against us are for us. The fact that the healer was acting in the name of Jesus also warrants our attention and reflection. The Holy Spirit can work in a mysterious way to share the grace of Christ with all human beings. God is not limited by our expectations or understandings when it comes to His mercy and love. All people are invited to know, love, and serve the Lord. This invitation is commonly known as the Universal Call to Salvation. It does not mean that all people will respond to this call or that all paths are equal. Rather, it acknowledges that God's grace can work in mysterious ways, even in the hearts of those who do not know Christ so that they respond to the voice of their conscience (Holy Spirit) and do what is good.

When Christians encounter goodness, charity, and other values of the Gospel in non-Christian environments, they should interpret these positive values as a cooperation with the Gospel. As such, these actions are good because they are done "in the name of Christ". This is an important principle for the Christian understanding of salvation. Namely, that all grace comes from Jesus Christ and that even those who "do not follow us" can participate in that grace, although in an imperfect and unknown way. According to our Lord's instruction, people of good will should be seen as co-workers in the mission of the Gospel, and their efforts should take place unhindered by Christians. This teaching does not in any way diminish the importance of evangelization which seeks to introduce all persons to Jesus who is the only source of the grace and life inspires their good actions. Rather, it acknowledges how those who do not know Christ can benefit from a real cooperation with the Holy Spirit and merit from their good efforts (see Mt 25:40). Ultimately, cooperation itself can become an effective means of evangelization in such circumstances.

Who is fulfilling the values of the Gospel today in a secular context or through a non-Christian religious environment? How can a person's good actions be an opportunity to introduce them to Jesus (evangelization)?

Who is healing, confronting evil, and alleviating the suffering of others?

The disciples of Jesus will be truly great when they can recognize and rejoice any time the mission of the Gospel is being carried out. How does this statement challenge you to become great?

How can people of a particular faith confession attempt to diminish and dismiss the good works that are being accomplished in other faith confessions?

The next area of greatness Jesus emphasizes is the faithful sacrifice needed to care for the little ones in our midst. To be a great disciple means both preventing the scandal that causes others to lose faith and being willing to make the necessary amendments of life to avoid occasions of sin. To demonstrate this point Jesus uses the dramatic example of removing one's hand, foot, and eye. There can be various levels on which this teaching can be interpreted. The image of a body can either refer to an individual person and the need to amend their personal causes of weakness, but the image can also refer to the corporate body of the Church and the need to remove or discipline members who are causing scandal and serious sin in the community (the image of a body was used as a communal and political metaphor in ancient times). This teaching on the necessity of sacrifice was commonly known in the time of Jesus. The Babylonian Talmud had similar metaphors involving amending one's hands, feet, and eyes so as to avoiding certain sexual sins.[32]

However one wishes to apply the images, it should be remembered that Jesus is speaking metaphorically and not about physical mutilation. The ancient audience would have known that our Lord was speaking in metaphors. Nonetheless, the Lord is addressing the need for real and ready sacrifice on the part of disciples when it comes to avoiding those things that lead us astray and into sin. Disciples who want to be great must be people who can humbly acknowledge their need to amend their lives so as to avoid those temptations, which play on their natural weaknesses. Greatness, then, is not in doing what we want but in living as God wants. Such a life inspires others' faith and strengthens the little ones, while a life of self-will and sin scandalizes little ones.

---

32. See *Babylonian Talmud: Translation and Commentary*, trans. By J. Neusner (Peabody, MA: Hendrickson, 2011).

How can people be tempted to retain un-Christian practices while claiming to be a disciple?

What sacrifices have you made as a consequence of your faith in Jesus?

What sin most scandalizes Christians today?

How can a faith community help its members have the courage and tools to identify occasions of sin, and amend their lives to avoid those occasions?

What other motivations might people have that cause them to sacrifice besides witness of Faith and discipleship?

The last thing Jesus addresses in this passage is the fundamental purpose of faith when He contrasts eternal life with Gehenna (an image for Hell). It is this stark alternative that motivates us to embrace sacrifice, especially the painful sacrifices necessary to avoid situations of sin on a personal, communal, and institutional level. It is also this contrast that motivates us to seek above all the mission of the Gospel rather than our own personal kingdoms. Finally, it is this contrast that ultimately reminds us why we follow Jesus and carry the cross of faithful discipleship. The purpose of the Christian life is to enter the Kingdom of God. If we settle for anything less than that goal for any reason, we have wasted the gift of faith and distorted the meaning of discipleship. There can be lots of reasons why people pursue religious experiences, membership in faith communities, and works of mercy, but if any of those reasons are anything less than eternal life with God, we have pursued a mistaken goal and lost the focus that is necessary to embrace difficult moments of sacrifice. Faith is not a sentimental ornament in a Christian's life; faith must be the primary driving principle that effectively leads us to God.

Is following Jesus Christ the core of your being and the fundamental motivation for your decisions and actions each day?

What else can a person choose as the core of their being or the fundamental motivation for their decisions and actions each day?

Why is a religion of convenience unable to lead a person to the greatness Jesus describes in this passage?

TWENTY-SEVENTH SUNDAY IN ORDINARY TIME

O ur Scripture passage comes from the Gospel of Mark 10:2–16. This reading presents Jesus' response to the Pharisees who question Him on the lawfulness of divorce. Rather than respond to their challenge with a simple answer, Jesus provides a teaching that offers guiding principles of discipleship for Christians of all times. Let's look more closely at this interesting passage to see what lessons it offers for us.

One of the first things to note is that the question posed to Jesus was clearly identified as a test. The Pharisees were attempting to draw Jesus into an issue that was pervasive, explosive and divisive especially in the political and cultural world of our Lord. Rather than shying away from the test, Jesus responds in a way that authentically and challengingly reveals the divine will of God. In order to understand the controversial intensity of the issue of divorce, we should remember that John the Baptist was beheaded for his verbal opposition to the divorce of Herod Antipas and his subsequent remarriage to his brother's (former) wife. Now the Pharisees were confronting Jesus on the same controversial issue while the Lord was still in Herod's dangerous territory!

There was no unified opinion on the issue of divorce in the ancient Jewish world, although some scriptural texts of the Old Testament do explicitly oppose it (see Mal 2:16). Some groups prohibited it (Essenes) while other groups did allow it and focused their discussion on the various possible grounds by which it could be allowed. The School of Hillel taught that a man could divorce his wife even if she burned his dinner, while the Rabbi Akiba taught that divorce was permitted if a man found another woman more beautiful.[33] Divorce in the Roman world was also pervasive and

---

33. Retrieved August 29, 2015 by J. Newmark, "The Benefit of Irreconcilable Differences": http://njjewishnews.com/article/28181/the-benefit-of-irreconcilable-differences#.VeHYGlbg5Vt

permissive. Seneca was quoted as saying, "Is there any woman who blushes at divorce, now that certain distinguished and aristocratic women reckon their years, not by consuls but by the number of their husbands? They leave home in order to marry, and marry in order to divorce."[34] It is in the context of this cultural and religious atmosphere that Jesus responds by reminding the Pharisees of the purpose of Moses' regulations regarding divorce: They were intended to reduce the harm already being caused rather than to endorse the acceptance of a practice. Moses required the writing of a decree of divorce in recognition of the people's hardness of heart and not in witness to the divine will (see Dt 24:1–4). In light of this controversial situation, it is worth reflecting on how our current society views marriage and how disciples are to respond.

> *What is the difference between something that is commanded, permitted, or regulated?*
> *How is our current secular world similar to the ancient world of Jesus and the Roman Empire when it comes to marriage and divorce?*
> *What aspects of marriage are controversial today and how are disciples "tested" to draw them into that controversy in an unfavorable way?*
> *How can disciples today safeguard their marriages against the destructive influences of the cultural world in which we live?*
> *How do disciples know when they have unwittingly accepted the destructive practices and perceptions of a secular world?*

After clarifying the reason why Moses regulated the practice of divorce (hardness of heart), Jesus then goes on to remind the audience of God's original intention and will. The texts of Genesis 1:27 and 2:24 form the basis of our Lord's response. It is important to note that this divine intention is expressed prior to the introduction of sin in Genesis 3:1–24. It is one thing for Moses to regulate what was happening because of the people's hardness of heart, but it is quite another thing to fulfill what God's perfect intention is for

---

34. Seneca, *On Benefits* 3:16—as quoted by Hopkins, K. *Death and Renewal: Volume 2: Sociological Studies in Roman History* (New York: Cambridge University Press, 1983), p. 94.

humanity. By answering in this way, Jesus is giving disciples of all times an important insight into how we are to act in the various circumstances we face. Rather than responding in a way that conforms to the practices around us, or settling for what is permissible, disciples should strive to fulfill in all things the ultimate will of God from the beginning. The presence of sin always weakens our ability to fully live out God's will for our lives, but the grace of Christ has the power to sustain us even in our weakness (see Rom 5:20).

When we pause in the midst of a crisis or controversy and seek God's original intention for humanity, it becomes easier to understand the ways in which we have deviated from the Lord's will. Our starting point for seeking resolution to any issue should be in the original (that is, Pre-Fall) will of God. It is only when we strive to fulfill God's will in its originality that we can hope to live as faithful disciples and be guided through the stormy waters of human weakness. This possible restoration and pursuit of the original will of God is one of the graces Jesus offers us as His disciples. The Gospel of Mark starts with the word "Beginning" (Mk 1:1, compare Jn 1:1), which alludes to the Book of Genesis and indicates that the ministry of Jesus will initiate a new creation so that those who follow the Lord (disciples) can share once again in the divinely intended way of life. Humanity, divided by sin, can become united with the grace of Christ, which overcomes all things. The union of husband and wife who become one flesh is the perfect symbol for the fullness of reconciliation and reunification our Lord desires for all people. Situations of human weakness may warrant pastoral accommodation and regulation, but such exceptions should not form the foundation or vision of Christian life or marriage.

How can the practice of remembering God's original intention help bring clarity to complex situations you are facing? In what ways are you tempted to live a faith life that is conformed to the practices around you, and how does the practice of recalling God's intention for your life challenge you to aspire for greater holiness?

For what situation in your life do you wish you could go back to "the beginning" and start over in the right way?

*How can a faith community show pastoral sensitivity for sit-
uations of human weakness and failure while also uphold-
ing the divine intention for human marriage?*

A further development in Jesus' teaching about the nature of marriage occurs when the Lord states, "What God has joined together
let no man separate." That statement reminds Christian disciples
that marriage is to be understood primarily as a manifestation
of divine will and not as mere human selection. This elevation of
the nature of marriage is something that surpassed the mindset
of Jesus' time. It should be remembered that marriage existed as
a natural bond between two people for thousands of years before
Jesus. This natural bond of human relationship was sometimes
used to seal national alliances, family economies and other strategic
partnerships. Most of these marriages were contracts arranged by
the parents with the bride and groom having little to do with the
process. The natural bond of marriage also can exist when a man
and woman freely choose to seal their love for one another as a
committed relationship. Such marriages expressing the natural
bond continue to occur throughout the world today with varying
frequency depending upon a specific culture.

What makes the marriage between two Christians unique and
distinct is that they share in a supernatural bond, not just a natural
bond. The marriage of Christians is the fulfillment and manifestation of God's will for two people. Thus, Christian marriage is
not so much based on human selection of a spouse but on human
participation in and discernment of God's selection of a spouse.
For this reason Christian marriage is both a vocation (calling from
God) and a Sacrament (sharing in God's grace). In a Christian
marriage the couple is called by God to manifest the very self-giving, creative, redemptive, sanctifying, and sacrificial love of Jesus
in their lives with one another. In doing so, the couple themselves
become the ministers of the Sacrament to one another as the love
Jesus has for the Church is mirrored in their marriage. This is an
understanding of marriage that exceeds that of the mere natural
bond. When Sacramental marriage truly exists as it is intended, it
is indissoluble. The permanence of marriage is not based on the
strength of the couple's commitment but on the unchanging will
of God who destined the spouses for each other.

By embracing and faithfully living out the commitment to love one another in the example of Jesus, a Christian married couple enters into an irrevocable covenant with one another and God. This covenantal understanding is very different from the contractual understanding involved in a marriage based only on the natural bond. Because a Christian marriage involves the presence of God, the couple is called to embody and reflect holiness in their lives and mission. Given the cultural atmosphere of divorce in Jesus' time, our Lord's insistence on the permanence of a Sacramental marriage was more radical and demanding then than it is now. Saint Paul reinforced this insistence on the permanence of marriage (see 1 Cor 7:10). The Church faces the great challenge of preserving the Lord's teaching on the permanence of Christian marriage and ministering to people who have suffered the painful and damaging effects of divorce. Jesus reveals that Christian marriage is a participation in the divine will so that those disciples preparing to marry will do so with awareness, prayerfulness, intentionality, honesty, and resolve.

> *What does a person look for in a spouse when they pursue marriage as a partnership?*
> *What does a person look for in a spouse when they pursue marriage as a loving union?*
> *What does a person look for in a spouse when they pursue marriage as a divinely-intended Sacrament?*
> *How can a faith community help couples understand marriage as a Sacrament (covenant with God) and not just a natural bond (contract)?*

The passage ends with what appears to be an unrelated scene of the disciples preventing children from coming to Jesus and of our Lord's acceptance and blessing of the little ones. However, the situational context of this teaching on the need to welcome children should not be underestimated in terms of its connection to the teaching on marriage. Namely, welcoming children is a natural part of the mission of Christian marriage. With this contextual interpretation in mind, we can better understand why our Lord grew "angry" with the disciples for preventing the children from coming to Him. We can also understand why our Lord embraced them and blessed them when others rebuked them. One of the essential missions of marriage is that of welcoming children into the world and bringing them to the Lord so as to become disciples. By fulfilling this mission, both the world and the Church are enriched. This teaching is important because not all married couples welcome children in acceptance of the divine will for Christian marriage. This was true in the ancient pagan world of the Roman Empire in which Mark's Gospel was written. One of the Roman poets wrote, "She who wants to appear beautiful, aborts" (Latin: *Nunc uterum vitiat quae vult formosa videri*).[35] This observation indicates that some Roman women considered children to be a threat to their beauty and terminated pregnancies rather than risk anything that might diminish their attractiveness. So predominant was this hedonistic attitude and destructive action against children that Seneca actually praised his mother for having three children when he wrote:

> Shamelessness, the greatest evil of our age has never attracted you, as it has the majority of women ... you have never been ashamed about the number of your children, as if they taunted you with your age; unlike other women whose beauty is their only recommendation, you have never tried to conceal your pregnancy as though it were an indecent burden; nor have you crushed the hope of children already conceived inside you.[36]

Musonius Rufus further commented in the first century AD, "What appears terrible to me is that some people, not even having the excuse of poverty, but being well-off and some even rich, nevertheless presume not to nurture their children, so that the children born previously may be better off. They impiously contrive the prosperity of their children by the murder of their siblings; that is,

35. Ovid, "Nux, 23" in *Art of Love and Other Poems,* Loeb Classical Library 232, Ovid vol. II, Trans. By J. H. Mozley (Cambridge, MA: Harvard University Press, 1929), p. 294.

36. Seneca. "To Helvia, 16" in *Minor Dialogues Together with the Dialog "On Clemency"* Book XI; Trans. by Stewart, A. (Cambridge: Trinity College, 1900), pp. 320–352; or see Hopkins, K. *Death and Renewal: Volume 2: Sociological Studies in Roman History* (New York: Cambridge University Press, 1983), p. 96.

they destroy their brothers and sisters, so that the earlier children may have a greater share of the inheritance."[37]

The actions of preventing children continued well into the early Church so that Ambrose of Milan (Easter Sermons 5:58) and Caesarius of Arles (5th century) both fought against the killing of children through exposure or abortion. These ancient testimonies bear witness that children were oftentimes falsely perceived as liabilities that threatened the superficial pleasures of life. The same restrictive attitude towards children can be present in our culture today when married couples falsely perceive children to be a threat to their freedom, pleasure, and finances. Jesus' words of anger and reprimand to such an attitude are a constant reminder that the most vulnerable in our midst warrant our greatest protection and care. This passage reminds us that children are an essential part of the divinely intended purpose of marriage and never separate from it. Indeed, disciples must let the children come to Jesus and be who are born into loving Christian families that welcome them and foster their growth in faith and virtue.

> *How do couples today perceive children as a threat to their desired lifestyle?*
>
> *How can a faith community help parents bring their children to Jesus so as to become disciples?*
>
> *What would Jesus say to our society regarding our attitude towards children?*
>
> *What are some of the obstacles that prevent children from effectively encountering Jesus today?*
>
> *As you pray over the above reflections, how do you think the Sacrament of Marriage and the openness to children have been diminished, undermined, and damaged by our current secular values of materialism, libertarianism, hedonism, consumerism, utilitarianism, relativism—and by our disposable society?*
>
> *What Christian values can serve as anecdotes for these infectious social ills?*

---

37. M. Rufus, Frag. 15b, Leipzig: Ed. O. Hense, 1905; as quoted by Hopkins, K. *Death and Renewal: Volume 2: Sociological Studies in Roman History* (New York: Cambridge University Press, 1983), p. 96.

TWENTY-EIGHTH SUNDAY IN ORDINARY TIME

O ur Scripture passage comes from the Gospel of Mark
10:17–30. The occasion of the rich man seeking eternal life
provides an opportunity for Jesus to present a radical and
enduring teaching on discipleship. This passage has a good deal to
say to us as we strive to progress along our own way of discipleship
even as Jesus met the man in today's reading while He was on His
way to Jerusalem.

The first thing to note about this passage is the well-developed
faith of the man seeking eternal life. The man's own journey of
discipleship was fairly advanced even as our Lord's journey was
advancing and He was drawing near to Jerusalem. This correlation
between Jesus' way and the man's way should not be overlooked.
We see the advanced state of the man's discipleship journey through
several key indications. For example, the man ran to Jesus, which
demonstrated that he was responding readily to the Lord's presence
and without regard to others' opinions (for adults in the ancient
world, running was something considered dishonorable). Also, the
man knelt before Jesus, which is a sign of reverence and homage.
Finally, the man addressed Jesus as "Good Teacher".

All these factors indicate that the man was responding correctly so far. Above all, he trusted that Jesus is the source of what is
"good" and not in his own ability to determine good for himself. The
man then posed his question to Jesus: "What must I do to inherit
eternal life?" This is a question he shouldn't have asked if he wasn't
prepared to receive the answer! The reader already knows from the
previous passage that eternal life is a gift and cannot be earned.
Here we have our first indication that something was disordered
in the man's discipleship: He was seeking to earn eternal life by
his own efforts. Still, his pursuit of eternal realities over temporal
realities is admirable and notable. Although he may be focused on
his own ability to achieve eternal life, at least he was focused on a

heavenly good as opposed to more wealth, the pursuit of power, or greater prestige in the eyes of others. Jesus then challenges the man to clarify why he addressed the Lord as "good" since God alone is good. Our Lord is most likely calling the man to deeper faith so that he will recognize in Jesus the presence of God and accept our Lord's response as the very Word of God.

When presented with the commandments, the man acknowledges that he has fulfilled all of these from his youth. However, fulfilling the commandments only means avoiding actions that harm others. Certainly it is good to avoid damaging actions towards others but it takes much more than that to be a disciple. At this point we see both how far advanced the man is in his discipleship and how far he has yet to go. He has already responded to the Lord's grace and diligently avoided harming others yet there is something that he lacks. It was in this moment that Jesus looked at him with love and invited the man to follow Him in a way that reflected our Lord's own way of life: sell what he has, give to the poor, and then engage in a life of ongoing radical discipleship. It is important to note that this invitation is made out of love and not harshness, indifference, or encroachment on the man's goodness. Jesus knows that the man is capable of greater and more profound discipleship, and our Lord readily invites him to that way of life. However, the man is unable to love as Jesus loves (by giving of himself in sacrificial generosity to others) and so he walks away sad.

His sadness was not caused by his many possessions but because he was not able to accept the challenging invitation Jesus had offered. Instead, the man clung to his sources of false security and chose to not love others (through sacrificial generosity to the poor) even as Jesus had loved him. Our Lord loves us in part because He desires to love others through us, and that requires our cooperation and sacrificial generosity to use the blessings we have received for the good of those in need. The man was able to avoid doing harm to others, but he could not bring himself to love others even as Jesus loved him. As a result his discipleship stopped and he no longer followed Jesus. This is a challenging story for all of us who are striving to follow the Lord. Like the man in this story, we may do well when following the Lord on our terms but falter when Jesus calls us to sacrificial generosity and radical discipleship. Such a moment is always decisive. Fortunately, God sometimes gives us second chances to do the right thing even when we initially falter.

> *As you think about this man's journey of discipleship, how does it help you to evaluate your own commitment to the Lord?*
>
> *How can disciples be tempted to settle for simply avoiding harm to others as the basis for their commitment to the Lord?*
>
> *When has Jesus invited you to leave behind something you treasure in order to follow Him?*
>
> *What are some of the false securities that can hold people back from being able to follow the Lord in freedom and radical commitment?*
>
> *How does the man's response of sadness (as opposed to joy) help you know when you are making the right decision of discipleship?*
>
> *When have you made great sacrifices to follow the Lord and experienced joy as a result?*

Next, Jesus offered a private instruction to the disciples on the danger of riches. It should be remembered that this teaching is a continuation of our Lord's instruction on the reversal of worldly standards of greatness that began in Mark 9:34 and has covered such themes as service (verses being served), relationships, and influence. Now our Lord addresses the inordinate attachment to wealth. In order to understand why the disciples were amazed by Jesus' teaching about the difficulty rich people will have entering the Kingdom of God, it is important to remember the religious and cultural view of wealth in the ancient Jewish world. Riches were commonly understood to be a sign of God's blessing, favor, and right relationship. The wealthy were the ones who had time and freedom to study the Law with leisure and to observe religious commandments in the smallest detail.

In light of that understanding, the disciples rightfully wondered who could be saved if not the wealthy since they seemed to have the greatest opportunity to live a life of study and faith practices. Jesus reminds the disciples that entering the Kingdom of God is difficult not only for the wealthy but for everyone. It is something that cannot be earned but can only be accepted as a gift. The reality is that no human can earn their admission into the Kingdom of God no matter what they do. As Saint James reminds us in his letter, "Every perfect gift is from above, coming down from the Father of lights (see James 1:17)." Whether wealthy or poor, admission to the Kingdom of God is a pure and gracious gift of God. What we can do is dispose ourselves to receive that good gift from God. The way in which we dispose ourselves properly is to reflect the values of the Kingdom in all parts of our lives. By conforming our lives to the Lord's will (including letting go of our false securities) we are opening ourselves to receive God's reign now and forever. However, when we resist God's reign and cling to our false securities, we are closing ourselves and cannot receive the Kingdom of Heaven now and forever. Thus, while we cannot earn the Kingdom, we can receive the Kingdom with the proper disposure. God can readily save anyone who is properly disposed to receive His grace.

> *Who are the people in our world whom we presume have privileged access to God's good graces?*
> *How do you know when someone is blessed by God (what external signs do you look for)?*
> *What does it mean for you to "reflect the values of the Kingdom of God" in your sacrificial generosity to others?*
> *In what parts of your life do you find it difficult to allow the Lord's reign?*
> *What values of our current society would the Lord challenge and reverse if He were to proclaim the Kingdom of God to us?*

The passage ends with Peter asking Jesus what will be the reward for those who have made a radical commitment to follow the Lord and have left behind their sources of security. Certainly Peter's question was motivated by his own sacrifice of leaving behind family and business on the shores of the Sea of Galilee. In response to this question about the rewards of discipleship Jesus offered a definitive teaching assuring Peter that his sacrifices were not in vain. In order to correctly understand our Lord's promises it is important to remember the situation of the early Church in which disciples saw themselves as members of the new Family of God. This new identity was important in light of the fact that many of Jesus' earliest followers had to face rejection by their own families in order to be the Lord's disciples. The Church was the environment in which disciples became a new family for one another as brothers and sisters. The Acts of the Apostles also relates how the early Church held all things in common (Acts 2:44 and 4:32).

It is in light of the situation of the early Church that we can interpret Jesus' response to Peter. Indeed, for those who leave behind everything to become our Lord's disciples, they will receive many more brothers and sisters and mothers in the Church as the Family of God. It is interesting to note that Jesus does not promise more "fathers"; some Scripture scholars think this exception is because disciples will have only one Father who is God. Also, because the Church is a community of love that holds all things in common, disciples will not only have one house but hundreds of houses as they share their belongings with each other. Jesus is assuring Peter that his sacrifices are not in vain; rather, Peter will be rewarded with a new family and common goods. In addition to these blessings, Jesus also assures Peter that he will receive persecution as part of his reward. This promise may strike us as strange, but it is important to remember that Mark's Gospel was written during the time of the first Christian persecutions under the Emperor Nero. True disciples will receive a new family, and they will also be given the courage and strength to bear the cross of suffering. Anyone can receive rewards that are pleasant, but only a truly committed person can accept consequences that are sacrificial. The acceptance of persecutions, then, is a sign of true discipleship and that a person is authentically following Jesus. Jesus states that such an experience is actually a reward that lets a person know they are on the right path. In the second century, before he was martyred, St. Polycarp approached his earthly end with these words, "I bless you Father for judging me worthy of this hour, so that in the company of the martyrs I may share the cup of Christ."[38]

---

38. P. Pirlo, "St. Polycarp" in *My First Book of Saints* (Paranaque City: Sons of Holy Mary Immaculate—Quality Catholic Publications, 1997), pp. 58–59.

When have you experienced persecution or rejection as a confirmation that you were on the right path of discipleship?
What relationships have you had to leave behind in order to follow the Lord?
What new relationships has God opened in your life as a result of your discipleship?
How do Christians today hold things in common as a sign of their communal love and care for one another?
What is most rewarding for you as a disciple?
What do you think was Peter's reaction when Jesus Promised persecution?

TWENTY-NINTH SUNDAY IN ORDINARY TIME

Our Scripture passage comes from the Gospel of Mark 10:35–45. In order to understand this passage, it is necessary to remember that, in the verses immediately preceding it (Mk 10:32–34), Jesus issued the third prediction of His pending Passion, Death, and Resurrection in Jerusalem. It is, then, immediately following the announcement of suffering, that the disciples James and John seek privileged positions of honor. Let's look at this passage to see what instruction we can gain for our lives of faith.

This passage is located at a very significant place in Mark's Gospel. As such, the very context of the story contributes to its understanding and becomes an important interpretive key with which to unlock its meaning. In particular, this story is a continuation of previous teachings regarding the damaging pursuit of mistaken greatness. Because there are several significant lessons to be gained from this account, it is worth considering each element in detail.

- The request for privileged positions of honor by James and John follows immediately after Jesus' third prediction of His Passion. As we saw in the reflection on Mark 9:30–37, this contextualization is a commentary on how the Passion of Jesus continues when members of the Church give in to similar competitive ambitious pursuits of exclusive and privileged positions. James and John demonstrated an unhealthy ambition that sought inordinate honor at others' expense. This passage is a warning to the Church reminding us that those who pursue such ambitions can cause the Body of Christ (the Church) to suffer. While Pope Francis and his predecessors have spoken strongly against such manifestations of ambition, like careerism, clericalism, and other "diseases" that afflict the Body of

Christ,[39] we need to remember that the inordinate thirst for prestige and honor through positions of ministry can afflict the Church at all levels—from the volunteers who coordinate coffee and donuts to the members of ministry teams and advisory councils. No one is immune from this temptation whether they be parishioners, deacons, priests, bishops, or even the Pope himself. When anyone seeks a position of ministry or leadership because of how it honors or benefits them personally then destructive ambition has entered their soul and the Body of Christ always suffers.

- It is also significant that James and John approach Jesus twice in their request. First they ask the Lord to do whatever they ask and then they ask for selfish pursuits. Faith is always distorted when we try to convince God to do what we want rather than seeking God's will for our lives so we can do what the Lord wants. At this point in Mark's Gospel Jesus has drawn close to Jerusalem, and His journey is almost fulfilled. We see in the question of James and John that the disciples have much to learn before their journey of discipleship is completed. In particular, they still have not yet learned the proper relationship of faith and disposition of servanthood that will allow them to bear the Cross with Jesus. Disciples are to follow the Lord's lead and not try to lead the Lord where they want to go. We can be tempted in our faith to approach God in the same way that James and John approached Jesus. This passage reminds us that authentic growth in discipleship is marked by increased surrender to God and not the desire for increased control over God.

- Although the request of James and John was for future glory (presuming they were referring to a heavenly place of honor similar to that described in Rev 4–5), they may have been seeking temporal glory as well. The Dead Sea Scrolls reveal that the Essene community had a highly-structured society that was based in part on how they believed the messianic banquet would be ordered in the Kingdom of God. The actual meals of the community and the relative seating of its members

---

39. Pope Francis, *Presentation of the Christmas Greetings to the Roman Curia* (22 Dec 2014).

reflected that heavenly order. James and John may have been hoping for similar places of temporal honor based on future positions in the Heavenly Kingdom. This reprimand may be a caution to the Church to avoid similar temptations of honor and prestige based on position and expressed in ceremony. As Jesus will make clear later in this passage, positions within the Church are for service to God's people and not for the benefit of the one who receives that position.

• The remedy Jesus offers for ambition is that of faithful suffering when He asks James and John if they can drink the cup He drinks and can be Baptized in the Baptism He will experience. That is the ultimate question of discipleship. It reminds the disciples that greatness is not found in the selfish pursuit of honorable positions or privileged status, but rather in the ability to faithfully endure hardship and suffering for the sake of Christ. The Old Testament uses the image of a cup as a symbol of suffering and wrath (Jer 25:15–29, Ps 75:8, Is 51:17, 22). Jesus will drink of this cup at the Last Supper in Mark 14:25 and in the Garden of Gethsemane in Mark 14:36. To drink from the cup of Jesus, then, is to share in our Lord's very suffering on Calvary rendered present to us in the Eucharist. This symbol of suffering is further developed because James and John asked to be placed, one at Jesus' left and one at Jesus' right, when our Lord enters His Kingdom. What they did not realize is that the Kingship of Jesus is established on the cross of Calvary, and in Mark 15:27 we are told that two bandits were placed "one on His right and one on His left". The lesson of this teaching is clear: Greatness for Christian disciples is in the ability to share in the Cross of Christ.

• Jesus' comment about Baptism is similar to that of the cup and connected to it. As Saint Paul reminds us in Romans 6:3–4, we were Baptized into the Death of Christ. Christian Baptism receives its life-giving sacramental power from the Cross of Christ. Jesus is asking James and John the fundamental question of discipleship: Can they follow the Lord in His suffering and not just in His glory? They approached the Lord with a desire for greatness and Jesus has taught them the standard of true greatness: Greatness is not based on where they sit but on how closely they can remain to the Lord when it involves suffering and persecution.

As you reflect on the exchange between James, John, and Jesus, which aspect challenges you in a particularly personal way and why?
How can positions of ministry today become a source of competition for power or prestige?
Why is suffering such an effective remedy for unhealthy ambition?
When do you pray for positions of power or prestige?

The next part of this passage conveys the indignant response of the other ten disciples towards James and John as well as Jesus' instruction on the necessity of serving others. We can easily understand the very human reaction of the other ten disciples towards James and John. The two had just attempted to secure honor to the exclusion of the rest and their request was rejected. In a certain sense, James and John may have been humbled by Jesus but the other ten were seeking to humiliate them. Sometimes people can be frivolously fascinated by the shortcomings and failures of others and that disordered interest can become a sinful exploitation of other people's difficulties. In a recent interview with the Belgian magazine *Tertio*, Pope Francis referred to such an unhealthy fascination with the descriptive term "coprophilia". That's what the ten were doing to James and John. That unhealthy and uncharitable fascination with another person's failure continues our Lord's suffering in the Body of Christ just as much as the inordinate ambition of James and John.

As a Church, we need to remember that Jesus desires our unity and charity towards others, especially in moments of personal weakness and failure rather than division and humiliation. It is interesting that in vs. 41 we are told that the disciples "began" to be indignant. Notice that we are never told that their indignation stopped. Mark's Gospel has many such beginnings most of which are constructive initiatives in the ministry of Jesus but some of which are negative actions and influences that harm and weaken the Church and individual disciples (see also Mk 8:32 where Peter "began" to rebuke Jesus following our Lord's first prediction of His

Passion). Influences in the life of the Church, both positive and negative, began during the time of Jesus and continue even today.

Jesus then addresses the damaging response of the ten disciples by contrasting how greatness and authority are expressed in the secular world with how they are expressed in the Kingdom of God. The Romans governed by brutal force and relied upon tactics of intimidation to coerce their subjects into absolute submission and loyalty. Jesus used His authority to heal the sick, free those oppressed by evil spirits, and confront the disordered priorities of the religious leaders of His time. Our Lord, then, used His authority in service to others rather than in domination of them. When Jesus sent the disciples on mission in Mark 3:15 and Mark 6:7 we are told that the Lord shared His own authority with them so that they could continue His works of healing, liberation, and service to the truth. By exercising their authority in the right way (selfless, sacrificial service to others in imitation of Jesus), the disciples will be able to avoid temptations to that false worldly greatness that divides and weakens the Body of Christ. Not only are they to be servants to one another but Jesus also tells them that they must become slaves to all. That is a very powerful term; a reminder that all people—not just some people—have a right to receive the Gospel.

The disciples and the Church cannot rest until the whole world has effectively received the Gospel of Jesus. This is not so much a task we complete as it is a life-long mission we fulfill. When we drink the cup of Christ and are Baptized into our Lord's Death and Resurrection, we belong to God who has complete and utter claim on our whole lives. Disciples, then, are ultimately slaves of the Lord who make no claim for reward, recompense, or recognition. We owe the Lord and others our service and commitment as a life condition.

> *When have you seen or heard one group of people celebrating someone else's failure, and what do you think would have been a more Christian response to that situation?*
> *Who are people with authority in our secular world, and how do they make their authority felt?*
> *How are authority and power exercised appropriately in a faith community?*

*What ministries most authentically manifest the authority
and power Jesus entrusted to the Church?
How does the image of being a slave of Christ inform and
challenge your discipleship?*

The passage ends with a single, very powerful statement of Jesus in
vs. 45 that the Son of Man came to serve, not to be served, and to
give His life as a ransom for many. The ultimate service that Jesus
will offer us is His Death on the Cross. It is then that the Lord
"redeems" us, "saves" us, and "ransoms" us. These are all terms
that we use in our prayer, yet we may not fully understand them.
It's worth reflecting for a moment on what Jesus means when He
speaks of ransoming the many because it is rare in today's world
that we hear of someone being ransomed. Occasionally pirates may
seize a ship and require ransom for those held captive. Sometimes
we might read about a person being kidnapped and held for ransom
as well, but in the time of Jesus this practice actually occurred more
frequently than it does today. To ransom (or redeem) means to pay
a price for someone's freedom from captivity. It is most likely this
aspect of freeing captives that Jesus wants us to focus on. The entire
mission of Jesus was to lead us to freedom in the Kingdom of God.

Jesus began this journey of freedom when He identified Himself with sinful humanity and received the Baptism of repentance
from John. In His life and ministry, Jesus shows us how to overcome
the forces of sin and violence through forgiveness and peace. Ultimately, Jesus definitively saved us from the power of death itself
by His own Death and Resurrection in which He opened the gates
of eternal life to those who believe. It is our Lord's great ministry
on Calvary that ransomed us from captivity to our sin and the
consequence of death. As disciples, we have been ransomed by
the Blood of Jesus so that we can live in the freedom of Christ. We
accept this freedom and ratify this ransom in every Eucharist we
celebrate when the grace of Calvary is offered to us sacramentally in
the Body and Blood of the Lord. This belief in redemptive suffering
for others (that is, suffering which "pays the price" for others) was
expressed in the Old Testament through the Suffering Servant of
Isaiah 53:11–12 and 2 Maccabees 7. Jesus is the true Servant of God
whose suffering justifies many, bears their guilt and takes away
their sins while gaining pardon for their offenses. This is what we

mean when we profess our belief in Jesus as our Redeemer and Savior. In the normal poetic style of the mystics, St. John of the Cross described this ransom on the wood of the cross by relating it to the Fall and the wood of the Tree of Knowledge in the Book of Genesis, "Beneath the apple tree: there I took you for my own, there I offered you my hand, and restored you, where your mother was corrupted."[40]

> *How does it make you feel when someone else pays for a cost that you have incurred?*
>
> *How does this teaching of Jesus change the way you look at a Crucifix?*
>
> *When have you "ransomed" or "redeemed" someone else and what was their response?*
>
> *How does this teaching affect the way you receive Communion as the moment in which you receive the redemption Christ gained for you on Calvary?*

---

40. St John of the Cross, "Spiritual Canticle v. 23" in *Complete Works* (Washington: ICS Publ., 1991), p. 474.

THIRTIETH SUNDAY IN ORDINARY TIME

Our Scripture passage comes from the Gospel of Mark 10:46–52. This is the final scene on Jesus' journey to Jerusalem, and the healing of the blind man Bartimaeus serves as a model of ideal discipleship (very similar to the model of discipleship exemplified by Zacchaeus in Luke 19:1–10). The healing of Bartimaeus offers many rich insights that can assist us in fostering discipleship both as individuals and as a faith community.

The passage begins by noting that Bartimaeus sat by the "roadside". The actual term used in Greek (*odon*) is more properly translated as "way" and also referred to the Christian way of life. While beggars did often position themselves next to common thoroughfares so as to have maximum access to the passing populace, this initial detail indicates that the story will function on both a literal (surface) and a symbolic (deeper) level. The statement that he is blind referred not only to physical impairment but more importantly to lack of spiritual insight and faith. Bartimaeus, then, represents all those people who do not know Christ but whom Christian disciples encounter on their way as they follow the Lord.

We are also told that Bartimaeus was "sitting", which indicates he was not moving either in a physical sense or in a spiritual sense. Bartimaeus was waiting, not only for assistance with his physical need but more importantly for the gift of faith to satisfy his spiritual need. It is in this moment that the blind beggar calls out to Jesus for mercy. The Greek word for mercy is *eleison* and is a root to the Greek word for alms (*eleimosyni*). Because of this etymological connection, it is probable that Bartimaeus was initially seeking alms more than a relationship with Jesus. The reality is that people are oftentimes drawn to the Lord due to a temporal need which can become the opportunity for a more profound encounter with the Lord. God can use any circumstance of life to lead us to Himself just as He used the blindness and poverty of Bartimaeus to call out for Jesus. As we follow the Lord, we should not be surprised when we encounter people who are blind (without faith) and sitting along the way. Rather, this passage invites us to see them as potential disciples and to serve their temporal needs as an opportunity to awaken the gift of faith.

> *How has the Lord awakened the gift of faith within you by first satisfying your physical or material needs?*
> *For what part of your life did you feel like you were just sitting by the roadside as others passed by on their journey of faith?*
> *How can a faith community evangelize others by first caring for their physical needs?*
> *Is there someone with whom you interact each day who is sitting by the way and waiting to be introduced to Jesus?*

The initial response of the disciples was less than helpful. Instead of reaching out to Bartimaeus, they first tried to silence him. This may strike us as an odd response, but it warrants our reflection so we can learn to act properly towards those whom we meet. This is not the first time the disciples tried to silence someone who was calling on Jesus, as we were told in Mark 9:38. They tried to stop a man who was casting out demons in Jesus' name because the man did not follow them. Now we see the disciples trying to silence Bartimaeus who also was not part of their group. This repetitive attempt to prohibit others from calling on the name of Jesus because they were not yet disciples demonstrates an unhealthy and unhelpful attempt to limit and restrict access to the Lord.

Basically, it is the temptation to think that someone must first become "one of us" before they can encounter the Lord. The reality is that sometimes it is only because someone has encountered the Lord that they can become a disciple with us! This first response of the disciples cautions us to be careful about the ways in which we can be exclusive or restrictive in our attitude towards others. Any time we think that others don't have a right to call out for God's mercy, we become obstacles to that mercy and to the encounter Jesus wants to have with all who seek Him. It is important to note that Bartimaeus was undeterred by their rebuke and shouted even louder.

How can people today become possessive and controlling when allowing others access to God's mercy?
What are practical ways in which people in a faith community are told to "be silent" or "you're not part of our group"?
What are some of the obstacles you have had to overcome in order to encounter Jesus in your life, and how can you help others overcome similar obstacles because of your experience?

It is at this moment that Jesus responded. We are told that the Lord stopped and ordered the disciples to call Bartimaeus. It is significant that Jesus works through the agency of the disciples because it shows how those who had been obstacles to Bartimaeus' quest for faith can become facilitators when they listen to the Lord. It is important that all disciples learn this lesson! Jesus wants to work through us so as to bring others to Him. The disciples invited Bartimaeus with very specific words: Take courage, Arise, and He is calling you! These are significant phrases that have deep meaning in the Gospel and in Mark's community. Courage was required of the disciples in Mark 6:50 when Jesus walked on the water in preparation to bring the message of the Gospel to the Gentile community of Gennesaret. Courage was also required of Mark's community when they faced the fierce persecutions of the Emperor Nero in Rome. Indeed, those who called out for Jesus needed courage in order to become disciples. The second phrase used is "arise" (Greek: *egeire*) and is the same verb used to describe the Resurrection of Jesus. It is the verb also used in previous passages of discipleship in Mark's Gospel (especially Peter's mother-in-law in Mk 1:31, the healing of the paralytic in Mk 2:11, and the raising of Jairus' daughter in Mk 5:41). The use of this verb indicates that Bartimaeus was being called to share in the risen life of Jesus.

This invitation to faith was from Jesus and ministered through the disciples. The way in which Bartimaeus will share in our Lord's risen life becomes clear when we are told that he threw off his outer garment and came to Jesus. This interesting detail of discarding the garment is significant and alludes to the Sacrament of Baptism. In the time of Jesus, a person's clothing was a symbol of their identity. To cast off one's clothing was a way of saying that a person was leaving behind their former identity so as to become a new reality.

For Christians, this new reality is received in Baptism when we are incorporated into the very person of Jesus who is the Resurrection and the Life. Bartimaeus was called by Jesus and now courageously approaches the Lord as someone who is sharing resurrected life, having left behind the trappings of his former life.

All these elements have a great deal to say to us in our lives as disciples. When we authentically and faithfully listen to the Lord, we can be instruments of Christ's mercy reaching out to effectively bring others to Him. We, too, need to remember that it takes courage to live the Gospel and profess our faith in Jesus in the midst of a secular world. We may not face fierce persecutions like so many Christians in other parts of our world, but we do face the resistance of a culture that does not readily welcome or value religious expression, the sanctity of human life, the dignity of the human person, and other values of our faith. Finally, we need to remember that it is Jesus who is calling us to Himself and offering us a sharing in His very life which alone can overcome the forces of sin and death. Our response to that invitation, and a demonstration of our courage, is to freely and eagerly cast off the trappings of a former life so as to embrace our new identity as a Baptized member of the Body of Christ. The reality is that discipleship requires a transformation of life, and change is not always easy when it involves letting go of habits and attitudes that are contrary to the Gospel while learning to sacrificially love God and neighbor.

> *What situation are you facing and for which you need courage in order to witness your faith in the midst of it?*
> *What are the typical trappings of a former life that people have to leave behind as they draw close to Jesus?*
> *How have you experienced the life of the Risen Lord filling you, and what has been the effect of that experience?*
> *How is God asking you to help bring someone to Him?*

When Bartimaeus came to Jesus the Lord asked him one of the most important questions of his life: What do you want me to do for you (Mk 10:51). This is the real moment of decision for Bartimaeus and his truly big chance in life. As he stands before the Lord he can ask for anything—Bartimaeus could have asked for the gift of money that would simply help him get by, but instead he asked for the transforming gift of God's grace that would restore his sight and change his life. It takes a lot of courage to ask for that kind of gift because it means learning to live in a new way and leaving behind familiar settings (begging by the roadside), expectations of others, and fulfilling new responsibilities. Sometimes when we pray for God's grace we seek only that gift which will get us by from one momentary need to another rather than the grace that will change our lives so we can follow the Lord as faithful disciples. Perhaps the greatest miracle in this story is that Bartimaeus knew what to ask for when he was given the chance and knew that he had the courage to actually seek it. Each of us experiences certain impediments in our efforts to faithfully live out our discipleship. It may be our inability to see clearly with the gift of faith, our inability to hear clearly the message of the gospel or to confess our faith to others, or our inability to walk in the way of the Lord because of the paralysis of sin and weakness. Rather than praying for a momentary grace that only gets us through a tough moment, we should have the courage of Bartimaeus to seek that enduring grace that will truly transform our lives and prepare us for the new challenges we will face as a result of that sharing in Christ's life. Prayer is the work of the Spirit; therefore, we need to pursue the grace of prayer so we can ask God what we really need. For this reason, Saint Paul reminded the Romans, "The Spirit helps us in our weakness; for we do not know how to pray as we ought, but that very Spirit intercedes with sighs too deep for words" (Romans 8:26).

> *What are examples of things we pray for that simply keep us comfortable the way we are and what are examples of things we can pray for that transform our lives?*
> *If Jesus said to you, "What do you want me to do for you today?" how would you respond?*
> *Do you know people who are struggling to live a new life because they have experienced God's transforming grace, and how can you help them learn to live that new life?*

The passage ends with Jesus commanding Bartimaeus to "go" because his faith has "saved" him. The commandment to "go" is not just a dismissal indicating that Bartimaeus should leave that area; rather, it is a command to Bartimaeus that he is to now start

living a new mission. Interestingly, the only time in the Gospel of
Mark that anyone other than Jesus issues the command to "go" is
in Mark 16:7 when the young man in the tomb commissioned the
women to bring the message of the resurrection to Peter and the
disciples (for previous scenes of discipleship in which Jesus commissions people to "go", see Mk 2:11, Mk 5:19, Mk 5:34, Mk 6:38, Mk
7:29). The comment about saving faith is worthy of note. It is not
often in the Gospels that Jesus identifies someone as having saving
faith (see Jesus' comment to the woman with the hemorrhage in
Mk 5:34 where "healed" and "saved" are actually the same word in
Greek). Bartimaeus demonstrated saving faith by his persistent
pursuit of Jesus in the face of opposition, his courage and willingness to transform his life through Baptism, and his request for the
enduring gift of sight rather than the temporary gift of alms. In
response to Jesus' commission to "go", we are then told that Bartimaeus followed the Lord on the "way". This is a beautiful statement
that Bartimaeus used his gift of sight to become a disciple of Jesus
and follow the Lord as He draws near to Jerusalem (as indicated
in the very next verse of Mk 11:1) where He will experience His
Passion, Death, and Resurrection. Bartimaeus could have used his
gift of sight to return to his former life or follow his own pursuits
instead. By using his gift to follow Jesus he is showing us what true
and authentic discipleship looks like when one commits his life to
Christ and lives out his Baptism by accompanying the Lord on His
way. Bartimaeus has become a missionary disciple entrusted with
the commission to "go" and witness the Resurrected Jesus to all
whom he meets, especially those people whom he will find sitting
along the way waiting for someone to bring them to the Lord.

> *How is every encounter with Christ meant to be an expe-*
> *rience that sends us on mission?*
> *What gifts has the Lord given you that can become the*
> *means for you to follow Jesus more closely in the Christian*
> *way?*
> *What part of Bartimaeus' faith inspires you most and why?*

THIRTY-FIRST SUNDAY IN ORDINARY TIME

Our Scripture passage comes from the Gospel of Mark 12:28b–34. (A very similar passage is recorded in the Gospel of Matthew 22:34–40 and additional insights are contained in that reflection located in the Liturgical Year A edition of *Come Follow Me*.) This Gospel passage is especially important for our reflection because the discussion between Jesus and the Scribe concerning the "First Commandment" is an instruction for disciples of all times and places.

One of the first things to note about this passage in Mark's Gospel is that the Scribe who poses the question concerning the First (or greatest) Commandment does not do so in an attempt to trap or test Jesus (compare Mt 22:35 and Lk 10:25). Rather, we are told that the Scribe only approached Jesus after he heard and saw our Lord's controversial discourse with the Pharisees and Sadducees. There are two important things to note about this observation of the Scribe.

First, it reminds us that there are always people watching what we say and do, and as disciples it is important to be good witnesses so that others will be inspired by our comments and actions. That is what happened to the Scribe in this passage: He first took time to observe Jesus' actions and to hear Jesus' teaching before approaching the Lord with his own question of faith. People will rarely approach us with sincere questions of faith until they trust us. Trust is the most fundamental step of discipleship and one that should not be overlooked. The Scribe was drawn to Jesus because he saw the Lord responding with insight, authority, understanding, and integrity. The same is true for us today: A life of authentic discipleship always attracts others, but we may only know of their interest after they have watched us act and listened to us speak for some time. Disciples bear the awesome responsibility of being such authentic witnesses of faith so that others are drawn to Jesus through us.

The second point to be taken from the response of the Scribe concerns our need to be open to all people when it comes to seeking potential disciples. It would have been easy for Jesus to dismiss the Scribe and to presume that his inquiry was antagonistic, but that was not the case. The Scribe was sincere and open to the Lord's teaching. If Jesus or His followers had rejected the Scribe because of his association with the Pharisees and Sadducees, they would have been rejecting a potential disciple. Sometimes it is easy for us to make judgments about people based on their associations with others. The action of the Scribe in this passage cautions us to give every person the benefit of the doubt and to avoid generalizations. We can never know for certain how a particular person will respond to the Gospel, but we do know that there can be no response if we do not present the Gospel to them. The Holy Spirit can move in the hearts of all persons of good will to awaken within them the gift of faith, and Jesus wants us to be welcoming, encouraging, and cooperative instruments in facilitating their conversion.

> *Who do you influence each day with your words and actions?*
> *Who gained your trust and opened the way for you to seek Jesus and become a disciple?*
> *What social, political, or other groups do you automatically presume will not respond positively to a message of faith?*
> *When have you been surprised by someone's growth in discipleship because they were part of a group that you did not think would be responsive?*

When Jesus answered the Scribe's question about the First Commandment, our Lord drew on two familiar and important sections of Scripture regarding love of God (see Dt 6:5) and love of neighbor (see Lev 19:18b). The quotation from Deuteronomy is particularly important because it was part of Jewish daily prayer life and reminded the faithful of the need to seek God in all things and above all things. The Scribe's response not only emphasized the unity of God ("He is one") but also the universality of God's reign over all peoples ("there is no other but He"). It is the universality of God's reign that redefines what it means to love our neighbor. God is not the Lord of only one people or nation but of all peoples and all nations. Because of God's all-encompassing dominion, Christians cannot restrict or limit their love for others based on whom they want to be their neighbor. The universality of God's reign means that all peoples in all places are our neighbors. It can be tempting for us to comfort our own consciences by reflecting on times when we do love God and neighbor.

This passage challenges us to be even more aware of those times when we do not love God and neighbor. It is only when we reflect on our lack of love that we can recognize ways in which we have limited and restricted the universality of God's reign in our own lives and our neighborly care for all people. This commandment particularly challenges us to seek the Lord in all things and above all things. God's reign is not only universal in terms of geography but also in regards to all dimensions of a disciple's life. To love God is to serve God with our entire mind; that is, in our thoughts, decisions, conversations, and entertainment. It means to serve God with all our soul by our attentiveness and devotion to the Lord's presence with us throughout the entire day, not only in momentary times of established prayer. It also means serving God with all our heart by conforming every one of our affections and attractions to what is Holy and seeking God in our relationships, hobbies, and other interests. Loving God also means to serve the Lord with the strength we exert through our daily tasks and involvement in the larger community. Any activity of a disciple's life that cannot be reconciled with the presence of God is an action contrary to love of God and an indication that we have failed to fulfill this great commandment. It is only when a person loves and seeks God in this way, with every aspect of their whole being, that they can love all others as God loves them.

> How can people today be tempted to think that God is not the Lord of all peoples but only of some special peoples?
> Who is the neighbor that you find it difficult to love?
> In what activities of your mind, soul, heart, or strength do you find it difficult to seek the Lord's presence?
> Which area of your life do you most need to submit to Christ's reign?

As we reflect on this great commandment, it is an opportune time to consider what it means to "Love". There were four words in the Greek language that were used to describe love, and each of these four terms had a different meaning. The specific kind of love that Jesus commands for God and neighbor is that of *agape*, which is the highest and most demanding of all loves. Let's consider the other three kinds before reflecting on agape. First, there is the kind of love described by the Greek word *storge*, which referred to the mutually affectionate relationships between family members or even with a person's pets. It is a love based on enjoyment of one another's company and mutual reward. This type of love may be more properly translated by the English word "like". Second, there is the kind of love described by the Greek word *eros*, which referred to the physical, sensual love of husband and wife and is expressed in sexuality (it is from this term that we derive the English word "erotic"). This love is an expression of mutual self-giving and commitment. While it is an intense kind of love, it is also limited by its very nature. Third, there is the kind of love described by the Greek word *philos*, which referred to the brotherly love between very good friends. This love involves loyalty, mutual support, encouragement, and even sacrificing for the good of the other. This was one of the highest forms of love in the ancient world. The fourth and most demanding type of love was that of *agape*. This type of love is the very love that God has for us and is not only emotional or sentimental but also active.

God's love is expressed in the Ministry, Life, Death, and Resurrection of Jesus. God's love is unconditional because the Lord loves us even when we reject it, fail to return it, or do not appreciate it. God's love is selfless because the Lord seeks what will benefit us in the pursuit of salvation. God's love is sacrificial and is demonstrated by Jesus' death on the Cross. God's love forgives those who commit wrongs even when they don't seek that forgiveness or even know their need of it. God's love is not limited only to some people in some places but to all people in all places. God's love is for both friend and foe. When we exercise sacrificial love, we easily defeat the shallow waters of our own selfishness as St. Francis de Sales reminds us, "Self-love deceives us...". We leave charity for a moment, and this imperfect habit of human love is thrust on us, and we content ourselves with it as if it were true charity, till some clear light shows us that we have been deceived."[41] It is this fourth kind of love, *agape* love, that Jesus commands us to live in our relationship with God and neighbor. As disciples, we are to become living witnesses of God's love in the world.

> *How does this four-fold understanding of love challenge*
> *you to grow deeper in your discipleship?*
> *For whom do you express philos and agape love?*
> *What does a disciple need before they can live agape love?*

One final note about this passage concerns the Scribe's comment that love of God and neighbor is greater than all burnt offerings and sacrifices (Mk 12:33). The priority of love over cultic sacrifice was already expressed in the prophetic and Wisdom writings of the Old Testament (see 1 Sm 15:22, Hos 6:6, and Prv 21:3). There were various religious groups in the time of Jesus, and each of those groups would have had a different opinion about how to best demonstrate love of God. The burnt offerings and sacrifices would have most likely been references to cultic worship in the Temple of Jerusalem. The Sadducees in particular would have promoted Temple sacrifice. The Pharisees would have emphasized daily purity laws, observance of the Sabbath, synagogue participation, separation from Gentiles and those considered unclean as ways in which a person should express their love of God. The Essenes (Qumran Community near the Dead Sea) would have promoted more extreme practices of prayer, fasting, and purity as part of their expression of love of God.

The response of Jesus in joining together love of God and love of neighbor challenges us to never separate one from the other. We cannot exempt ourselves from our responsibility to care for those in need because of our engagement in religious practices. Religious practices are meant to foster within us a greater awareness and commitment to all our brothers and sisters throughout the world. Any time we choose to perform religious practices instead of caring for our neighbor, whoever they may be, we have misinterpreted the purpose of those religious actions and have failed in both our love of God as well as our love of neighbor. The Scribe in this passage

---

41. St Francis de Sales, *Treatise on the Love of God*, Book IV, chap. 10 (London: Burns & Oates, 1910).

properly understood the necessary interconnectedness between our religious and charitable actions: Our obligation to God can only be fulfilled when we also care for our obligation to others. The debt of love that Christian disciples owe to their neighbor can never be fully repaid (Rom 13:8).

> *What are some of the ways in which people today express their love of God?*
>
> *How can those expressions be used as a false exemption from the obligation of charity to neighbor?*
>
> *What happens when a faith community focuses only on love of God?*
>
> *What happens when a faith community focuses only on love of neighbor?*
>
> *What leads a disciple to think they already fulfilled their obligation to love their neighbor?*

THIRTY-SECOND SUNDAY IN
ORDINARY TIME

Our Scripture passage comes from the Gospel of Mark 12:38–44. This story is commonly known as the "Widow's Mite" and is often interpreted as a teaching on the virtue of generosity. However, there are additional elements in this passage that offer other challenging insights and cautions for us as disciples. In order to properly interpret this passage, it is necessary to read this story of the widow in context of our Lord's reprimand of the Scribes who "devour the households of widows" (Mk 12:40). The negative example of the Scribes who use their resources to seek their own gain is presented in stark contrast to the example of the widow who gives of her resources in a sacrificial religious offering.

The first thing Jesus does is to caution against following the example of the Scribes. Their actions, such as wearing long robes and giving greetings in market places, were intended to draw public attention to themselves. The first seats in Synagogues and first couches at dinners were places of honor that enhanced the reputation of those who occupied them. These actions may sound harmless and may be perceived as mere trappings of an honor-based society. The Gospel of Mark has already given several teachings against seeking such honors (Mk 9:35, 10:31, 10:43–44) and so this warning would be understandable in itself as a caution against pursuits of false greatness. However, Jesus then goes on to state an even more serious charge against the Scribes: They devour widows' households and for a pretense make long prayers (Mk 12:40). This accusation goes beyond that of self-seeking and implies deception as well as manipulative insincerity. This combination of actions (self-promotion, misrepresentation, and securing power over widows' households) implies that the Scribes may have been using their religious and public standing in order to secure a position of management (trusteeship) over the inheritance of widows.

Once in such a position, dishonest Scribes would have the power to unjustly appropriate a share of the estate for themselves. In doing so, they could easily "devour" the households of widows. This is a serious charge and is not just a matter of self-seeking. The implication is that the Scribes are using their public and religious status (best seats in the Synagogue, best seats at banquets, and greetings in the market place) to promote themselves in positions of power over the vulnerable and powerless (widows) for the sake of self-gain at another's expense. This act of exploitation reveals that the Scribes were acting as wolves in sheeps' clothing and were preying on the powerless of their society. Jesus harshly condemns these actions as a direct violation of Love of God and Neighbor (see the preceding pericope of Mk 12:30–31). Our Lord ends His teaching with a warning that such persons who use religious pretense for self-gain will be harshly judged. The reason for this particular harshness is because they used religion as a platform from which they could abuse others for the sake of self-gain. This is a strong condemnation of anyone who would invoke God as a justification or disguise for harmful and selfish pursuits.

> *How do people today use religion as a means to build up their personal reputation for the sake of self-gain and self-promotion?*
> *How does this passage challenge disciples to be cautious when relating to the poor and vulnerable in our midst?*
> *When have you been tempted to use your religious affiliation and involvement as a source of public respect and trust?*
> *How has the mission of the Gospel been hindered by people who use respected religious positions to do harmful things?*

The second thing Jesus does is to comment on the actions of the widow who makes a contribution into the Temple treasury. In the ancient world, temples often served a mixed combination of economic, political, and religious functions. For this reason, temple treasuries were sometimes pillaged by invading armies much like banks might be robbed in today's world. Ancient accounts indicate that the Temple of Jerusalem contained an inner area known as the "Court of the Women" in which the treasury was located. The

Mishnah in Middoth 2, 5 further indicates that there were thirteen trumpet-shaped metal chests in which people were to leave financial donations. Larger and more valuable coins would have made a different sound that that of smaller and less valuable coins. Thus, the amount of benefaction would have been readily known by anyone in the Temple area at the time a donation was made due to the noise. Widows were particularly vulnerable in the ancient world because they had no inheritance rights. In the absence of a social charitable system, widows had to rely on their families for support and care. The fact that the widow in this story is described as being poor indicates that she did not have such a supportive family and lived at the mercy of public charity.

Although poor and relatively destitute, this widow offered the little she had by giving two *lepta* coins, which was one of the smallest possible donations. Such a gift was clearly a sacrificial act and Jesus summarizes it as representing "her whole life savings" (Mk 12:44). It is the quality of her sacrifice rather than the size of her gift that forms the basis of our Lord's comments to the disciples. It is true that the wealthy may make larger gifts but the widow gives out of her poverty (need) rather than her abundance, and so the sacrifice of the poor is greater than that of the rich. This religious action of the widow's generosity stands in stark contrast to the deceptive, pretentious, and self-serving actions of the Scribes. The widow put her effort and resources into a sacrificial gift of pious generosity while the Scribes put their efforts and resources into self-promotion for the sake of self-gain.

It is important to note that Jesus does not make a qualitative comment on the widow's action but only an observation of the contrast between a faith that leads to self-giving as opposed to a faith that leads to self-promotion. Some Scripture scholars detect a note of lament in our Lord's final words about the widow giving everything she had. This lament may be an indication that while Jesus praised the sacrificial generosity of the widow, our Lord was also saddened by the actions of misguided religious leaders who manipulated the pious attitudes of the poor in order to secure funds for a physical building. (It should be remembered that the very next passage, which follows this section, contains a prediction of the Temple's destruction.) Indeed, what the widow did remained a virtuous statement of her faith and generosity even if her donation may have been promoted and encouraged by the deceptive actions of the religious leaders and Scribes. Our Lord's tone of lament may also have been in reference to the social system that created such an unjust plight for widows, which effectively reduced them to destitute poverty. With this second interpretation of our Lord's lament, Jesus may have been praising the woman who responded with generosity even in the midst of unjust suffering. Certainly that description described our Lord on the Cross who forgave those who crucified Him.

> *How do you know when you are giving from your surplus or giving from your need?*
> *How is God calling you to be sacrificial in your generosity now?*
> *Why do you think the Gospels speak so much about the importance of sacrifice for disciples?*
> *How can sacrificial acts be used as a source of self-promotion?*
> *How can people's pious attitudes be manipulated today for the purpose of securing charitable donations?*
> *How do you know when someone is sincere and worthy in their request for financial assistance?*

This Gospel passage is often used to encourage charitable giving. As disciples, we are called to be responsible and responsive in how we address situations of need as well as how we invite others to be generous as an expression of their faith. There are several important points for reflection that we can gain from this reading which can help guide us in our efforts.

- First, this passage can serve as a caution against pursuing religious maintenance at the expense of religious mission. Buildings and facilities are intended to promote the Gospel and never to contradict it. When the maintenance of institutional buildings becomes an undue burden or impediment to the work of evangelization (including charitable concern for the poor), there exists the danger of misplaced religious values.
- Second, great caution must be taken to never use the values and teachings of faith in a way that manipulates people's generosity

for the sake of self-gain or disordered priorities. As disciples, we are inevitably involved in various charitable endeavors. It can be easy to find ourselves in a blind competition for limited resources and to seek the support of our own charitable causes without regard for the charitable causes of others. When asking someone to support a particular charity, it is important to take care lest such a request actually diminish charitable outreach to more important causes. Sometimes the media will report obvious frivolous charitable causes that provide for the purchase of private jets, expensive homes and grandiose salaries. However, it is more difficult to assess the relative importance of charitable causes in the absence of such obvious distinctions. It is then that disciples must prayerfully discern with responsibility and accountability both the reasonableness and faithfulness of the charitable requests they pose for others.

• Third, this passage of the contrast between the Scribe and the widow follows the previous passage containing the great commandment to love God and neighbor. This contextualization invites us to consider who are the poor and vulnerable ones whose sacrificial efforts sustain our way of life. They, too, are our "neighbors", and if we love them with the *agape* love of God then we will seek to raise them from the oppressive economic and social conditions in which they live. This love will challenge us to see them as brothers and sisters and to work so that they can experience the same dignity of life and have the same opportunities for their families that we enjoy. Jesus may have been implicitly criticizing the social conditions that reduced the widow to a life of destitute poverty. Our Lord might very well criticize contemporary economic structures that exploit the poor in our world as well.

As you reflect on these three points, which one offers a particularly helpful insight to assist or challenge you in your discipleship?

How do you know when a ministry has become too "maintenance"-focused and is no longer "mission"-focused?

What criterion can you use to determine which charitable causes are of greater importance and which are of lesser importance?

Who pays the price for your lifestyle?
Why should disciples care about the economic and social
conditions of people they have never met or will never see?
What social or economic structures do you think Jesus
would confront if He spoke in your world?

The Church proposes the Seven Principles of Catholic Social Teaching to assist disciples in discerning how their love of God should affect their love of neighbor. The Seven Principles are intended to serve as a checklist to help us know whether we have considered all relevant priorities and factors as we make decisions that affect others and the world around us. The Seven Principles are as follows:

1. The protection of the life and dignity of the human person
2. The call to family, community, and participation in the social order
3. The rights and responsibilities of each person
4. The preferential option for the poor and vulnerable in a given situation
5. The dignity of work and the rights of workers
6. The realization of solidarity with the situation of others
7. The care of God's creation

How can these principles help you to live this Gospel passage in a more effective way?
What can you do to embrace these principles in your daily life?

THIRTY-THIRD SUNDAY IN
ORDINARY TIME

Our Scripture passage comes from the Gospel of Mark 13:24–32. This section of Mark's Gospel contains a type of literature known as "apocalyptic" because of the cosmic references and future realities that take place as part of the "end times". Special care must be taken when interpreting apocalyptic writings to avoid bizarre understandings or false expectations. This text does contain several important lessons for discipleship and so our reflection will focus primarily on those elements that can benefit us in our efforts to faithfully follow the Lord.

Chapter thirteen of Mark's Gospel is often referred to as the "Little Apocalypse" as compared with the more extensive writing in the same style known as the Book of Revelation (or the Book of the Apocalypse). The word apocalypse comes from Greek and means to "un-veil" or to "remove the veil", allowing a person to see clearly what was previously obscured. In order to properly understand this style of literature it is important to remember that the word "apocalypse" is singular, not plural, and refers to the revelation of one great hidden truth: The manifestation of Jesus Christ as Victor over the forces of sin and death and who now reigns as supreme Lord and judge of Heaven and Earth. That one great revealed truth gives meaning to all experiences of the Christian life, especially moments of difficulty, persecution, and even martyrdom at the hands of oppressive earthly powers.

This one great timeless revelation is portrayed in a variety of different ways and can be applied in multiple historical contexts ranging from the persecutions of the Emperor Nero in AD 64–68 to the destruction of Jerusalem and the Temple by the Romans in AD 70. Throughout history persecuted Christians have found encouragement, hope, consolation, and challenge in the apocalyptic writings of the New Testament and have interpreted their experiences through those writings. However, apocalyptic literature is interpreted quite differently if a person reads it as though it were intended to communicate multiple revelations (plural) rather than one great singular revelation. Such a divergent interpretation gives rise to tabloid articles about prophetic fulfillment, "end times" books, and other attempts to guess the exact day and hour of particular events. The singular victory and exaltation of Jesus Christ is meant to be a source of enduring hope, life, and encouragement to help Christians of all time face the challenges and obstacles presented in their faith lives.

Apocalyptic literature functions in much the same way as a preview of a movie's closing scene; once you know how the movie ends then you can watch with calmness and confidence the many trials and tense challenges faced by the various characters because you have sure and certain knowledge that all will be well in the end. Apocalyptic literature provided much the same type of consolation for Christians of the first century who were experiencing fierce persecutions. Their faith in the victory of Jesus was strengthened, and they were able to embrace difficulties and martyrdom with confidence, hope, and even joy because of the assurance of Christ's ultimate triumph.

> *When you read the Book of Revelation or other apocalyptic passages, how does it change your understanding to know that these texts are communicating one fundamental revealed truth rather than a multitude of future happenings?*
>
> *What forms of persecution do Christians face today from powerful entities forcing them to act contrary to their faith?*
>
> *The good news of apocalyptic literature is that it reveals God's effective salvation for those disciples who have no earthly recourse for help. How is the Church called to be an instrument of that salvation and how can the Church effectively carry out that ministry?*

One of the important elements revealed in this apocalyptic passage is the new authority of the Son of Man. Jesus announces that He, as the Son of Man, will ride on the clouds of heaven (Mk 14:62). Through this statement, the Son of Man (Jesus) is being revealed as the Lord of heaven and earth since in Psalm 68:4 it is God who rides on the clouds. Also, the new authority of Jesus is further revealed when He announces that the Son of Man will send His angels to gather the elect from the four winds. This act of gathering the faithful was previously attributed to God in Deuteronomy 30:4. In each of these passages it is clear that Jesus, as the Son of Man, now does what God does in the Old Testament. This new authority revealed in Jesus means that a new kingdom is emerging, and with it, the old kingdoms are passing away. Kingdoms rarely pass peacefully or quietly and so the image of a violent transition is oftentimes a part of apocalyptic literature. The passing away of former kingdoms and powers is indicated by the sun and moon being darkened, the stars falling from heaven, and the heavens being shaken.

The coming kingdom (new order) of the Son of Man and these other realities cannot coexist for a couple of reasons. First, the sun and moon were the sources of light that helped us see the world around us. In the new order it is the Son of Man who will shed light on the events of our lives and allow us to see and understand them clearly through the values of the Gospel (Rev 21:23, "The city has no need of the sun or of the moon to shine on it, for the glory of God has illumined it, and its lamp is the Lamb"). Second, the stars were used as stable points from which people could determine their relative position on Earth and navigate to new destinations. Stars, then, gave guidance and stability. This image takes on further significance because of the ancient belief that earthly kings were identified by a corresponding heavenly counterpart (star). It is for this reason that the Magi followed the star that rose with the birth of Jesus in order to find the newborn King of the Jews. The falling of the stars, then, means more than just a change in guidance and direction in the new order. The falling of the stars primarily refers to the demise of worldly kingdoms (especially those that opposed Jesus) so that the new order, the Kingdom of God, can reign unhindered and supreme.

These earthly kingdoms included the Roman Empire as well as the leading families of Jerusalem who cooperated in the Crucifixion of Jesus. These temporal kingdoms will have no more authority in the new order. The greatest kingdom to fall, however, will be the kingdom of Satan that was manifested most graphically on Calvary.

The Death and Resurrection of Jesus definitively crushed that kingdom of evil once and for all. Indeed, every other power in heaven and on earth will give way to that of the Son of Man. Those who place their hope in the passing kingdoms of this world are doomed to be disappointed and frustrated while those who place their hope in the Crucified and Risen Lord will be cared for as His faithful subjects (elect). This image challenges us to be clear about what power or authority we allow to give us direction, to determine the meaning of our life events, to guide us through every day decisions, and to be the source of our hope for future stability.

> *To what earthly powers or agencies do you turn for direction, understanding, stability and security?*
> *How does this reading challenge you to seek these gifts in Jesus Christ?*
> *How do great people today seek to make themselves immortal, and what does this passage teach us about the real source of immortality?*
> *What can a faith community do to reveal Jesus as the only true and eternal authority who can direct, interpret, guide, and give stability to our lives?*

Jesus goes on to instruct the disciples on the need to faithfully interpret the signs of the time by using the image of a fig tree that sprouts at the end of winter so as to announce the beginning of spring. This is a very beautiful image and offers a rich opportunity from which to understand the new order of God's Kingdom. The fig tree is barren in winter and seemingly lifeless. It appears dead due to the lack of foliage. However, the barrenness is only a precursor to the abundant and new life that bursts forth each spring around the time of Passover. This connection between the "new life" that bursts forth from barrenness around the time of Passover, Crucifixion, and Resurrection of Jesus at that same time should not be missed. The deeper meaning of this symbolism, when interpreted through the Death and Resurrection of Jesus, is this: What we think is the end is really the true beginning of a new and greater reality.

Christians of the early Church had a wonderful way of expressing this belief in the power of God to bring life out of death and good out of evil. They expressed their firm faith in two ways. First, when a martyr died, they referred to that day as the "Birthday" of the martyr since it was the day when their true life began even as their earthly life ended. For those who are faithful, the end is really only the beginning. Another way they professed this confidence was with graffiti written near the tombs of the martyrs. Sometimes they would juxtapose the Greek letters Alpha/Omega (meaning "beginning and end") so that they instead read Omega/Alpha indicating that the end is actually the beginning. This beautiful expression of faith manifested the early Church's belief in the power of Jesus' Death and Resurrection to become the pattern for the trials and persecutions disciples experienced as well. What appeared to be the "end" of Jesus on Calvary was actually the "beginning" of His new Kingdom and resurrected life!

This mystery gives disciples hope when they face every obstacle, every closed door, every failed effort, and every organized attempt to thwart the Christian mission. There will always be difficulties in carrying on the mission of the Gospel. These difficulties occur because of the resistance of existing kingdoms to relinquish power and authority to the Kingship of Christ. It's that simple. Jesus threatened the existing powers in His religious and political world and those powers resisted Him with all their might. There is no room in the Kingdom of God for coexistence with evil. The ongoing clash of kingdoms is a futile last effort of the lesser kingdoms of this world to retain their power and influence. In Mark 13:3 when our Lord sat opposite the Temple, Jesus gave warning that the kingdoms of this world must submit. His posture of opposition was a declaration that the kingdoms of this world were soon to be destroyed and His more powerful Kingdom was soon to emerge.

> *What does the statement "The end is really the beginning" mean to you and how have you experienced that through various situations in your life?*
>
> *How does the image of the fig tree bursting forth with new life inform your understanding of the Cross and Resurrection of Jesus?*
>
> *Christians of the early Church used graffiti and intentional images such as "birthday" to profess their faith in the power of Jesus' resurrection to overcome all things. What are symbols or actions that can profess that same faith today?*

The passage ends with Jesus making two very important and interpretative statements. The first statement is when the Lord says that
this generation will not pass away until these things have taken
place, and the second statement is made when Jesus says that no
one knows the day nor the hour. These two statements create a
certain tension between a part of our Lord's revelation that has
already been fulfilled and another part that is awaiting whose fulfillment we still await. What has already taken place is the definitive
victory Jesus won over the forces of sin and death that sought to
destroy Him, and by that victory Jesus is rightfully established as
the eternal Lord and judge of Heaven and Earth. What has not yet
been fulfilled is the full manifestation of that kingdom on Earth.

To use a familiar image, the war may already be won but the
battles rage on. We continue to experience manifestations of the
power of evil in various ways throughout history on global, communal, and personal levels. These battles are real, but they cannot
overcome the definitive victory Jesus has already won for us. The
challenge for a Christian disciple when confronted with such a
battle is to remain faithful to the Lamb of God who sacrificed
Himself for our Salvation and who lives forever. By our fidelity
and unwavering commitment to Jesus in the face of seemingly
hopeless situations, we already share in His victory. This passage
teaches us that the Lord will gather those who remain faithful (the
elect) from across the face of the Earth. The Church, born from
the foot of the Cross, is that faithful gathering (also known as the
"Holy Remnant") who are called to witness the new order of God's
reign even as we deal with the archaic vestiges of former reigns.
Christ's definitive victory gives us confidence that good will always
ultimately triumph. The coming of God's Kingdom, then, is not a
cause of fear or concern or even curiosity for a faithful disciple but
a cause of hope, confidence, and encouragement.

> *How does the unveiling (revelation) of Jesus' ultimate vic-
> tory in this passage give you hope, confidence, and encour-
> agement for the situations you face?*
> *How can a faith community help disciples remain faithful
> when they are engaged in a struggle with evil?*
> *In what settings do you experience opposition when you try
> to live out the values of the Kingdom of God?*

How does this understanding of the Church, as the Holy Remnant that is called to live faithfully in the Kingdom of God, challenge you to extend the Lord's reign into other parts of your life and what are those parts?

The French Jesuit author Pierre Teilhard de Chardin once wrote:

> Above all, trust in the slow work of God. We are quite naturally impatient in everything to reach the end without delay. [...] Only God could say what this new spirit gradually forming within you will be. Give Our Lord the benefit of believing that his hand is leading you, and accept the anxiety of feeling yourself in suspense and incomplete.[42]

---

42. P. Teilhard de Chardin, *Hearts on Fire*, Edited by M. Harter (Chicago: Loyola Press, 2004), p. 102.

SOLEMNITY OF CHRIST THE KING

Our Scripture passage comes from the Gospel of John 18:33b–37. In this extraordinarily profound scene we read about the kingship of Jesus proclaimed in the context of our Lord's dialogue with Pilate. This passage offers some important insights into what it means for us to be the Lord's loyal and faithful subjects.

One of the first things to notice about this passage is how quickly the trial of Jesus actually turns into the trial of Pilate! This change in perspective is accomplished by the initial exchange of questions between Our Lord and the Roman Procurator. Pilate begins by asking Jesus a simple and objective question: "Are you the King of the Jews?" Jesus responds by challenging Pilate with a personal question: "Do you say this on your own or have others told you about me?" The Gospel of John contains several moments when Jesus asks questions, and all of these occasions represent ongoing causes of reflection and discernment for the Christian life. These questions began with Jesus' inquiry of Andrew and another disciple (Jn 1:38) and continue throughout the Gospel. Each of these questions is meant to clarify and focus our faith as disciples just as it did with the faith of those to whom Jesus first addressed them.

In this passage our Lord is asking Pilate to decide between a faith that is based on hearsay (what others have told him about Jesus) and a faith that is based on personal encounter and response (what he can say about Jesus on his own). Pilate has heard a lot about Jesus, but this is the moment when he meets Jesus for the first time and our Lord is offering him the relationship of faith. For this reason it is really the trial of Pilate rather than the trial of Jesus because the question to be resolved is how Pilate will respond to this opportunity: whether he will remain distant from Jesus and limit his knowledge to objective titles of faith or whether he will enter into a personal relationship with the Lord and make His own profession of faith.

As the story unfolds we see Pilate distance himself from the Lord by stating the source of His knowledge as being that of others ("your own nation and the chief priests"). Pilate further demonstrates his distance from Jesus by insisting that our Lord answer his question (Are you the King of the Jews?) rather than following the discussion Jesus has initiated (His Kingdom is not of this world). That reluctance of Pilate to follow Jesus in the conversation can be symptomatic of a mistaken discipleship in which we sometimes expect Jesus to follow our lead rather than following the Lord's lead. As disciples today, we inherit a great tradition of faith and benefit from what others have told us about Jesus. Like Pilate, we are called to make these objective statements of faith our own in a subjective (personal) commitment to the Lord.

While our personal relationship is always guided and informed by objective statements, it is the subjective encounter with Jesus that animates and makes concrete those statements. Being a disciple isn't just a matter of knowing what others have said about Jesus, it also requires that we make those statements our own and in doing so, recognize and respond to the presence of the Lord Who is active and present in each moment of our lives. That responsiveness and obedience is what it means to be a loyal subject of Christ the King. The Saints give great examples of what it looks like when a disciple integrates objective statements of faith into a personal (subjective) response to Jesus Christ. Pilate gives us an example of what happens when we resist such integration.

> *What have other people told you about Jesus?*
> *What can you say about Jesus from your own life experience?*
> *When have you felt like you were on trial for your faith and how did you do?*
> *In what ways are we tempted to set the agenda for our prayer?*
> *How might you seek God's agenda for your prayer?*

Jesus responds to Pilate's question by speaking about the nature of His Kingdom rather than His identity as a King. In all four Gospels there is a high frequency of royal language in the Passion accounts which indicates that this moment serves as our Lord's most explicit enthronement as King (Mk 15:2, 9, 12, 18, 26, 32; Mt 27:11, 29, 37, 42; Lk 23:2, 3, 37, 38; Jn 18:33, 37, 39; Jn 19:3, 12, 14, 15). Although John's Gospel does not have many references to the Kingdom of God, the Kingship of Jesus has already been introduced and alluded to in previous chapters (see Jn 1:49 and 6:15, 12:13). When we study John's rare references to the Kingdom of God, we find that both of them are in the context of our Lord's conversation with Nicodemus in John 3:3 and John 3:5. This use of the same term ("Kingdom") means that the conversation with Nicodemus and the trial before Pilate (Jn 18 and Jn 3) should be read together so as to give a deeper understanding to the dialogue now taking place with the Roman Procurator.

In the conversation with Nicodemus, Jesus specified that those who wish to enter the Kingdom of God must be born again of water and the Spirit. This process involves both a visible and an invisible action and suggests the moment of Baptism when a person is incorporated into the Body of Christ, the Church. Jesus has made no other reference to the Kingdom in John's Gospel until He stands before Pilate. This tells us that our Lord's pending Passion, Death, and Resurrection (Paschal Mystery) not only continues the conversation with Nicodemus, but actually fulfills it. The Spirit that regenerates humanity through the Sacrament of Baptism will be handed over by Jesus from the Cross and entrusted to the newborn Church (Jn 19:30) gathered to Him at that moment (Jn 12:32) The Cross is the saving event Jesus described to Nicodemus when He spoke of that faith which would give eternal life (Jn 3:14–15).

Beginning with the instruction of the Mother of Jesus at the Wedding in Cana (2:5) and continuing throughout John's Gospel, John the Evangelist has repeatedly described the necessary relationship between the internal and external manifestation of faith for a disciple: namely, what a person believes interiorly must be lived out in their actions (see Jn 10:27–28 Jn 14:15, 21, 23 Jn 15:5, Jn 15:7–8 Jn 15:14, Jn 21:15–17). Such integrity between faith and action is what it means to be a loyal subject of the Kingdom of God. Therefore, to be a loyal subject of Christ the King and part of His Kingdom requires both an internal experience of faith and love for God as well as an external transformation of life conforming us to the will of God. This integrated and committed act of faith is what brings us into an abiding relationship with Jesus and the

Father and that relationship is eternal life. Jesus' response to Pilate cautions us, however, to realize that while His Kingdom is present in the world through the lives of faithful disciples, His Kingdom is never something that is "of" the world.

Rather, His Kingdom is always from above and is a gift of the Father through the Son and in the Spirit. This caution is to prevent us from thinking that we are ever the origin of the Kingdom or that the Kingdom receives its authority and success through our efforts. We can only cooperate with God's reign in our lives but we are never the authors of it. Jesus demonstrates in His own Passion and Death what it means to live a life that is completely conformed to the will of the Father. He is the King of Love who reigns supremely and principally from the Cross of Calvary. For this reason, it is on the Cross that Pilate actually proclaims Jesus as the Universal King of the known world by giving Him the title "King of the Jews" in the three major languages of ancient civilization; that is, Latin, Greek, and Hebrew (see Jn 19:19–20).

Disciples must have the eyes of faith that can recognize Jesus as our King in this moment and the obedience of spirit to imitate His love as a faithful member of our Lord's Kingdom. Disciples must also have the integrity of faith to not only hear our Lord's voice but to follow Him with a life conformed to His teaching. The Kingdom of Jesus stands in stark contrast to the kingdoms of this world which tempt us to pursue only what has meaning in our limited experience of the current moment; it is both necessary and difficult to recognize and dismiss our attachment to any earthly desire that tries to influence our decisions or actions and to seek a life of sacrificial selfless love even as Jesus witnessed it for us on Calvary.

> *It is in light of these insights that we must ask the question: Is Jesus really our King and are we truly His loyal subjects? If someone were to put you on trial for being a citizen of the Kingdom of God, what evidence could they put forth? How does the kingship of Jesus over both the internal and external dimensions of your life challenge you?*
>
> *In Baptism we become a member of Christ's body. How does this truth inspire and challenge your discipleship when you see the Body of Christ on a Crucifix?*

The final element of this passage offered for our reflection concerns our Lord's statement that truth is the motivating purpose for His birth, mission, and witness. In order to understand what Jesus is saying we have to recall how truth has already been used in relationship to Jesus in the Gospel of John. We were first told in John 1:14 that the Word became flesh and dwelt among us and the Word was full of "grace and truth". A few verses later in John 1:17 it states that we receive from Jesus the "grace and truth" which He embodies. This phrasing is important because it relates to the two qualities of God in Exodus 34:6–7. Thus, John is telling us from the beginning of his Gospel that Jesus is the presence of God among us and that we have access to the life, truth, and grace of God through Him. That is the reason for Jesus' birth: To reveal God, who is love, so that we can be in eternal communion with Him.

The question that remains concerns how Jesus will accomplish this mission. As the Gospel unfolds we are reminded that truth is a fundamental element of Jesus' mission. We see these reminders in the description of John the Baptist's ministry (Jn 5:33) and in our Lord's statement when He identified Himself as the "Way, the Truth, and the Life" (Jn 14:6). Truth, then, is not an intellectual concept or proposition to which we assent. Truth is first and foremost a person: the presence of God incarnate in Jesus Christ. The mission of Jesus, the reason for His birth, is to reveal the truth of God's love for the world and in doing so to make God known to all people. The dialogue before Pilate indicates that the moment of Jesus' ultimate revelation of truth has begun: He is about to bear full witness to God, who is love, so that the truth of God can be revealed to the world. This witness will take place on the Cross of Calvary, and that is why Jesus' final words in John's Gospel (Jn 19:30) are a proclamation that the reason for His birth, mission and witness are now "finished" (the Greek term *tetelestai* more properly means "accomplished, perfected, or fulfilled").

Our Lord's revelation of God's love is offered to everyone, including Pilate. The question remains as to how each of us will respond to this great gift and invitation. Jesus knows that not everyone will accept His truth, and for that reason He goes on to say that everyone who does belong to truth listens to His voice. The act of "listening" means more than just hearing; it means to respond with acceptance and obedience. This is an important statement because it connects the interior act of believing ("belongs to the truth") with an exterior conformity of life ("listens to my voice"). The text of 1 John 3:18–19 reminds us of this necessary connection between belief and practice when we are cautioned to love not only in word or speech but in deed and truth. It is only by the conformity of our life to the voice of Jesus that we can truly know if we belong to the truth of God's love. Jesus is the only one who can reveal the true nature of God because He alone knows God since He has come from above (see Jn 3:31, Jn 5:19 and Jn 8:26).

In the verses that follow this passage we read of Pilate's dismissal of Jesus' witness when he says, "What is truth?" (Jn 18:38). Jesus has offered Pilate the same invitation He offers us: to accept that truth of God, which is eternal and from above. Pilate responded by dismissing our Lord's offer of revelation and rejecting truth as an eternal reality. In doing so, Pilate demonstrates that attitude present in our own world, which rejects any claim to objective truth in favor of subjective opinions. For Pilate, a decision (or judgment) does not need to be based on the objective revealed truth of right and wrong but can be made according to the subjective goal of whatever is the most expedient or profitable solution to a momentary problem. We see Pilate demonstrating this rejection of truth when he declares Jesus innocent (Jn 18:38) yet allows our Lord's fate to be determined by the unjust public opinion of the crowd. Pilate doesn't want a world that is governed by revelation and subject to God's values; instead, he wants a world that is self-determined where right and wrong can change according to the fickle whims of human desire. Such a world is fundamentally opposed to the revelation of Jesus who offers Himself as the only "Way, Truth, and Life".

This choice for self-determination and self-definition of right and wrong demonstrates not only the unbelief of Pilate but is a caution for all disciples to consciously avoid these same tendencies in our secular world and culture. By turning away from the invitation Jesus offered, Pilate condemned himself. We cannot remain indifferent to our Lord's claim that He Himself is the embodiment of the eternal truth of God. We must either accept that claim and choose to live by it, or we will reject it in favor of self-determination and self-definition based on the expediency of each situation. It is our response to the truth of Jesus that will determine whether we pass the trial of faith or not. When Pope Pius XI established the Feast of Christ the King, he stated, "When once men recognize, both in private and in public life, that Christ is King, society will at last receive the great blessings of real liberty, well-ordered discipline, peace and harmony."[43]

> *What forms of liberty, order, peace, and harmony do we try to establish in today's society without appealing to the objective truth of God's revelation?*
> *How do these values differ from Jesus' values?*
> *Which values in today's society could help realize the ideals of God's Kingdom?*
> *How can you promote the blessings of liberty, well-ordered discipline, peace, and harmony in your own personal life, family, and faith community?*
> *What is the truth about God that you most appreciate when you see a Crucifix?*

---

43. Pope Pius IX, *Quas Primas* (11 Dec 1925).

BIBLIOGRAPHY

AAVV., *Rite for the Baptism of One Child*, May 15, 1969, (1970 Missal).

AAVV., *Babylonian Talmud: Translation and Commentary*, Trans. By J. Neusner. Peabody, MA: Hendrickson, 2011.

AAVV., *The Mishnah*, Trans. by Herbert Danby, Oxford: Oxford Univ. Press, 1933.

Aelred of Rievaulx, St, *Spiritual Friendship*. Collegeville, MN: Liturgical Press, 2010.

Anonymous, "Didache" in *Apostolic Fathers Series,* I-II, Translated and Edited by J. B. Lightfoot. London: MacMillan and Co., 1885–1891.

Anonymous, "Acts of Peter" in *The Apocryphal New Testament*, Translation and Notes by M. R. James. Oxford: Clarendon Press, 1924.

Augustine, St *Sermon 272 on the Nature of the Sacrament of the Eucharist in Sermons*, Trans. Edmund Hill, O.P. Hyde Park: New City Press, 1993.

Augustine, St *Confessions*. New York: Cosimo Classics, 2006.

Benedict XVI, Pope, *Homily at the Beginning of the Petrine Ministry of the Bishop of Rome* (2005).

Catherine of Siena, St, "Treatise on Divine Providence" in *The Dialogues*, Mahwah, NJ: Paulist Press, 1980.

Flavius Josephus, *Antiquitates Judaicae* (Jewish Antiquities). London: Wordsworth, 2006.

Francis of Assisi, St, *Sacrum Commercium sancti Francisci cum domina Paupertate*, Ed. Stefano Brufani. Assisi: Edizioni Porziuncola, 1990.

Francis de Sales, St, *Treatise on the Love of God*. London: Burns & Oates, 1910.

Francis, Pope, *Misericordiae Vultus* (2015).

Francis, Pope, *Presentation of the Christmas Greetings to the Roman Curia* (2014).

Hopkins, K., *Death and Renewal: Volume 2: Sociological Studies in Roman History*, New York: Cambridge University Press, 1983.

Ignatius of Antioch, St, *Epistle to the Romans*. Mahwah, NJ: Paulist Press, 1946.

John Paul II, Pope St, *Dies Domini* (1998).

John Paul II, Pope St, *Ecclesia de Eucharistia* (2003).

John of the Cross, St, "The Dark Night of the Soul" in *Collected Works*. Washington DC: ICS Publications, 1991.

John of the Cross, St, "Spiritual Canticle" in *Complete Works*, Washington D.C.: ICS Publications, 1991.

Lewis, C. S., *Mere Christianity*, London: Collins, 1952.

Newmark, J., "The Benefit of Irreconcilable Differences": http://njj-ewishnews.com/article/28181/the-benefit-of-irreconcilable-differences#.VeHYGlbg5Vt

Ovid, "Nux" in *Art of Love and Other Poems*, Loeb Classical Library 232, Ovid vol. II, Trans. By J. H. Mozley. Cambridge, MA: Harvard University Press, 1929.

Pirlo, P., "St. Polycarp" in *My First Book of Saints*, Paranaque City: Sons of Holy Mary Immaculate—Quality Catholic Publications, 1997.

Pius IX, Pope, *Quas Primas* (1925).

Pliny the Elder, *Natural History*, New York: Penguin Classics, 1991

Rufus, M. Frag. 15b. Leipzig: Ed. O. Hense, 1905. As quoted by Hopkins, K. *Death and Renewal: Volume 2: Sociological Studies in Roman History*, New York: Cambridge University Press, 1983.

Sacrum Commercium sancti Francisci cum domina Paupertate, Ed. Stefano Brufani, Assisi: Edizioni Porziuncola, 1990.

Seneca. *On Benefits*, Chicago: The University of Chicago Press, 2011.

Seneca. "To Helvia" in *Minor Dialogues Together with the Dialog "On Clemency,"* Trans. by A. Stewart. Cambridge: Trinity College, 1900.

Spurgeon, C. H. *The Evidence of Our Lord's Wounds*, (Sermon No. 2061 in the Spurgeon Archives), Delivered at the Metropolitan Tabernacle in Newington, Dec. 2, 1887.

Teilhard de Chardin, T., "Prayer" in *Hearts on Fire,* Edited by M. Harter, Chicago: Loyola Press, 2004.

Teresa of Avila, St, *Life,* Trans. By E. Allison Peers. Garden City: Image, 1960.

Thomas Aquinas, St, *Summa Theologiae.* New York: Cosimo Classics, 2007.

Twain, M., *Pudd'nhead Wilson and Those Extraordinary Twins.* New York: Harper and Brothers, 1894.

Vatican II, *Dei Verbum* (1966).

Zauzmer, J., "Pope Francis compares media that spread fake news to people who are excited by feces." In: *The Washington Post* (7 December 2016).

CPSIA information can be obtained
at www.ICGtesting.com
Printed in the USA
BVOW09s1717301117

501440BV00001B/68/P